Business Analysis for

The Institute of Marketing

Marketing means Business

The Institute of Marketing was founded in 1911. It is now the largest and most successful marketing management organisation in Europe with over 20,000 members and 16,000 students throughout the world. The Institute is a democratic organisation and is run for the members by the members with the assistance of a permanent staff headed by the Director General. The Headquarters of the Institute are at Moor Hall, Cookham, near Maidenhead, in Berkshire.

Objectives: The objectives of the Institute are to develop knowledge about marketing, to provide services for members and registered students and to make the principles and practices of marketing more widely known and used throughout industry and commerce.

Range of activities: The Institute's activities are divided into four main areas:
    Membership and membership activities
    Corporate activities
    Marketing education
    Marketing training

Other titles in the series

Essentials of Statistics in Marketing
C. S. Greensted, A. K. S. Jardine and J. D. Macfarlane

Glossary of Marketing Terms
N. A. Hart and J. Stapleton

Legal Aspects of Marketing
J. L. Livermore

A Modern Approach to Economics
F. Livesey

The Fundamentals and Practice of Marketing
John Wilmshurst

Management Controls and Marketing Planning
R. M. S. Wilson

Business Analysis for Marketing Managers

L. A. ROGERS

Dip.M., M.Inst.M., M.I.M.C., B.A., M.Sc., Ph.D.

Published on behalf of the Institute of Marketing and the CAM Foundation

HEINEMANN: LONDON

William Heinemann Ltd
10 Upper Grosvenor Street, London W1X 9PA
LONDON MELBOURNE
JOHANNESBURG AUCKLAND

© L. A. Rogers 1978
First published 1978
Reprinted 1981, 1984, 1986

ISBN 0 434 91738 9

Text set in 10/11 pt IBM Press Roman, printed and bound
in Great Britain at The Bath Press, Avon

Preface

This book is based on the use of the case study as a tool for learning. It may be studied by the individual reader or used in group work with a tutor. The cases cover a wide range of business activities and each is accompanied by an analysis that draws on a number of different techniques, many of them quantitative. The aim is to expose the various aspects of each case and thus prepare the ground for rational decision-making. These analyses are intended to be used primarily as departure points for the reader's own investigations, although it will be clear from the text that too extensive an analysis can lead into highly conjectural areas. Self-examination questions are included throughout the analyses and answers to them follow.

In addition to the specific analyses there is an introductory chapter setting out a systematic approach to analysis followed by a chapter devoted to the relevant quantitative techniques.

Ability in decision-making can only be learned from experience, although the process may be helped by practice and by understanding the experience of others. This book is no substitute for experience but, in providing a methodology and practice in applying selected techniques, it should go some way towards helping those who wish to develop their analytical decision-making skills, whether as manager or student.

In my business life I have constantly to consider reports from colleagues and decide what resources should be applied to support their proposals. To such report compilers and evaluators I hope that this book will be of value. In my academic life I have read and graded more than 25,000 case-study scripts over the past eleven years and know at first hand the problems that confront the student. I offer this volume to them in the belief that it will help them to surmount some of the obstacles they will meet.

All the cases in the book are based on my own experience over the last thirty years although, to preserve confidences, the names of the companies and individuals have been altered and the financial data and statistics amended where necessary. On the other hand, dates and prices have been left unchanged to correspond with the actual political and economic events of the time although, for convenience, prices have been decimalized.

Contents

		page
Preface		v
Chapter 1	Introduction	1
	1.1 Marketing	1
	1.2 Cases	1
	1.3 Analysis and Synthesis	2
Chapter 2	Techniques of Business Analysis	13
	2.1 Estimating Trends	13
	2.2 Non-linear Trends	18
	2.3 Complexity Analysis	25
	2.4 Game Theory	28
	2.5 Correlation Analysis	33
	2.6 Financial Analysis	40
	Bibliography	50
Chapter 3	Medway Appliances Ltd.	56
	3.1 Data	56
	3.2 Analysis	70
	3.3 Report	78
Chapter 4	Soloran Ltd.	86
	4.1 Data	86
	4.2 Analysis	93
	4.3 Report	110
Chapter 5	Owen and Davies	114
	5.1 Data	114
	5.2 Analysis	123
	5.3 Report	134
Chapter 6	Upton, Vance and Wells Ltd.	137
	6.1 Data	137
	6.2 Analysis	160
	6.3 Report	170
	Index	173

1. *Introduction*

1.1 Marketing

The word 'marketing' has, in recent times, come to be widely used and widely accepted, and yet it means different things to different people; it suffers from a surfeit of definitions, and is widely misunderstood and misinterpreted. As soon as one finds a definition that appears to be satisfactory, one reads of another that tends to erode one's confidence in the belief that marketing will eventually become a universal term or at least a readily understood present participle. One of the earliest descriptions of marketing was made by Adam Smith, who, in 1776, stated that consumption should be the objective reason for all production. Other writers have coined phrases indicating that marketing delivers, or possibly creates, standards of living; and that marketing is a business process which may be observed by considering channel transactions or understood from the study of the institutions engaged in it. Marketing has been regarded as a business philosophy, or, more academically, as a concept, and the word has even been applied to organizations whose primary function is not geared to the making of profit in the usual day-to-day sense.

As this book is about the analysis of business activities for marketing managers, it is important that you understand the view of marketing taken by the author in the preparation of the cases and their analyses. Marketing is the creation of satisfied customers at a profit. It is tempting to add the constraint, 'at a profit to the organization', but marketing should have a much broader outlook than the mere development of profitable companies. Marketing should have social responsibilities in addition to responsibilities for the profitable pursuit of customers, and profit itself must be defined, because it is not restricted to cash profit or even 'book' profit. The organization that develops its employees by expanding their experience and supplying adequate training is creating 'profits' that will not be found in the final accounts. The company, by paying its rates, taxes and other dues, is making a 'profit' for the community. The company that processes its waste materials before disposal is contributing its part in creating a 'profit' of non-pollution for society. When studying the cases that follow, you should be prepared to accept this wider meaning of profit and the consequent broader scope of marketing when it is 'creating customers at a profit'.

1.2 Cases

The use of cases in helping students and scholars to improve their skills is not a recent innovation; they have been used for a very long period of time in both the medical and legal professions. However, the use of case material in business studies is, by comparison, modern, dating from the early 1900s. Since 1950 the use of cases has escalated so much that now there is an impressive array of case material of every variety, located in several different countries, and differing in length and quality. What is sometimes confusing is the mass of material that is grouped under the general description of 'case study'. For this reason the following definitions are offered in the hope that they will be of help to student, scholar and tutor in making better use of this method of investigating business operations. Irrespective of length and depth, cases may be classified in three categories: case histories, case studies and case projects.

A *case history* is an event, or series of events, described in some detail and set in an organizational framework with or without a related environment. These events are well documented, with the main and subsidiary points highlighted. Actions taken by the subjects in the case are described; reactions, responses and the effects on other subjects are related; and events are taken to a conclusion or to a point that is irreversible. (Medical cases are typical of the case-history category.)

A *case study* also describes events in a framework and within an environment, but the problems are not always highlighted or even made clear to the reader; they emerge only as the case material is subjected to analysis. A conclusion is not necessarily reached nor is the position arrived at irreversible. The student is usually able to 'take over' operations at a suitable entry point of his choice, often in the position of an external omniscient adviser, although he is sometimes placed in a specific position by an accompanying brief. Most business case studies fall into this category.

The *case project* is a comparatively recent innovation, and is sometimes combined with field work by the student, so that it becomes a practical piece of investigation. The case project is a series of diverse continuous events, usually set in a well illustrated organizational framework, and leading the student to a specific point in time and circumstance at which he becomes a 'participant' in the case. He may be asked to assume the role of a person in the case, or to play the part of the person appointed to a particular vacancy. Alternatively he may be asked to take on the role of an external consultant. Whatever part the student is asked to play, it is usually made explicit, and it is from this particular viewpoint that he must present his arguments. For example, if the student is placed in the position of the newly appointed sales manager, he will be expected to deal with the case material in quite a different manner from that he would adopt if he were appointed as a consultant to the board.

Each of the cases and its analysis is self-contained, so that they may be studied in any order to suit the reader's aims. The need to refer to sources external to the cases has been eliminated, as all the data necessary are contained in the cases.

1.3 Analysis and Synthesis

Case-study work, which is best conducted in small groups, consists of two distinct elements: analysis of the case material into its constituent parts, which are then assessed and compared with each other in terms of importance; and the synthesis of those analysed constituents into an acceptable form. These elements are illustrated in Exhibit 1.1.

The eventual report and its recommendations must be approved by those in charge and also by those who have to carry out the recommendations. In real life this situation is readily understandable: a report on the courses of action recommended requires management approval and authorization to be activated; and the specific actions proposed have to be accepted by employees and others before they can be implemented. There is a link between achieving acceptance by management in real life and achieving acceptance by one's colleagues in a case-study exercise. Action plans propounded in the boardroom must be soundly based and well presented to win acceptance; and plans formulated in the training situation must be presented in a similarly persuasive vein to win approval and adoption. Battles in the market place have first to be won in the boardroom, just as arguments in plenary training sessions have first to be tested in small groups. In this respect case studies contain real-life situations and are invaluable in tempering executive enthusiasm. There is no substitute for experience in learning to gain consensus of

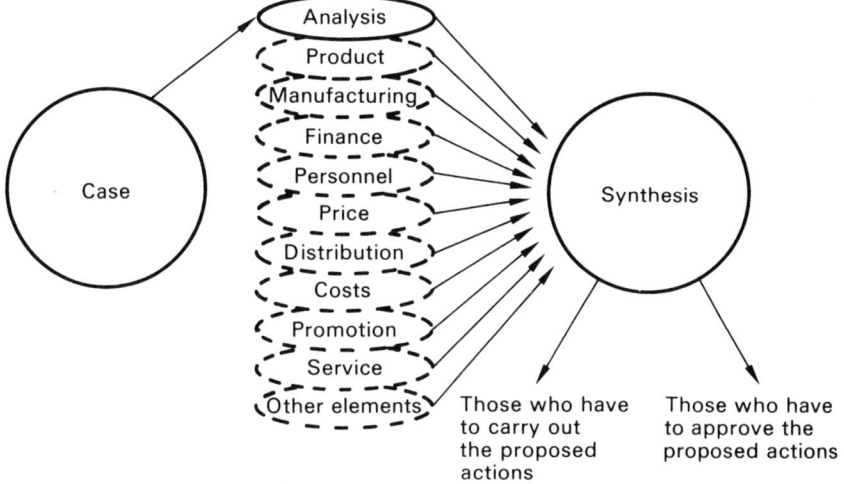

Exhibit 1.1 Analysis and synthesis

opinion, although, as Bismarck is alleged to have stated: 'Only a fool learns from experience — the wise man learns from the experience of others.' Gaining acceptance from those who have to carry out the proposals is often absent in case-study work, but the proposer can confidently expect, and wisely anticipate, role identification of case personalities by individuals in his audience ready to judge whether or not they would be prepared to carry out the actions he recommends.

All the cases can be analysed in depth, although not all to the same depth in all areas. Statistical analysis will usually yield a rich volume of information for consideration, while, in some cases, organizational and procedural analysis must precede decision-making. In all cases there is a requirement of financial analysis to underline the point that all decisions have a cost, usually in money — a vital point overlooked by some managers.

The situations in the cases are all from real-life business experience and, as with those actual situations, it is not always clear where the problem or problems are

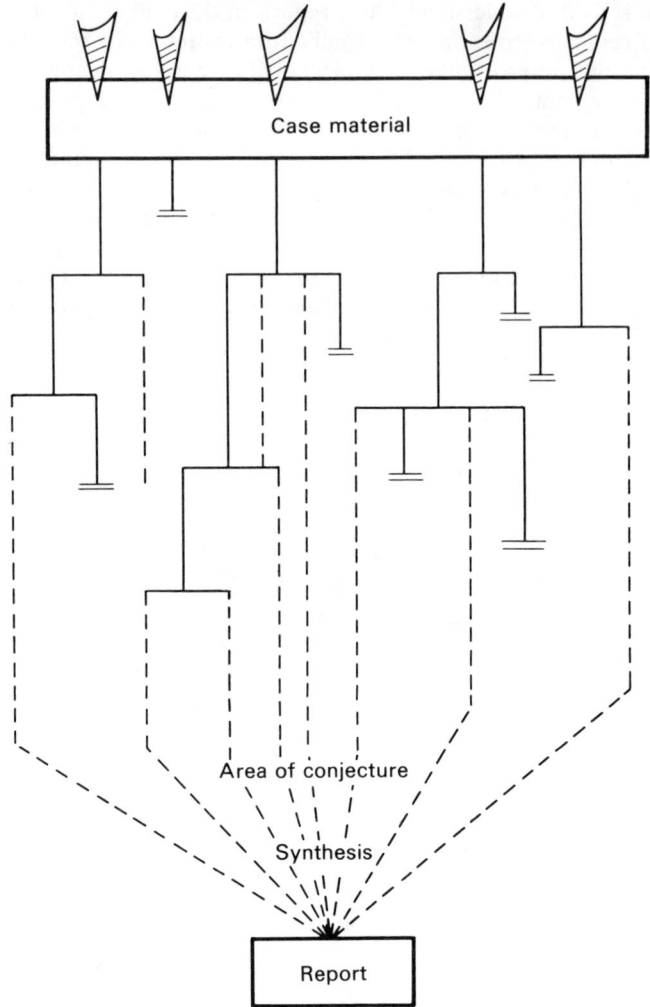

Exhibit 1.2 Schematic representation of case analysis

rooted, or indeed, whether there is a problem at all. Mostly only the symptoms are observed, and frequently, actions are suggested in ignorance of the nature of the disease; such well intentioned actions may assuage the symptoms but leave the root cause untouched. A whole range of effects often stems from one cause, and, occasionally, a single effect is created by a combination of several causes.

Weak analysis can follow from two main shortcomings: first, insufficiently detailed investigation, and, second, a failure to locate the source or sources of problems. Exhibit 1.2 illustrates the method recommended for case or situation analysis. Entry points are selected by the investigator, who should look into all quantitative aspects first. Such analysis is taken as far as is judged necessary, and certainly into the area that can be described as 'conjectural analysis'. Some lines of investigation soon come to a stop; others tend to fade as incomplete reference data are encountered. When the area of conjectural analysis has been as fully explored as is thought desirable, relevant data are synthetized to form a report.

Exhibit 1.3 illustrates a general approach to problem location, which can be in one or more of four possible areas. This concept is useful for organizational or procedural analysis, and can also be applied to, say, a market research problem, as is illustrated in Exhibit 1.4. When it is thought that the root problem has been located (this is mostly subjective judgment), appropriate measures to deal with matters can be considered.

While analysis must, of necessity, restrict itself to parts of the whole, it is imperative to keep the whole in mind and see it as composed of interlinking elements of a total system. Changes in any one element will affect others in the system.

A guide to a structured report based on the analysis can take the following form:

1 Aim of the company.
2 Purpose of operations.
3 Objectives to be achieved.
4 Actions proposed.
5 Assessment of actions proposed.
6 Selection of actions to be undertaken.

1.31 *Aim of the Company*

The aim of a company is the general direction in which the company is heading. It may include (1) increasing the size of the company in its industry, (2) making the company more widely known in overseas markets, (3) increasing the number of customers, and (4) diversifying the product range into the industrial market.

1.32 *Purpose of Operations*

The purpose behind these aims may be made up of an almost infinite number of different purposes. Examples include increasing company profits, using up spare manufacturing capacity, keeping the labour force intact, preventing redundancies, achieving a better harmony between the work force and management, achieving a better balance between consumer and industrial sales, reducing expenses, and so on.

1.33 *Objectives to be Achieved*

The determination of objectives is a more difficult task because an objective should be stated in terms of the results to be achieved, and these are often not known until an extensive analysis of the situation has taken place. Even when objectives appear to be reasonably clear and precise, they sometimes need to be modified in the light of experience. It is here that case analysis and company analysis diverge sharply, because, with case analysis, there can be no subsequent evaluation of one's

6   Business Analysis for Marketing Managers

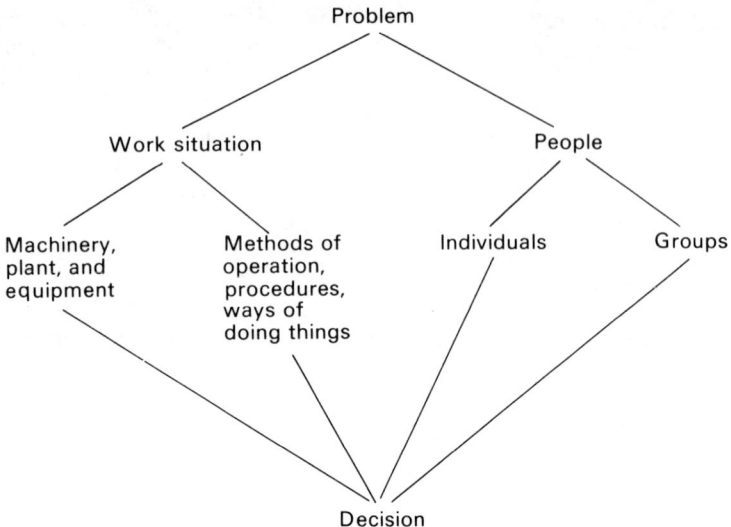

Exhibit 1.3 Location of problems scheme for organizational and procedural analysis

Exhibit 1.4 Location of problems scheme for market research

Introduction

decisions, whereas, with company operations, the results of decisions will eventually become known. This emphasizes an important characteristic of decision-making: the quality and effectiveness of a decision can only be judged in retrospect. It may therefore become incumbent on the investigator to adopt proxy objectives until such time as more is known about company operations.

1.34 Actions Proposed

The actions proposed will depend on the perceived location of case problems and how they are identified. To some extent problem location and identification will be influenced, if not determined, by selected entry points of investigation (see Exhibit 1.2). Problems may remain deeply imbedded and undetected, not necessarily because of one's inability or lack of skill in handling such problems but because one has not ventured in that direction. Actions proposed will therefore be largely subjective and a function of investigation rather than a definitive and exhaustive set of corrective possibilities.

Analysis may indicate that the problems have root causes in areas outside, as well as within, company control, and that two kinds of actions are necessary. For example, a problem resulting from an absolute decline in market demand may be dealt with by company action in response to the situation; a problem resulting from a falling market share may be dealt with by company action directly controlling the situation. To illustrate the former, suppose that the company has been manufacturing such products as radio valves, motor-car running boards, gas mantles, acetylene bicycle lamps, rubber proofed rainwear, steel pen-nibs, or domestic black iron kettles (not all at once of course!); then, a declining market demand that causes a fall in sales for such products cannot be combated with a more dynamic, more vigorous, marketing mix. Neither will the investing of more capital in research and development in an attempt to obtain an improved product win customers or influence the market. In such a situation the most appropriate action is to phase out the product over a period as long as it continues to return a profit, provided, of course, that the declining demand is due to market change and not just a transient occurrence.

The main factors that affect a company's operations but over which it has no control are (1) the markets, (2) competition, (3) the political environment, and (4) economic conditions. Where falling sales have been due to a decreasing market share and the cause *is* within the company's control, then, when the cause has been located, appropriate action might be to reduce price, increase discounts, step up promotion, motivate the sales force, improve advertising, give the product a greater degree of differentiation or greater utility, change the distribution scheme, and so on. Sometimes we can observe a combination of both types of root causes — external forces and internal shortcomings — occurring at the same time or maturing during the same period and combining to create problems for an organization. This was the situation in which the British Steel Corporation has found itself since 1975, when there was not only an absolute decline in demand for steel but internal problems of overmanning, poor industrial relations and aged uneconomic equipment combining to produce losses of many millions of pounds each week. Similarly, the problems of U.K. motor-car marketing in the 1970s are not rooted in a unique location.

Another very important consideration when actions are to be proposed is the degree of responsibility and authority possessed by the person carrying out the investigation. A manager with low hierarchical status or too narrow a functional responsibility is likely to be at a disadvantage if he locates major problems requiring fundamental actions he is unable to authorize. This particular dilemma is often identified in case analysis, where the subsequent report must be constructed in diplomatic as well as business terms.

An appreciation of the areas where proposed actions might be made can best be indicated by a marketing audit or marketing checklist. While no list can be really exhaustive, the following is suggested as a guide to possible courses of action.

The first consideration is the *current position*, as follows:

A Return on capital employed (ROCE).
   Sales as a percentage of capital employed.
   Profit as a percentage of sales.
   Liquidity ratio.
   Working capital.
   Shareholders' interest ratio.
   Debtors' ratio.
   Creditors' ratio.
   Stock as a percentage of sales.
   Stockturn.
   Fixed assets profitability.

B Total sales in value and in volume.
   Total gross profit, expenses and net profit.
   Sales expenses, advertising, etc. as percentages of sales.
   Percentage of sales in each market segment.
   Value and volume sales by area, month, model, size, etc.
   Sales per 1,000 consumers, population, per factory, in segments.
   Market share in total market and in segments.

C Number of actual and potential buyers by area.
   Characteristics of consumer buyers, e.g. income, occupation, education, sex, size of family, etc.
   Characteristics of industrial buyers, e.g. primary, secondary, tertiary, manufacturing, distribution, service; type of industry, size, etc.
   Characteristics of users if different from buyers.
   Locations of buyers, users.
   When purchases made (time of day, week, month, year), frequency of purchase, size of average purchase or typical purchase.
   How purchases made: specification or competition; by sample, inspection, impulse, rotation, system; cash or credit.
   Attitudes, motivation to purchase; influences on buying decision; the decision-making unit in organizations.
   Product uses — primary and secondary.

The second consideration is the *product*. Check the following:

A Quality: materials, workmanship, design, method of manufacture, manufacturing cycle, inputs-outputs.

Technical characteristics, attributes that may be considered as selling points, buying points.
Models, sizes, styles, ranges, colours etc.
Essential or non-essential, convenience or speciality.
Industrial equipment, materials, supplies, services.
Similarities with other company products.
Relation of product features to users' needs, wants, desires.
Development of branding and brand image.
Degree of product differentiation, actual and possible.
Packing and packaging, functional and promotional.
Materials used in packing: sizes, shapes, construction, closure, re-use.

B Competitive and competing products.
Main competitors and leading brands.
Comparison of design and performance differences with leading competitors.
Comparison of offerings of competitors, images, value, etc.

C Likely future product developments in company.
Likely future, or possible future, developments in industry.
Future product line or mix contraction, modification, expansion.

The third consideration is *distribution*. Check the following:

A Current company distribution structure.
Channels and methods used in channels.
Total number of outlets (consumer or industrial) by type.
Total number of wholesalers or industrial middlemen broken down into areas and by types.
Percentage of outlets of each type handling product broken down into areas.
Attitudes of outlets, by type, size, area.
Degree of cooperation; current and possible.
Multi-brand policy; current and possible.
Strengths and weaknesses in distribution system, geographically and functionally.
Number and types of warehouse; location of warehouses.
Transportation and communications in the market.
Stock control, delivery periods, control of information flow.

B Competitive distribution structure: strengths and weaknesses.
Market coverage and penetration.
Transportation methods used by competitors.
Delivery periods and reliability of competitors.
Specific competitive selling conditions.

C Future likely and possible developments in industry as a whole or from one or more competitors.
Probable changes in distribution system of company.
Possibilities of any future fundamental changes in outlets.

The fourth consideration is *personal selling and promotion*. Check the following:

A Size and composition of sales force.
   Calls per day, week, month, year by salesmen.
   Conversion rate of orders to calls.
   Selling cost per value and per volume of sales achieved.
   Selling cost per customer.
   Average size/value of orders.
   Internal and external sales promotion.
   Recruiting, selection, training, control procedures.
   Methods of motivation of salesmen.
   Remuneration schemes.
   Advertising appropriation and media schedule, copy themes.
   Cost of trade, technical, professional, consumer media.
   Cost of advertising per unit, per value of unit, per customer.
   Advertising expenditure per 1,000 readers, viewers, listeners, of main and of all media used.
   Methods and costs of merchandising.
   Public and press relations, exhibitions.

B Competitive selling activities and methods of selling and advertising, strengths and weaknesses.
   Review of competitors' promotion, sales contests, etc.
   Competitors' advertising themes, media used.

C Future developments likely in selling, promotional and advertising activities.
   Possibilities of legislation affecting future promotions.

Fifthly, check *price*, as follows:

A Pricing strategy and general methods of price structuring in the company.
   High or low price policies, reasons why for particular products.
   Prevailing pricing policies in industry.
   Current wholesaler, retailer margins in consumer markets or middlemen margins in industrial markets.
   Discounts: functional, quantity, cash, reward, incentive.
   Pricing objectives, profit objectives, financial implications such as breakeven figures, cash budgeting.

B Prices and price structures of competitors.
   Value analysis of own and competitors' products for comparisons.
   Discounts, credit, offered by competitors.

C Future developments in costs likely to affect price structures.
   Possibilities of more/less costly raw materials or labour that would affect prices.
   Possible competitive price attacks.

Lastly, check *service*, in the following areas:

A Extent of pre-sales or customer service and after-sales or product service required by company's products.

Introduction

    Survey of customer needs.
    Installation, education in use, inspection, maintenance, repair, accessories provision.
    Guarantees, warranties.
    Credit facilities required by market and offered by company.
    Methods, procedures of carrying out service.
    Returned goods, complaints.

B Services supplied by competitors and service organizations.
    Types of guarantee, warranty, credit, given.

C Future possible developments that might require revision of service policy.

As problems will be seen by different people to have root causes in different locations, then actions proposed will also differ, so that it is seldom possible to propose a course of action that will receive unanimous agreement. This is as true of real life as it is of case-training situations, and therefore the case analyses that follow contain few explicit proposals for action. Instead, by the way in which such analyses are developed, courses of actions are implicit in the aims and objectives suggested.

1.35 *Assessment of Actions Proposed*

It is almost too obvious to state that assessment of actions proposed must be made before actions are selected, but 'assessment' in this context has two aspects. The techniques used in the analysis and construction of measures to be taken must be assessed; similarly, the results and the implications of those results must be assessed. If an extrapolation of a time series has been made with different trend extension techniques to estimate a new sales turnover, then the techniques used must themselves be compared and assessed when considering the proposed actions based on those extrapolated sales figures. In this book I distinguish between 'assessment' and 'evaluation' — the former is used in the sense of pre-event judgment, the latter as a post-event judgment. Thus decisions can be assessed but not evaluated before they have been taken and implemented. We cannot say, 'That is a good decision', only 'That *was* a good decision'.

It is not normally necessary to employ a large number of different analytical techniques when investigating business situations and case material because, as is illustrated in Exhibit 1.2, one is sooner or later in the area of conjectural analysis. Any technique that is applied to data and succeeds in creating statistical prognostications correct to two decimal places should be considered with reservations, for such 'accurate' figures are almost certain to be conjectural.

The techniques used in the analyses in this volume are evident from those analyses and, where necessary, explanations are given on the construction and application of the technique. Chapter 2 is devoted to a selection of techniques and the way in which they can be linked sequentially. This sequential linking is of use when assessing the proposed action based on the techniques selected. For example, a market factor that has a causal relation with a sales figure may be observed and isolated in a case. An appropriate correlation analysis method can be used to determine the strength of the statistical association and then a financial analysis and projection applied to determine likely profit margins. When assessing actions that might be taken in this example, one then possesses evidence on a slightly wider, connected base to support such proposed actions. The more analytical links that are thus sympathetically connected, the surer a basis one has in assessing proposed actions.

1.36 *Selection of Actions to be Undertaken*

The action or actions recommended after an analysis has been made must inevitably be subjective, for there is no 'right' way of managing a business and it is possible to achieve the same objectives by adopting quite different courses of action. Because of the subjective nature of these decisions, and to avoid implying that any recommended measures are best, specific courses of action are not given in the case analyses. However, it is made clear what needs to be achieved, and this usually in quite explicit terms. It is left to the reader to choose how it shall be done.

Once you are familiar with the kinds of technique used in business analysis (Chapter 2), you should start with the cases and their analyses. Quickly scan the case to obtain an appreciation of its length, general content and split between text and exhibits, pausing here and there to consider specific matters of interest. Next, a first reading should enable you to make a mental, if not a written, note of the product, distribution scheme, selling and promotion, price structure and service given. Cases and business situations have different sets of elements with varying emphasis. In one case there may be a wealth of information on the various product lines and total mix and adequate information about price structures, but less data on the company's financial history. Another situation might have extensive financial history of the company and sufficient details about prices and price structures, but no detail about the company's distribution system. Where one case may possess copious data on its distribution system and a fairly extensive distribution cost analysis is possible, another case will offer no such possibility, and we are required to construct extrapolated sales estimates for a difficult and largely unknown market.

Deeper analysis should be retained for a closer reading of those areas you have chosen to investigate further. The checklist already given will be useful in this deeper analysis, and will enable you to probe the text and exhibits in a systematic way.

2. Techniques of Business Analysis

In this chapter we explore some of the statistical, financial and other techniques that can be used in analysing case material to isolate problems and prepare the ground for decision-taking. The search for, and identification of, any particular trends in data is one of the first approaches that may be made in case analysis, although the extent to which mathematical trend fitting can be attempted in the cases is limited to elementary treatment.

2.1 Estimating Trends

Suppose the following data for four years are stated in a case:

Year	Sales in Units
1	500
2	700
3	1,500
4	1,700

What is the trend and what would be a reasonable estimate for year 5? The increase in unit sales between year 1 and year 4 (3 years) is 1,200, and 1,200/3 = 400 a year. It would be possible to argue that sales for year 5 might be expected to reach 1,700 + 400 = 2,100. A more sophisticated approach is to calculate the percentage rate of increase per year with the following formula:

$$r = \left\{ \left(\sqrt[m]{\frac{X_n}{X_t}} \right) - 1 \right\} 100$$

where r is the rate of growth per year, m is the difference in periods between the first and last periods, X_n is the value of the last period, X_t the value for the first period. Thus, with the above data:

$$r = \left\{ \left(\sqrt[3]{\frac{1,700}{500}} \right) - 1 \right\} 100 = +50 \cdot 369 \text{ per cent p.a.}$$

From which we can calculate that year 5 might be in the region of 1,700 plus 50 per cent — approximately 2,550. Another approach is to find the line of best fit using the method of least squares.

A simple method of calculating the formula for the straight line of best fit to data is to tabulate the data for the periods and the differences of these data from the mid-point of the series. A third column shows the differences squared and a final column for the original data multiplied by the differences.

Let Y = the items of the data,
  d = the differences before and after the mid-point of the series,
  d^2 = the individual differences squared,
  Yd = each item in the data multiplied by its difference.

The information may be set out as in Table 2.1.

Table 2.1

Year	Y	d	d^2	Yd
1	500	−1·5	2·25	−750
2	700	−0·5	0·25	−350
3	1,500	0·5	0·25	750
4	1,700	1·5	2·25	2,550
	$\Sigma Y = 4,400$		$\Sigma d^2 = 5\cdot00$	$\Sigma Yd = 2,200$

The formula for a straight line is of the form:

$$Y = a + bx$$

where a is the intercept (that is the point where the curve cuts the y-axis) and b is the slope of the line. For the above data we may substitute d for x, and use the formula,

$$Y = a + bd$$

Now a and b are constants and may be found by calculating the simple mean of the data for a, that is $\Sigma Y/n$, which is 4,400/4 = 1,100; b is found by the formula $\Sigma Yd/\Sigma d^2$, which is 2,200/5 = 440. Therefore, the formula for the straight line of best fit is,

$$Y = 1,100 + 400d$$

For year 5, d is +2·5 and Y is found to be,

$$Y = 1,100 + (440 \times 2\cdot5)$$
$$= 2,200$$

Compare the trends with each other and with the yearly figures (Table 2.2).

Table 2.2

Year	Actual sales	Simple trend	Percentage trend	Straight-line trend
1	500	500	500	440
2	700	900	752	880
3	1,500	1,300	1,131	1,320
4	1,700	1,700	1,700	1,760
5	–	2,100	2,550	2,200

If there is no further information in the case, then you must apply commonsense and judgment to arrive at an estimate for the fifth year of between 2,100 and 2,550 – a sizeable difference of 450. You will encounter many problems similar to this, where the emphasis is on the qualitative nature of your argument. You would be wise to adopt a minimum-maximum approach in such instances and employ a flexible budgetary control system. However, crude figures such as these should persuade you to look more closely at the case material, and it is always possible that elsewhere in the text or tables additional information can be extracted. Assume you find such supplementary information relating to the quarterly sales as that given in Table 2.3.

Table 2.3

Year	Qtr	Unit sales	Year	Qtr	Unit sales
1	1	100	3	1	290
	2	130		2	380
	3	120		3	360
	4	150		4	470
2	1	130	4	1	400
	2	190		2	430
	3	150		3	380
	4	230		4	490
			5	1	520

The data from Table 2.3 (notice that there is additional information for the first quarter of the fifth year) can now be plotted on a graph, as in Exhibit 2.1, where the growth pattern can be seen quite distinctly, although with a number of marked variations from quarter to quarter. With the additional information on the first quarter for year 5, deducting this figure (520) from the lowest and highest estimates already calculated, and dividing by three to obtain the average for the subsequent three quarters, gives us averages of 526 and 676 per quarter. This seems to underline the need for a much more vigorous analysis of the situation.

You can establish another line of best fit, which may then be extrapolated to provide quarterly estimates. As the number of items is odd ($n = 17$) the mid-point of the series will be item nine and the differences from this mid-point will be whole numbers (Table 2.4).

Table 2.4

Y	d	d^2	Yd
100	−8	64	−800
130	−7	49	−910
120	−6	36	−720
150	−5	25	−750
130	−4	16	−520
190	−3	9	−570
150	−2	4	−300
230	−1	1	−230
290	0	0	0
380	1	1	380
360	2	4	720
470	3	9	1,410
400	4	16	1,600
430	5	25	2,150
380	6	36	2,280
490	7	49	3,430
520	8	64	4,160
$\Sigma Y = 4,920$		$\Sigma d^2 = 408$	$\Sigma Yd = 11,330$

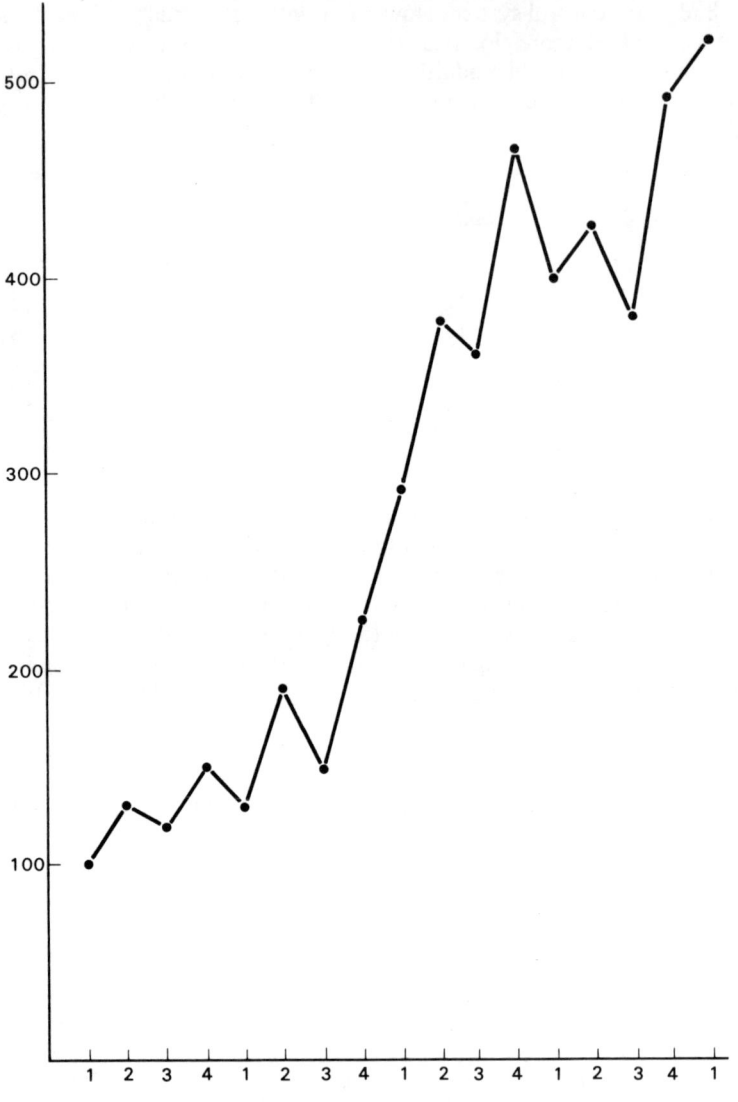

Exhibit 2.1 Graph of quarterly unit sales

As before, a is the simple mean of the data $\Sigma Y/n = 4{,}920/17$, which is 289·41, and the simplest formula for b is $\Sigma Yd/\Sigma d^2$, $11{,}330/408 = 27\cdot77$.

Using the formula for the line of best fit

$$Y = a + bd$$
$$Y = 289\cdot41 + 27\cdot77d$$

Therefore the trend for the first quarter of the fifth year (actual unit sales are 520) is $Y = 289\cdot41 + (27\cdot77 \times 8) = 512$ (rounded) and for the next three quarters

Table 2.5

(1) Qtr	(2) Unit sales	(3) Sum in 4s	(4) Sum in 2s	(5) Trend ÷ by 8	(6) Deviation (2) − (5)	(7)* Estimate of cycle	(8) Irregular factor (6) − (7)
1	100						
2	130						
3	120	500	1,030	129	−9	−35	+26
4	150	530	1,120	140	+10	+22	−12
1	130	590	1,210	151	−21	−11	−10
2	190	620	1,320	165	+25	+24	+1
3	150	700	1,560	195	−45	−35	−10
4	230	860	1,910	239	−9	+22	−31
1	290	1,050	2,310	289	+1	−11	+12
2	380	1,260	2,760	345	+35	+24	+11
3	360	1,500	3,110	389	−29	−35	+6
4	470	1,610	3,110	409	+61	+22	+39
1	400	1,660	3,340	418	−18	−11	−7
2	430	1,680	3,380	423	+7	+24	−17
3	380	1,700	3,520	440	−60	−35	−25
4	490	1,820					
1	520						

*The estimate of the cycle is calculated by adding the quarterly deviations and finding their average deviation for the quarter, as follows:

	Quarter			
	1	2	3	4
Year 1			−9	10
2	−21	25	−45	−9
3	1	35	−29	61
4	−18	7	−60	
	−38	+67	−143	+62
Average	−12·67	+22·33	−35·75	+20·67

The sum of these averages is −5·42, so that 5·42/4 = 1·36 is added to each of the quarterly average deviations to make them sum to as near zero as possible, after which they are rounded for ease of calculation:

1	2	3	4
−11	+24	−35	+22

the estimates are 539, 567 and 595, making a total estimate for the fifth year of 2,213 (if the 512 for the first quarter is included) or 2,221 (if the actual figure of 520 is included).

Further analysis may be based on the assumption that turnover is a trend component, plus a cyclical or seasonal component, plus an irregular or incidental factor. This is set out in Table 2.5.

Column 8 in Table 2.5 is the irregular factor that cannot be accounted for statistically and is quite substantial. The estimate of the cycle is fairly pronounced, and illustrates a downward movement in the first and third quarters and an upward movement in the second and fourth quarters. The difficulty of this particular method of establishing the trend is that some estimates are not available for the few quarters at the start and the end of the series.

2.2 Non-linear Trends

It is often more illuminating to determine a non-linear trend, as with logarithms, with the added advantage that the method does not lose data at the beginning and end of the series. This is set out in Table 2.6.

From Table 2.6, $\Sigma \log Y = 40{\cdot}7910 \qquad \Sigma X^2 = 408 \qquad \Sigma X \log Y = 19{\cdot}1631$

$$\log a = \Sigma \log Y / n$$
$$= 40{\cdot}7910/17 = 2{\cdot}3995$$
$$\log b = \Sigma X \log Y / \Sigma X^2 = 19{\cdot}1631/408$$
$$= 0{\cdot}0470$$
$$\log Y = \log a + (\log b) X$$
$$= 2{\cdot}3995 + 0{\cdot}047 X$$

For Y = 5th year 1st quarter, X = 8 and therefore $\log Y = 2{\cdot}3995 + (0{\cdot}047 \times 8) =$ = 2·7755, from which the value is 596 (instead of 520, the actual figure). For Y = 5th year 2nd quarter, X = 9 and the value of the trend will be found to be 664. You can see the difficulties of using a logarithmic-based trend when the original data does not fit that trend. In the above case the indications for the fifth year are too high. You will also appreciate that the cyclical trend and the irregular component in Table 2.6 are to be distrusted. In several of the cases you may find it more accurate to fit a logarithmic curve to the data rather than to fit a simple, linear $y = a + bx$. Occasionally it is helpful to explore a little more deeply into the data (certainly in real-life situations) and the pattern of quarterly sales indicates that an exponential curve might be a better fit. Consequently, a simple modified exponential is attempted first and then a Gompertz curve. The simple modified exponential formula is,

$$Y = a - br^t$$

and the Gompertz is,

$$\log Y = a - br^t$$

where a, b and r are the parameters, derived from averages of logarithms of sales, with r less than 1 and t the relevant quarter in the series.

Table 2.6

Qtr	Y	Log Y	X	X^2	X log Y	Log trend	Value	Dev. +	Est. of cyc.	Irrg. fctr
1	100	2·00	−8	64	−16·00	2·0238	106	−6†	−15	+9
2	130	2·11394	−7	49	−14·7976	2·0708	118	+12	+28	−16
3	120	2·07918	−6	36	−12·4751	2·1177	131	−11	−31	+20
4	150	2·17609	−5	25	−10·8805	2·1648	146	+4	+19	−15
1	130	2·11394	−4	16	−8·4558	2·2118	163	−33	−15	−18
2	190	2·27875	−3	9	−6·8363	2·2588	181	+9	+28	−19
3	150	2·17609	−2	4	−4·3522	2·3058	202	−52	−31	−21
4	230	2·36173	−1	1	−2·3617	2·3528	225	+5	+19	−14
1	290	2·4624	0	0	0	2·3998	251	+39	−15	+54
2	380	2·57978	1	1	2·5798	2·4468	280	+100	+28	+72
3	360	2·5563	2	4	5·1126	2·4938	312	+48	−31	+79
4	470	2·67209	3	9	8·0163	2·5408	347	+123	+19	+104
1	400	2·60206	4	16	10·4082	2·5878	387	+13	−15	+28
2	430	2·63347	5	25	13·1674	2·6348	431	−1	+28	−29
3	380	2·57978	6	36	15·4787	2·6818	481	−101	−31	−70
4	490	2·69019	7	49	18·8313	2·7288	536	−46	+19	−65
1	520	2·716	8	64	21·7280	2·7758	596	−77	−15	−62

$\Sigma \log Y = 40·791$ $\Sigma X^2 = 408$ $\Sigma X \log Y = 19·1631$

Of the various methods that are available to establish the three parameters a, b, and r, the one selected here is the 3-point method, so-called because the data are divided into three equal parts, or sets, and an average found for each set. It is not necessary to have three exactly equal sets, but the guiding principle is that sufficient numbers of items are included in each set. If, for example, there are twenty-nine items in the series, then the first two items may be ignored and the data divided into three nines; if there are only twelve items in the series, averages of the three fours may not provide such well fitting parameters as, say, the first five (items 1 to 5), the middle six (items 4 to 9), and the last five (items 8 to 12). A slight overlapping of items in more than one set is permissible: thus, in a series of twelve, items 4 and 5 would be included in both the first and second sets, and items 8 and 9 would be included in the middle and last sets (Table 2.7).

Table 2.7

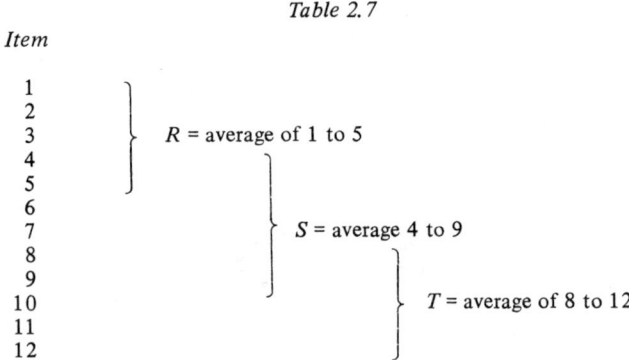

An inspection confirms that if four is too small a number of items for a set to provide an adequate average, and five is taken as an acceptable minimum, then a set of five cannot be taken from the exact middle because it would leave three items on one side and four on the other. Therefore, a set of six is taken from the middle.

In the data being investigated there are seventeen items and we may therefore take three sets of five, seven and five items and determine the averages as follows:

$$R = 1/5 \, (Y_1 + Y_2 + Y_3 + Y_4 + Y_5)$$

$$S = 1/7 \text{ (middle set of seven items)}$$

$$T = 1/5 \, (Y_{n-4} + Y_{n-3} + Y_{n-2} + Y_{n-1} + Y_n)$$

The parameters a, b, and r are determined by inserting the values for R, S, and T into the following general formulae, with x being the number of items selected to compute the average of R and T ($n = 17$, $x = 5$).

$$r^{(n-x)/2} = \frac{T-S}{S-R} \left\{ \text{or,} \log r = \frac{2}{(n-x)} \log \frac{T-S}{S-R} \right\}$$

$$a = \frac{S^2 - TR}{2S - T - R}$$

$$b = \frac{x}{(r + r^2 + \ldots + r^{x-1} + r^x)} \times \frac{(S-R)^2}{2S - T - R}$$

From the data in Table 2.8 we may calculate R, S, and T:

Techniques of Business Analysis

Table 2.8

Item	Sum	Divided by	Average
100, 130, 120, 150, 130	630	5	126 = R
190, 150, 230, 290, 380, 360, 470	2,070	7	295·71 = S
400, 430, 380, 490, 520	2,220	5	444 = T

Therefore $r^{(17-5)/2} = \dfrac{444 - 295 \cdot 71}{295 \cdot 71 - 126} = 0 \cdot 8738$

$r^6 = 0 \cdot 8738$ {or, $\log r = 1/6 \log 0 \cdot 8738$}

$r = \sqrt[6]{0 \cdot 8738}$

$= 0 \cdot 977767$

$a = \dfrac{S^2 - TR}{2S - T - R}$

$= \dfrac{295 \cdot 71^2 - (444 \times 126)}{(2 \times 295 \cdot 71) - 444 - 126}$

$= 1,470 \cdot 6071$

$b = \dfrac{5}{(r + r^2 + r^3 + r^4 + r^5)} \times \dfrac{(S - R)^2}{2S - T - R}$

$= \dfrac{5}{4 \cdot 676227} \times \dfrac{28,801 \cdot 4841}{21 \cdot 42}$

$= 1 \cdot 069238 \times 1,344 \cdot 607101$

$= 1,437 \cdot 705$

Thus, the simple modified exponential

$$Y = a - br^t$$

applied to the data with the parameters calculated becomes,

$$Y = 1,470 \cdot 6071 - 1,437 \cdot 705 \, (0 \cdot 977767)^t$$

where t is the appropriate quarter. Putting $t = 1$, $t = 2$, and $t = 3$, the first three trend figures are as follows:

$$Y_1 = 1{,}470 \cdot 6071 - 1{,}437 \cdot 705(0 \cdot 977767)^1 = 64 \cdot 8666$$
$$Y_2 = 1{,}470 \cdot 6071 - 1{,}437 \cdot 705(0 \cdot 977767)^2 = 96 \cdot 1271$$
$$Y_3 = 1{,}470 \cdot 6071 - 1{,}437 \cdot 705(0 \cdot 977767)^3 = 126 \cdot 6793$$

Continuing the calculations up to $t = 17$, we can establish the simple modified exponential trend, as in Table 2.9.

Table 2.9

Year	Qtr	S.M.E. trend	Year	Qtr	S.M.E. trend
1	1	65	3	1	296
	2	96		2	322
	3	126		3	348
	4	157		4	373
2	1	186	4	1	397
	2	214		2	421
	3	242		3	445
	4	270		4	467
			5	1	490

The Gompertz is calculated similarly, but R, S, and T are the averages of the logs of sales (Table 2.10).

Table 2.10

Qtr	Y	Log Y	
1/1	100	2·00	
1/2	130	2·11394	
1/3	120	2·07918	$10 \cdot 4831/5 = 2 \cdot 0966 = R$
1/4	150	2·17609	
2/1	130	2·11394	
2/2	190	2·27875	
2/3	150	2·17609	
2/4	230	2·36173	
3/1	290	2·4724	$17 \cdot 0872/7 = 2 \cdot 4410 = S$
3/2	380	2·57978	
3/3	360	2·5563	
3/4	470	2·67209	
4/1	400	2·60206	
4/2	430	2·63347	
4/3	380	2·57978	$13 \cdot 2216/5 = 2 \cdot 6443 = T$
4/4	490	2·69019	$n = 17$
5/1	520	2·716	

The formula for the Gompertz curve is,

$$\log Y = a - br^t$$

and the parameters a, b, and r are established as before by the general formulae:

$$r^{(n-x)/2} = \frac{T-S}{S-R} \left\{ \text{or,} \log r = \frac{2}{(n-x)} \log \frac{T-S}{S-R} \right\}$$

$$a = \frac{S^2 - TR}{2S - T - R}$$

$$b = \frac{x}{(r + r^2 + \ldots + r^x)} \times \frac{(S-R)^2}{2S - T - R}$$

where x is the number of items taken for the average of R, S, and T, but here is taken to be 5. Therefore,

$$r^{(17-5)/2} = \frac{2 \cdot 6443 - 2 \cdot 441}{2 \cdot 441 - 2 \cdot 0966} = \frac{0 \cdot 2033}{0 \cdot 3444}$$

$$r^6 = 0 \cdot 5903$$

$$r = \sqrt[6]{0 \cdot 5903}$$

$$= \underline{0 \cdot 915895}$$

$$a = \frac{(2 \cdot 441)^2 - (2 \cdot 6443 \times 2 \cdot 0966)}{(2 \times 2 \cdot 441) - 2 \cdot 6443 - 2 \cdot 0966}$$

$$= \frac{0 \cdot 4145}{0 \cdot 1411}$$

$$= \underline{2 \cdot 9376}$$

$$b = \frac{5}{(0 \cdot 915895 + 0 \cdot 915895^2 + \ldots + 0 \cdot 915895^5)} \times \frac{(2 \cdot 441 - 2 \cdot 0966)^2}{0 \cdot 1411}$$

$$= \frac{5}{3 \cdot 87127} \times \frac{0 \cdot 1186}{0 \cdot 1411}$$

$$= 1 \cdot 291566 \times 0 \cdot 8405$$

$$= \underline{1 \cdot 0856}$$

Thus the Gompertz formula based on the data is

$$\log Y = 2 \cdot 9376 - 1 \cdot 08556(0 \cdot 915895)^t$$

where t is the appropriate quarter. In the first three quarters, $t = 1$, $t = 2$, and $t = 3$, the Gompertz formula gives the following three trend figures:

$\log Y_1 = 2 \cdot 9376 - 1 \cdot 0856(0 \cdot 915895)^1 = 1 \cdot 94334 \quad Y_1 = 87 \cdot 76$
$\log Y_2 = 2 \cdot 9376 - 1 \cdot 0856(0 \cdot 915895)^2 = 2 \cdot 02693 \quad Y_2 = 106 \cdot 4$
$\log Y_3 = 2 \cdot 9376 - 1 \cdot 0856(0 \cdot 915895)^3 = 2 \cdot 10355 \quad Y_3 = 126 \cdot 92$

We can now calculate the rounded trend of unit sales (Table 2.11).

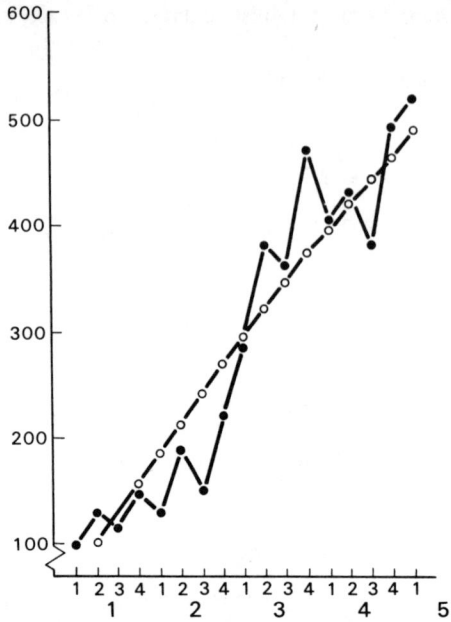

Exhibit 2.2 Original data and simple modified exponential

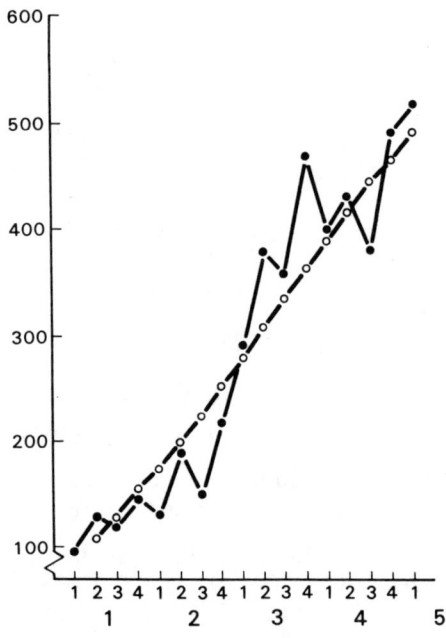

Exhibit 2.3 Original data and Gompertz

Table 2.11

Year	Qtr	Gompertz trend	Year	Qtr	Gompertz trend
1	1	88	3	1	279
	2	106		2	307
	3	127		3	335
	4	149		4	363
2	1	173	4	1	390
	2	198		2	417
	3	224		3	444
	4	251		4	469
			5	1	494

The estimates for the second quarter of year 5 are now compared, as follows:

Line of least squares	539 units
Simple modified exponential	511
Log trend value	664
Gompertz	518

We have now illustrated a number of ways in which a time series can be analysed in the cases and, doubtless, you will be able to apply other techniques to the data. The various trends established with the actual data are shown in Exhibits 2.2 to 2.5. One fact appears to emerge — straight-line projections offer the considerable advantages of simplicity to operate, reasonable accuracy for the data being investigated and ease of recalculating. For example, you may decide that only the last few data in the series have any appropriate impact on unit sales and a straight-line projection of the last few quarters might be useful. We have projected the line of best fit of the last seven terms in Table 2.12.

Table 2.12

Y	d	d^2	Yd
360	−3	9	−1,080
470	−2	4	− 940
400	−1	1	− 400
430	0	0	0
380	1	1	380
490	2	4	980
520	3	9	1,560
$\Sigma Y = 3,050$		$\Sigma d^2 = 28$	$\Sigma Yd = 500$

$a = \Sigma Y/n = 3,050/7 = 435 \cdot 71$
$b = \Sigma Yd/\Sigma d^2 = 17 \cdot 86$
$Y = 435 \cdot 71 + 17 \cdot 86d$; and Y for 5/2 = $435 \cdot 71 + 17 \cdot 86 \times 4 = 507$ units.

2.3 Complexity Analysis

What has been done so far is to demonstrate that logical analysis tends to highlight the difficulties rather than to simplify them. The situation is, in fact, very much more complicated than it appears to be on the surface, and the wide fluctuations of the irregular factors in the trends emphasizes this. The method of investigation

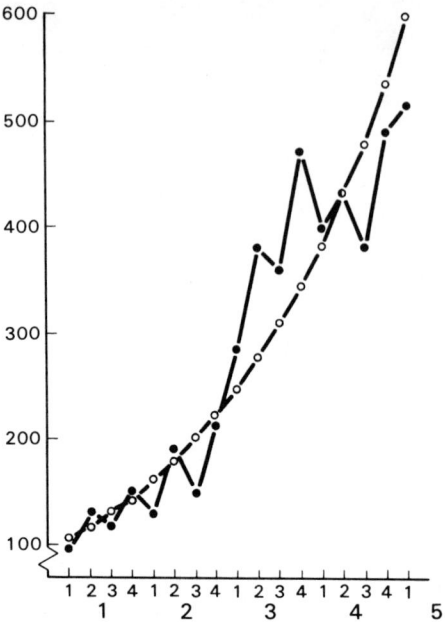

Exhibit 2.4 Original data and logarithmic trend

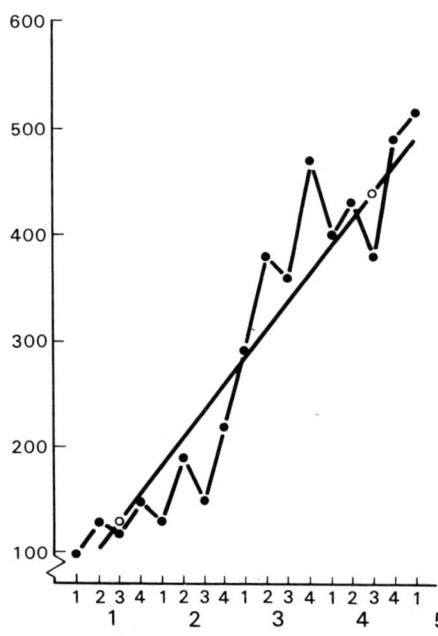

Exhibit 2.5 Original data and the line of best fit, using least squares method

called for may be described as 'complexity analysis', because it is aimed at uncovering the complexities of a situation and showing the manager the real position. In effect, it is attempting to diagnose the disease. It produces no startling revelations, no magic formulae that can substitute for qualitative management decisions, but a suggestion that, when all possibilities have been considered and analysed, it may make good sense to base decisions on the most salient but simple criteria. You will find in practically all analytical explorations that continual linear projections using new data as soon as they are available offer a strong tool for management operations; but the sad truth is we usually have to conduct a fairly deep analysis to establish this. There are other areas of business analysis, notably finance, where complexity analysis reveals a state of affairs that cannot be treated by simple methods, and amelioration requires fundamental constraints on company operations.

With regard to the data we have been investigating, let us now suppose that we have made an estimate, which must necessarily be a qualitative one based on the quantitative analysis, for the second quarter of the fifth year. This estimate is 540 units and, if these are priced at £20 less 10 per cent, we have the following:

Sales 540 @ £20	£10,800
Less 10 per cent discount	1,080
Net turnover	£9,720

To maintain the same net turnover but offering $12\frac{1}{2}$ per cent discount,

$$\frac{9{,}720}{0{\cdot}875 \times £20} = \frac{9{,}720}{17{\cdot}50} = 556$$

That is, to achieve the same net turnover of £9,720, we have to sell 556 at this higher rate of discount:

Sales 556 @ £20	£11,120
Less $12\frac{1}{2}$ per cent discount	1,390
Net turnover	£9,730

A sales manager might feel confident in granting the extra $2\frac{1}{2}$ per cent discount if he knew that he could sell another sixteen or even twenty units. Let us analyse this further. Suppose the manufacturing costs are £10 each unit and that the selling expenses (apart from the discount) will be £3,000 for the period. Therefore,

Sales 540 @ £20		£10,800	Sales 556 @ £20		£11,120
Less manufacturing cost		5,400	Less manufacturing cost		5,560
		5,400			5,560
Less expenses	£3,000		Less expenses	£3,000	
Discount 10 per cent	1,080		Discount $12\frac{1}{2}$ per cent	1,390	
		4,080			4,390
Net profit		£1,320	Net profit		£1,170

The position is quite clear — £150 less profit will be made. The question is: How many units must be sold at the higher rate of discount ($12\frac{1}{2}$ per cent) to maintain the profit at a level of not less than £1,320?

The calculation is based on the following:

$$0.9 \times (540 \times £20) - (540 \times £10) - £3{,}000 = £1{,}320$$

and by putting N for the number to be sold and 0·875 instead of 0·9, because we are receiving 87·5 per cent of the price and not 90 per cent, we have,

$$0.875 \times (N \times £20) - (N \times £10) - £3{,}000 = £1{,}320$$
$$17.5N - 10N - £3{,}000 = £1{,}320$$
$$7.5N = £4{,}320$$

from which $N = 576$ which we can check:

Sales 576 @ £20		£11,520
Less manufacturing cost at £10		5,760
		5,760
Less expenses	£3,000	
Discount 12½ per cent of £11,520	1,440	4,440
	Net profit	£1,320

2.4 Game Theory

It is very important to follow through any particular analysis to calculate the effects in other areas. We have seen how trend analysis can be linked with discount and profit assessment; now let us consider another connexion between statistical analysis and profit. In the determination of likely strategies that may be adopted by a company there is the interesting exercise of 'game theory', which is concerned with general situations of conflict over time. The technique can be demonstrated with two people, X and Y, who can adopt various strategies, such as high price or low price, heavy promotion or light promotion, restricting sales to appointed dealers or operating through discount and cash and carry stores, TV advertising or press advertising and exhibitions, and so on. Labelling the strategies that X can adopt as A and B, and the strategies that Y can adopt as C and D, it may be possible to determine that if X adopts strategy A and Y adopts strategy C, then X gains 20 per cent of the available market — let us call this 'wins 20'. Assuming that the other likely outcomes are known by both X and Y, the resulting wins and losses can be arrayed in the form of a matrix:

		Y	
		Strategy C	Strategy D
X	Strategy A	X wins 20	X wins 30
	Strategy B	Y wins 10	Y wins 20

The question now is, who will play first — that is, who makes the first move in the market? If X makes the first move, he will adopt strategy A because he always wins; if he adopts strategy B, he always loses. If Y makes the first move, he knows that whichever strategy he adopts, C or D, X will win, because the situation is biased against Y. To minimize his losses Y will play strategy C. Therefore X always adopts strategy A and Y always plays strategy C. This situation can be reduced to the universal language of game theory as in the following matrix:

$$X \begin{pmatrix} & Y & \\ 2 & & 3 \\ -1 & & -2 \end{pmatrix}$$

The figures have been reduced to units for ease of calculation and are always signed for X's wins (positive) and X's losses (negative). Here are some other games:

$$X \begin{pmatrix} & Y & \\ 2 & & -2 \\ -1 & & 3 \end{pmatrix}$$

If X plays row 1, Y will play column 2 and win 2 (−2 means that X loses 2); if X plays row 2, Y will play column 1 and win 1. If Y plays first and plays column 1, X will play row 1 and win 2; if Y plays column 2, X will play row 2 and win 3. In the following game,

$$X \begin{pmatrix} & Y & & \\ -3 & 4 & & 2 \\ 1 & 1 & & -3 \\ -2 & 2 & & 1 \end{pmatrix}$$

Y observes that if he plays column 2, X will win every time; if he plays column 1, the most that X can win is 1; if he plays column 3, X can win 2. Y will therefore want to play column 1. If X plays first, and plays row 1 or row 2, this will enable Y to make the appropriate response and win 3 each strategy; if X plays row 3, Y plays column 1 and wins 2.

An interesting feature of these three situations is that in only one, the first one, is there a strategy that is always adopted irrespective of who makes the first move. If we look at the first game again and *underline the lowest figures in each row* and *encircle the highest figure in each column* we have,

$$X \begin{pmatrix} & Y & \\ \underline{\textcircled{2}} & & \textcircled{3} \\ -1 & & \underline{-2} \end{pmatrix}$$

The 2 is both underlined and encircled and, with the assumption that X and Y are intelligent people, this is the strategy played every time, provided the matrix remains unaltered. This is termed a 'saddle point', and is also the 'solution' to the game because 'pure' strategy is adopted. If you underline and encircle the other games, you will find no saddle points. When no saddle point exists, mixed strategies are adopted by the participants, which means that both X and Y will play strategies a certain proportion of the time in an endeavour to optimize their winnings. Consider the following game with no saddle point:

$$X \begin{pmatrix} & Y & \\ 4 & & 2 \\ 1 & & 3 \end{pmatrix}$$

It is biased in favour of X but there are still the decisions to be made by X and Y on the adopting of various strategies for proportions of the time. Let q be the proportion of time that X plays row 1 to optimize his winnings, so that $(1-q)$ is the proportion of the time he will play row 2. Similarly, for Y, let p be the proportion of the time playing column 1 and $(1-p)$ the proportion of time playing column 2. The solving of this situation of mixed strategies is therefore that given in Table 2.13.

Table 2.13

	If Y plays column 1	If Y plays column 2
X plays row 1 q of the time	X wins 4 q of the time	X wins 2 q of the time
X plays row 2 $(1-q)$ of the time	X wins 1 $(1-q)$ of the time	X wins 3 $(1-q)$ of the time
X's expected winnings	$4q + 1(1-q)$ when Y plays column 1	$2q + 3(1-q)$ when Y plays column 2

To optimize X's winnings, irrespective of whether Y plays column 1 or 2, we put,

$$4q + 1(1-q) \text{ equal to } 2q + 3(1-q)$$
$$4q + 1 - q = 2q + 3 - 3q$$
$$4q - q - 2q + 3q = 3 - 1$$
$$4q = 2$$
$$q = \tfrac{1}{2} \quad (1 - q = \tfrac{1}{2})$$

Therefore X should play row 1 50 per cent of the time and row 2 50 per cent of the time to optimize his winnings. This is best decided by a random selection, such as with tossing a coin, because the probability of a 'head' or a 'tail' is always 50/50 irrespective of how many times the coin is tossed. The algebra above can fortunately be quickly simplified, as follows:

$$X \begin{pmatrix} & Y & \\ 4 & & 2 \\ 1 & & 3 \end{pmatrix} \quad \begin{matrix} 4 - 2 = 2 \\ 1 - 3 = -2 \end{matrix} \quad \begin{matrix} 2 \\ 2 \end{matrix}$$

Along each row, subtract the figure in the second column from the figure in the first column; then reverse the results but ignore the signs. X plays row 1 twice out of four times, and row 2 twice out of four times (50 per cent each). Using this simplified method, we can now solve for Y's optimum play:

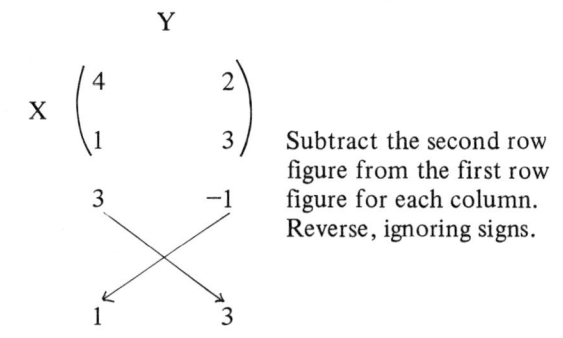

$$X \begin{pmatrix} 4 & 2 \\ 1 & 3 \end{pmatrix}$$

$$\begin{matrix} 3 & -1 \end{matrix}$$

Subtract the second row figure from the first row figure for each column. Reverse, ignoring signs.

$$\begin{matrix} 1 & 3 \end{matrix}$$

Therefore Y should play column 1 once out of four times (25 per cent) and column 2 three out of four (75 per cent).

The situation is biased in favour of X, who will always win, and, if the matrix remains the same and Y plays his optimum strategy, then X will always tend to win $2\frac{1}{2}$, as explained below:

$$X \begin{matrix} & \frac{1}{4} & \frac{3}{4} \\ \frac{1}{2} & \begin{pmatrix} 4 & 2 \\ 1 & 3 \end{pmatrix} \\ \frac{1}{2} & \end{matrix}$$

$$\frac{1}{4}[(4 \times \tfrac{1}{2}) + (1 \times \tfrac{1}{2})] + \tfrac{3}{4}[(2 \times \tfrac{1}{2}) + (3 \times \tfrac{1}{2})]$$
$$= \tfrac{1}{4}(2 + \tfrac{1}{2}) + \tfrac{3}{4}(1 + 1\tfrac{1}{2})$$
$$= 2\tfrac{1}{2}$$

Let us now apply this game theory to a situation where two companies have both carried out marketing research and possess similar information on the market with regard to demand for their products at various price levels. The market shares for each can be shown by the market share for A (Table 2.14).

Table 2.14

A's likely share of market

		B's price		
		£5.25	£5.00	£4.75
	£4.80	45 per cent	30 per cent	25 per cent
A's price	£4.50	65 per cent	60 per cent	50 per cent
	£4.20	70 per cent	65 per cent	55 per cent

32   *Business Analysis for Marketing Managers*

By underlining the lowest share in each row and encircling the highest in each column we can see that a saddle point occurs where both A's and B's prices are at their lowest. This would be optimum strategy for each to adopt if nothing is done to disturb the matrix values, *other things being equal*. However, linking this statistical investigation with financial considerations and assuming (for arithmetical peace of mind) that 100 products will be sold in the market, we can insert the turnover at the various prices and market shares (Table 2.15).

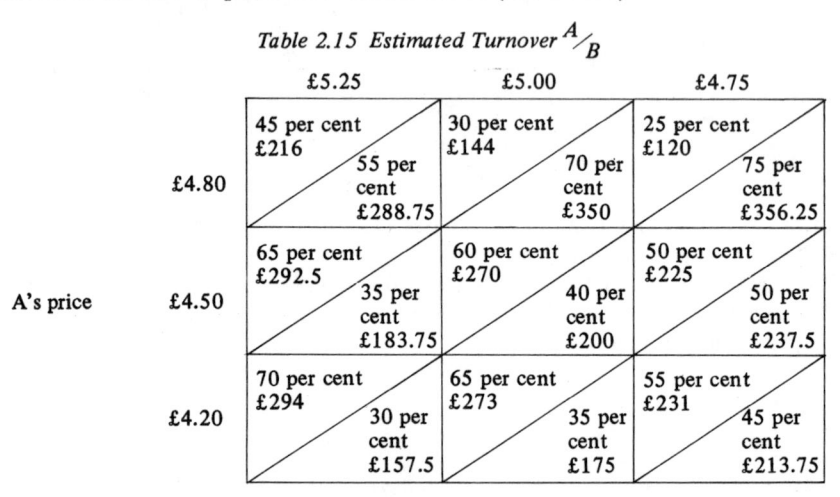

Table 2.15 Estimated Turnover A/B

		£5.25	£5.00	£4.75
A's price	£4.80	45 per cent £216 / 55 per cent £288.75	30 per cent £144 / 70 per cent £350	25 per cent £120 / 75 per cent £356.25
	£4.50	65 per cent £292.5 / 35 per cent £183.75	60 per cent £270 / 40 per cent £200	50 per cent £225 / 50 per cent £237.5
	£4.20	70 per cent £294 / 30 per cent £157.5	65 per cent £273 / 35 per cent £175	55 per cent £231 / 45 per cent £213.75

The pricing situation A £4.20 and B £4.75 still appears to give the optimum results. If A prices first, he will select £4.20 (to obtain £231 turnover), believing that B will price at £4.75 to achieve £231.75 turnover (the highest possible for B in that row). This is therefore still the saddle point, and a pure strategy optimizes returns to each. Table 2.16 shows another situation.

Table 2.16

A's likely share of market

		B's price		
		£4	£5	£6
A's price	£3	(55 per cent)	(65 per cent)	(70 per cent)
	£4	<u>50</u> per cent	60 per cent	65 per cent
	£5	<u>25</u> per cent	30 per cent	45 per cent

The saddle point occurs at A £3 and B £4. Extending Table 2.16 at the prices and market shares we have the turnovers of Table. 2.17 (assuming that 100 products are available).

A different situation emerges now because the saddle point that was originally indicated (A £3 and B £4) gives A 55 per cent of the market but less turnover. A is unlikely to price at £3; he is more likely to price at £4 because he is assured of a minimum of £200 turnover, which is more than he secures by pricing at £3 and

Table 2.17 Estimated Turnover A/B

		£4	£5	£6
A's price	£3	55 per cent £165 / 45 per cent £180	65 per cent £195 / 35 per cent £175	70 per cent £210 / 30 per cent £180
	£4	50 per cent £200 / 50 per cent £200	60 per cent £240 / 40 per cent £200	65 per cent £260 / 35 per cent £210
	£5	25 per cent £125 / 75 per cent £300	30 per cent £150 / 70 per cent £350	45 per cent £225 / 55 per cent £330

getting 55 per cent of the market. But if A does price at £4, will B price at £4 or £5 to achieve £200 turnover at each price, or £6 to achieve £210 turnover? If B does price at £6, going for the higher turnover, A achieves an even higher turnover of £260.

We have now moved into the area of judgment — qualitative judgment based on quantitative analysis. More factors will doubtless have to be taken into consideration. As far as game theory is concerned, it is possible to reduce this 3 x 3 situation by assuming that A will never price at £5 because he would allow B to secure too high a market share and turnover; and B is unlikely to price at £6 because he does not want A to obtain too large a market share. This game is then reduced to a 2 x 2 situation, although there are still a number of variables to be considered, and you may care to explore further yourself.

Sufficient elementary treatment of game theory has been set out, and an indication of how it may be linked with market shares and turnover has been given. As it is unlikely that the two companies represented by A and B would be producing identical products or at identical costs, a consideration of profit would require more information than we have available in the examples.

2.5 Correlation Analysis

All the data we have looked at so far have been interval data, but, when we consider whether there is any statistical association between two or more sets of data, it is important to appreciate the limitations of various forms of correlation analysis. In a description of a particular market its outlets may be classified as 'large stores' and 'small stores', while turnovers might be graded as 'over £200,000 a year' and 'under £200,000 a year'. At one extreme we might have the position where eight stores are classified as large and all have a turnover in excess of £200,000 a year. If we further find that the size of the stores is graded according to whether they have more or less than 30,000 ft^2, then this data can be set out as in Table 2.18.

Business Analysis for Marketing Managers

Table 2.18

	Low Sales	High Sales
Small stores	4	0
Large stores	0	4

It is clear that there is perfect correlation, because the size of the store corresponds exactly with the size of turnover. The amount of quantitative analysis that can be undertaken with nominal data such as these is limited. The degree of association between two mutually exclusive categories can be determined with the help of the mean square contingency coefficient phi (ϕ). The calculation is based on the four cells labelled $a, b, c,$ and d (Table 2.19).

Table 2.19

	Low Sales	High Sales
Small stores	a	b
Large stores	c	d

The formula for phi is:

$$\phi = \frac{ad - bc}{\sqrt{(a+c)(b+d)(a+b)(c+d)}}$$

and inserting the data from above data,

$$\phi = \sqrt{\frac{(4 \times 4) - (0 \times 0)}{4 \times 4 \times 4 \times 4}} = \frac{16}{16} = 1$$

Thus the formula indicates perfect correlation.

However, it is more likely that store turnover will relate to floor space in other than a perfectly correlated manner, as in the Table 2.20.

Table 2.20

	Low Sales	High Sales
Small stores	4	0
Large stores	1	3

From Table 2.20 the formula indicates a high degree of correlation:

$$\phi = \sqrt{\frac{(4 \times 3) - (1 \times 0)}{5 \times 3 \times 4 \times 3}} = \frac{12}{13.42} = 0.89$$

If the eight stores were arrayed as in Table 2.21,

Table 2.21

	Low Sales	High Sales
Small stores	2	2
Large stores	2	2

phi would be,

$$\phi = \sqrt{\frac{(2 \times 2) - (2 \times 2)}{4 \times 4 \times 4 \times 4}} = \frac{0}{16} = 0$$

and there is no correlation whatsoever.

We may not possess actual figures but just the ranking of the eight stores in order of size and in order of turnover (Table 2.22).

Table 2.22

	Ranked in order of size	Ranked in order of turnover
A	1	1
B	2	2
C	3	4
D	4	3
E	5	5
F	6	6
G	7	7
H	8	8

In that case it is possible to measure the relation between two such ranked orders with the correlation coefficient called Spearman's rank order correlation, often abbreviated to Spearman's rho or the symbol r_s. It lies between +1 and −1.

The formula for Spearman's rank order correlation coefficient is,

$$r_s = 1 - \frac{6\Sigma d^2}{n(n^2 - 1)}$$

which, in words, means that r_s equals

one minus $\dfrac{\text{six times the sum of rank order differences}}{\text{total number of items times one less than itself squared}}$.

Therefore, with the ranked data from above, we get Table 2.23.

Table. 2.23

Size X	Turnover T	Rank difference X − Y = d	(Rank difference)² (X − Y)² = d²
1	1	0	0
2	2	0	0
3	4	−1	1
4	3	1	1
5	5	0	0
6	6	0	0
7	7	0	0
8	8	0	0

From this table it is clear that $n = 8$ and $6\Sigma d^2 = 12$ and, therefore,

$$r_s = 1 - \frac{12}{8(64-1)} = 1 - \frac{12}{504}$$

$$= 0.98$$

This is near to 1 and therefore indicates a high degree of statistical correlation between the rank order of store size and store turnover.

Suppose that we are now given the actual data concerning store size and store turnover, as in Table 2.24.

Table 2.24

Store	Selling space (000 ft^2) X	Annual sales (£000) Y
A	15	100
B	20	105
C	29	160
D	40	110
E	48	165
F	65	205
G	76	210
H	80	350

To calculate Pearson's coefficient of correlation we need n, ΣX, ΣX^2, ΣY, ΣY^2, and ΣXY.

$$\Sigma X = 373 \quad \Sigma X^2 = 21{,}771$$
$$\Sigma Y = 1{,}405 \quad \Sigma Y^2 = 294{,}575$$
$$\Sigma XY = 77{,}845 \quad n = 8$$

The formula for Pearson's coefficient of correlation is,

$$R = \frac{n\Sigma XY - \Sigma X \Sigma Y}{\sqrt{\{n\Sigma X^2 - (\Sigma X)^2\}\{n\Sigma Y^2 - (\Sigma Y)^2\}}}$$

$$R = \frac{8 \times 77{,}845 - 373 \times 1{,}405}{\sqrt{\{8 \times 21{,}771 - (373)^2\}\{8 \times 294{,}575 - (1{,}405)^2\}}}$$

$$= \frac{98{,}695}{\sqrt{(35{,}039)(382{,}575)}} = \frac{98{,}695}{115{,}780 \cdot 16}$$

$$R = 0.85$$

This is a reasonably high degree of correlation and indicates, by means of the coefficient of determination ($R^2 = 0.85^2 = 0.72$) that 72 per cent of the total variation between store size and store turnover is accounted for. This leads one to conclude that the two variables are closely related, and that a knowledge of selling space enables a prediction to be made of likely turnover.

Other data that are now worth searching for in the case material are the gross margin and any other expenses relating to the stores. By now you should be

Techniques of Business Analysis

expecting certain data to follow a pattern and, in this example, it is reasonable to expect that the larger the store (in terms of selling space and therefore buying ability) the less might be the percentage buying costs, since the larger the store the more orders it can place with suppliers. Table 2.25 shows gross margins and other expenses that may be used in our calculations.

Table 2.25

Store	Gross margin (per cent)	Other expenses (£)
A	40	24,000
B	41	28,350
C	42	48,000
D	41	36,300
E	42	52,800
F	43	69,700
G	43	79,800
H	45	143,500

With this further information, it is possible to extend the analysis, as in Table 2.26.

As a matter of interest, the correlation coefficient of store selling area and percentage profit may be calculated. See Table 2.27.

Table 2.27

Area (000 ft²) X	Percentage profit Y
15	16
20	14
29	12
40	8
48	10
65	9
76	5
80	4

$\Sigma X = 373$ $\Sigma X^2 = 21,771$
$\Sigma Y = 78$ $\Sigma Y^2 = 882$
$n = 8$ $\Sigma XY = 2,953$

$$R = \frac{8 \times 2,953 - 373 \times 78}{\sqrt{\{8 \times 21,771 - (373)^2\}\{8 \times 882 - (78)^2\}}}$$

$$= \frac{-5,470}{\sqrt{(35,029)(972)}} = \frac{-5,470}{5,835 \cdot 92}$$

$$= -0 \cdot 94$$

This indicates that $R^2 = -0 \cdot 94^2 = 0 \cdot 88$, so that 88 per cent of the variations are explained and a very high degree of inverse correlation exists between the size of selling area and the percentage profit obtained. It is here possibly where one might

Table 2.26

Store	Area (ft²)	Sales (£)	Sales per ft² (£)	Costs (per cent)	Gross margin (per cent)	Gross profit (£)	Other expenses (£)	Net profit (£)	Per cent profit
A	15,000	100,000	6·67	60	40	40,000	24,000	16,000	16
B	20,000	105,000	5·25	59	41	43,050	28,350	14,700	14
C	29,000	160,000	5·52	58	42	67,200	48,000	19,200	12
D	40,000	110,000	2·75	59	41	45,100	36,300	8,800	8
E	48,000	165,000	3·44	58	42	69,300	52,800	16,500	10
F	65,000	205,000	3·15	57	43	88,150	69,700	18,450	9
G	76,000	210,000	2·76	57	43	90,300	79,800	10,500	5
H	80,000	350,000	4·38	55	45	157,500	143,500	14,000	4

start a more extensive analysis of the data to discover whether there are reasons for the statistical relations between store size and store turnover, and between store size and percentage profit. These relations, which have been demonstrated statistically, are not necessarily causal, and to base decisions for future company operation on the erroneous assumption that correlation and causation are synonymous is likely to prove disastrous.

The higher the selling area the lower the net profit, and, assuming that all eight stores belonged to the same group and adequate data are available, further investigations could be made into sales-per-square-foot and expenses-per-square-foot of departments. Sales-per-square-foot of each store has already been calculated, and a widely dispersed pattern uncovered. The smallest store has the highest sales-per-square-foot, and the largest store the fourth highest.

The limitations of such statistical aids as correlation analysis for nominal, ordinal and interval data are important. Too much reliance must not be placed on one particular approach, and arbitrary divisions of data should always be suspected.

Previously we calculated hypothetical figures for phi based on 'large' and 'small' stores because we did not, at that time, possess data on the particular stores. Using 30,000 ft^2 and £200,000 p.a. as variables we have,

$$\phi = \frac{(3 \times 3) - (2 \times 0)}{\sqrt{(3+2)(0+3)(3+0)(2+3)}} = 0.6$$

and using 30,000 ft^2 and £150,000 p.a. as variables we have,

$$\phi = \frac{(2 \times 4) - (1 \times 1)}{\sqrt{(2+1)(1+4)(2+1)(1+4)}} = 0.467$$

There is a significant difference between these coefficients simply because we have used £150,000 p.a. and £200,000 p.a. as arbitrary divisions. If the variables are 50,000 ft^2 and £200,000 p.a., there is perfect correlation:

$$\phi = \frac{(5 \times 3) - (0 \times 0)}{\sqrt{(5+0)(0+3)(5+0)(0+3)}} = 1.00$$

The point to remember is that we are using the mean square contingency coefficient as a test of correlation on nominal data, and if we possess (as we do) ordinal and interval data, then more accurate statistical assessments can be made. We are merely pointing out the dangers of using phi. For example, the average size of store might be the acceptable division between 'small' and 'large' stores, and the average turnover the division between 'small' and 'large' turnover – these are 46,000 ft^2 and £175,000 p.a. respectively. Using these, phi can be calculated as follows:

$$\phi = \frac{(4 \times 3) - (1 \times 0)}{\sqrt{(4+1)(0+3)(4+0)(1+3)}} = 0.77$$

This, as we might expect, is a high degree of correlation, since the division between 'small' and 'large' turnover and size is either side of the average turnover and average size. This highlights the danger of relying too much on the mean square contingency coefficient phi, which is all that can be used with nominal data: an arbitrary division of the nominal data into two sets can introduce considerable bias. Phi is best used with nominal data when they are obviously dichotomous, such as smokers and non-smokers, and men and women. Suppose we have,

	Men	Women
Smokers	20	20
Non-smokers	29	31

Then, $$\phi = \frac{(20 \times 31) - (29 \times 20)}{\sqrt{(20 + 29)(20 + 31)(20 + 20)(29 + 31)}} = 0.02$$

A very low correlation between the variables indicates that there is practically no statistical significance between sex and the tendency to smoke. In addition, there is obviously no argument as to where the dividing line is for both variables. Let us now turn to a closer examination that may be made of any financial data contained in a case.

2.6 Financial Analysis

When looking into the financial operations of a company, one must consider the historical and control aspects. Historical investigation is only of value if it leads to bases for decision-making, although the usual historical management ratios are difficult to translate into action. For example, a company that has achieved a return on funds in the past three years of 10 per cent, 8 per cent and 9 per cent, might be expected to achieve 10 per cent or higher during the next year. But, any business analyst making that decision must translate it into specific objectives that can be agreed with the appropriate managers. It is not expected or even suggested that marketing managers should be financial analysts, but every manager who makes decisions must be aware of the financial implications of those decisions.

The primary ratios (profit/funds employed) and secondary ratios (profit/sales, sales/funds employed) are of very restricted value if only one or two years can be calculated. While it is possible to compare these ratios with other firms' results, by means of, say, an Interfirm Comparison Index, there are such wide variations possible in the same industry, and even between similar companies, that it is more useful to establish the company's particular trend of ratios over as long a period of years as is reasonably possible from the case data. It is not always possible to obtain all ratios from case material, and many gaps will become apparent. Most cases possess profit and loss accounts (or revenue accounts) and balance sheets, but, where these are not given, it is possible that financial analysis can only be undertaken after the data has been extracted from the case text. If the final accounts are available – especially if there are several years' accounts – then a start should be made to determine certain relations. Ratio analysis is instructive in so far as it indicates areas of good or poor management of a company, but you should concentrate on those ratios that are sensitive to direct control procedures. Obviously profit to funds is not one, as it is a historical aspect and can only be affected indirectly. Exhibit 2.6 shows a suggested arrangement of important ratios.

Exhibit 2.6 is intended to be used as a guide and not as a definitive statement of what must be investigated. The various totals will be found in the final accounts, and it may readily be seen that the ratios which can be affected by the marketing manager's decisions relate directly to selling costs and expenses in getting and filling orders, finished stock control, and control of debtors. The trend of such ratios is usually much more revealing than the individual ratios, although it is possible to determine certain single ratios and use these as a basis for making decisions. Debtors, for example, arise because of sales, and the application of a fairly crude

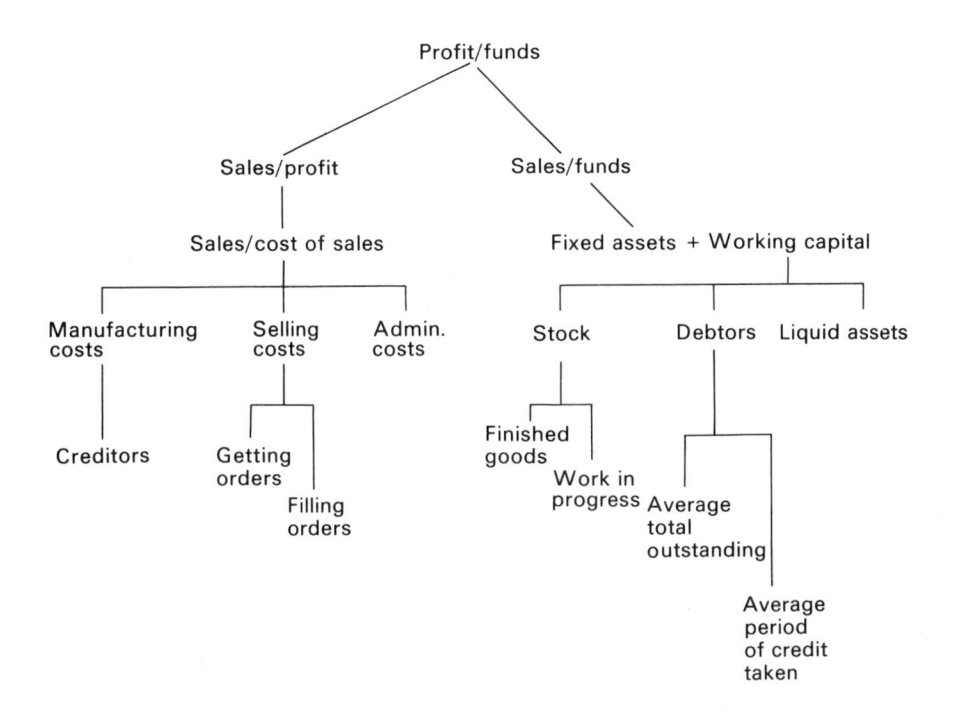

```
                           Profit/funds
                          /            \
                  Sales/profit        Sales/funds
                       |                    \
              Sales/cost of sales    Fixed assets + Working capital
         ┌──────┬──────┬──────┐      ┌──────┬──────┬──────┐
   Manufacturing Selling Admin.    Stock   Debtors  Liquid assets
   costs         costs   costs       |        |
        |          |                 |        |
   Creditors    Getting          Finished   Average
                orders           goods      total
                    |            Work in    outstanding
                 Filling         progress      |
                 orders                     Average
                                            period
                                            of credit
                                            taken
```

Exhibit 2.6 Ratios

formula will indicate the average number of weeks' credit taken by the company's customers, as follows:

$$\frac{\text{Debtors shown in the balance sheet} \times 52}{\text{Sales shown in the same year's profit and loss account}}$$

To illustrate this formula, if a company's sales for the year were £200,000 and in the balance sheet there were £61,500 debtors, then the average number of week's credit taken by customers is indicated by,

$$\frac{61,500 \times 52}{200,000} = 16 \text{ weeks}$$

What we do not know is what proportions of the debtors represent good payers, average payers, bad payers and potential bad debts.

The following formula shows the average number of weeks' credit taken by the company:

$$\frac{\text{Creditors shown in the balance sheet} \times 52}{\text{Purchases from the same year's profit and loss account}}$$

The value of finished stock usually has to be carried by the sales function in a company, so that if the sales manager schedules too great a quantity on production, the value of the quantity that remains excess to actual sales has to be carried by the sales department. Stock control is therefore an important activity to be instituted, and an analysis of a company's finished goods stock might indicate areas for management decisions. To optimize the quantity of stock held, the cost of carrying the stock is made to equal the costs of ordering the stock. This simple arithmetical analysis must not override such considerations as the type of goods being held in stock, because certain products (wood and wooden fabrications, for instance) have to season, spirits and wines have to age, and foodstuffs may need to mature. There are several formulae for determining optimum stock levels and orders. The formula given here is used to establish the optimum number of items that should be on each order placed with a supplier. Let N be the optimum number of items in each order, then,

$$N = \sqrt{\frac{\text{twice the annual usage rate} \times \text{cost of ordering}}{\text{price} \times \text{carrying cost expressed as percentage of average stock}}}$$

This formula is demonstrated particularly in the Upton, Vance and Wells case (Chapter 6). Such a tool, however, is only of use where conditions of certainty are expected, and, as the majority of situations in the cases are shrouded in uncertainty, we are making only an elementary analysis of these situations.

You will find certain approaches to elementary financial analysis helpful: first, the use of a projected revenue account for a certain future period, usually a year, and the projected balance sheet as at the end of that period; and second, the preparation of a cash budget to chart the financial waters between one period and another. Both are of vital importance to any manager charged with the responsibility of making decisions. You must accept that these are crude rule-of-thumb projections that bear a limited relation to normal financial accounting practices but help the non-financial marketing man to appreciate the impact of certain decisions on future results. Here is a simple example to start with.

A company's sales for the year were £1,000, and the cost of producing the goods was maintained at a level of 60 per cent of selling prices. Opening stock is valued at £100 and closing stock at the same figure. Expenses for the year amounted to £300, which comprised £250 for general distribution expenses and £50 for depreciation of assets. Taxation is assumed to be at a rate of 50 per cent, and a dividend has consistently been paid at a rate of 30 per cent. Debtors are assumed to be at a rate of 10 per cent of sales, and creditors at 10 per cent of manufacturing costs. The total value of the fixed assets is £500, and, up to the end of the previous year, they had been depreciated by a total of £150. The company has issued 100 £1 ordinary shares, which have been fully paid up, while the retained profit in the company amounted to £280 in the last balance sheet.

Here is the revenue account:

Sales		£1,000
Opening stock	£100	
Manufacturing cost (60 per cent of sales)	600	
	700	
Less closing stock	100	600
		400
Less expenses:		
Distribution	250	
Depreciation	50	300
		100
Taxation at 50 per cent		50
		50
Dividend (30 per cent on 100 shares of £1)		30
		20
Profit brought forward		280
		£300

A balance sheet as at the end of this period might be as follows:

Fixed assets				£500
Less depreciation (£150 + £50 for current year)				200
				300
Current assets	Stock	£100		
	Debtors	100		
	Cash (by calculation)	10		
			210	
Current liabilities	Creditors	60		
	Taxation	50		
	Overdraft (calculated)	—		
			110	100
				£400
Financed by:				
100 Ordinary £1 shares fully paid up				100
Retained profit				300
				£400

Several of the percentages have already been given in the problem, but if we were going to project a revenue account from these figures, we would be guided by the various percentages of sales from this account as an indication for the next year's figures. In addition, the figures in the balance sheet would be calculated from appropriate reference figures and used to project the picture as it might be at the end of the period.

Here is another, rather more complicated, example.

XYZ Ltd is a company with £10,000 ordinary share capital issued as 10,000 fully paid up £1 shares, and the total profit retained in the company up to the end of the previous year is £33,750. During the past year sales reached £105,000, and the value of the closing stock is £10,000. The company started the year with an opening stock valued at £15,000, and manufacturing costs were as follows: materials, £33,000; labour, £24,000; and overheads in the factory, £3,000.

Expenses are, for simplicity of calculation, grouped into four main categories: salaries, commission and travelling, £18,000; distribution, £5,000; financing, audit, and insurance, £5,000; and depreciation for the year £1,500. Taxation is assumed to be at the rate of 50 per cent, and 20 per cent is to be paid on the shares. During the past year the company has increased its assets to £50,000, and depreciation totalled £6,000 up to the end of the previous year. By the close of business this year the company has debtors of £25,000 and owed its creditors £10,000.

What is the company's cash position at the end of the year's operations?

Here is the suggested revenue account:

Sales					£105,000
Opening stock				£15,000	
Manufacturing costs:	Materials	£33,000			
	Labour	24,000			
	Overheads	3,000			
				60,000	
				75,000	
Closing stock				10,000	
					65,000
					40,000
Less expenses:	Salaries etc.	18,000			
	Distribution	5,000			
	Financing etc.	5,000			
	Depreciation	1,500			
					29,500
					10,500
Taxation (at 50 per cent)					5,250
					5,250
Dividend (say 20 per cent on £10,000)					2,000
					3,250
Profit brought forward					33,750
					£37,000

The balance sheet might look like this:

Fixed assets				£50,000
Less depreciation (£6,000 + £1,500 for this year)				7,500
				42,500
Current assets:	Stock	£10,000		
	Debtors	25,000		
	Cash	0		
			£35,000	
Current liabilities:	Creditors	10,000		
	Taxation	5,250		
	Overdraft	15,250		
			30,500	
				4,500
				£47,000
Financed by:				
10,000 ordinary £1 shares fully paid up				£10,000
Retained profit				37,000
				£47,000

Completion of the profit and loss account is fairly straightforward, but the preparation of the balance sheet is a little more difficult. It is best to calculate the total retained profit in the profit and loss account and add this total to the capital (£37,000 + £10,000) to make £47,000. From this total the fully depreciated fixed assets figure is deducted to arrive at the figure representing the difference between the current assets and current liabilities. Until the account has reached this stage, it is often impossible to decide whether there will be cash balance or overdraft required to make the account balance.

If this set of accounts is to be used as a basis for projecting the next year's figures, the various percentages would have to be noted for use. Salaries, commission etc. are 17 per cent of sales, distribution 5 per cent, and stock 10 per cent of sales. Debtors are 24 per cent of sales, and creditors are 30 per cent of purchases of materials.

Debtors of £25,000 are 12 weeks outstanding, using the formula already mentioned − (25,000 x 52)/105,000 = 12 (approximately). Creditors are 16 weeks outstanding − (10,000 x 52)/33,000 = 16 (approximately). The company is apparently taking 4 months' credit and giving 3 months' credit, while the level of stocks as indicated in the balance sheet represents 5 weeks' sales. Notice that £5,000 of sales were made from stock, which indicates that the manufacturing cost is about 60 per cent of sales.

The company has a number of problems to overcome, not the least of which is to reduce the overdraft of £15,250. Let us decide on a modest price increase, a more vigorous attack on the market next year, and aim for an increased turnover of £150,000. To project these figures (allowing for an increase in price), it can be decided that cost of materials is to be 30 per cent of sales (compared with 33 per cent last year), labour is to be 25 per cent, and overheads at 4 per cent. Closing

Sales				£150,000
	Opening stock		£10,000	
	Materials (30 per cent)	£45,000		
	Labour (25 per cent)	37,500		
	Overheads (4 per cent)	6,000		
			88,500	
			98,500	
	Closing stock		15,000	
				83,500
				66,500
Less expenses:	Salaries etc. (18 per cent)		27,000	
	Distribution (5 per cent)		7,500	
	Financing, etc.		5,000	
	Depreciation		1,500	
				41,000
				25,500
Taxation (50 per cent)				12,750
				12,750
Profit brought forward				37,000
				£49,750

stock will be kept to a maximum of £15,000, and we shall aim to get debtors down to 20 per cent of sales and creditors to, say, 25 per cent of materials purchased. Salaries, commission etc. may be set at an arbitrary level of 18 per cent, and distribution costs at 5 per cent of sales turnover, with financing and depreciation kept at the same figures for the time being. Projecting these into a revenue account, we have the result shown on p. 45.

We can project a balance sheet as at the end of this period as follows:

Fixed assets			£50,000
Less depreciation (£7,500 + 1,500)			9,000
			41,000
Current assets:			
Stock	£15,000		
Debtors	30,000		
Cash	0		
		£45,000	
Current liabilities:			
Creditors	11,250		
Taxation	12,750		
Overdraft (calculated)	2,250		
		26,250	
			18,750
			£59,750
Financed by:			
10,000 ordinary £1 shares fully paid up			10,000
Retained profit			49,750
			£59,750

Projected accounts such as these are of help in determining objectives. We have reduced the overdraft considerably and signposted the areas where control must be exercised — especially stock and debtors. At a deeper level of analysis a cash-flow estimate might highlight problems that are not yet in focus. The cash requirements from month to month (Table 2.28) can be forecast on the following assumptions:

1 Sales through the year are seasonal, with a peak from May through August.
2 Production costs are 60 per cent of selling prices.
3 Production is maintained at a level parallel to sales each month.
4 Expenses of £39,500 (£41,000 less £1,500 depreciation) are apportioned in twelve equal amounts.
5 Interest is charged at the rate of 1 per cent per month on outstanding balances.
6 Cash from sales is received 3 months after those sales. (January, February and March collections would be sales made in the previous year.)

The discrepancy between the cash balance of £2,403 at the end of the year and not only zero cash but also £2,250 overdraft depicted in the projected balance sheet is explained by variations as follows: different production costs; depreciation charge is not in the cash budget calculations; different costs for interest, financing, etc; different debtors, total — £30,000 in balance sheet but October, November, December total £21,000 in cash budget unknown total for creditors.

Table 2.28

	Jan (£)	Feb (£)	Mar (£)	Apl (£)	May (£)	June (£)
Sales	6,000	7,000	8,000	10,000	18,000	25,000
Production (60 per cent)	3,600	4,200	4,800	6,000	10,800	15,000
Expenses	3,292	3,292	3,292	3,292	3,292	3,292
Cash out	6,892	7,492	8,092	9,292	14,092	18,292
Cash in	8,000*	7,000†	6,000‡	6,000	7,000	8,000
Cash flow ±	1,108	(492)	(2,092)	(3,292)	(7,092)	(10,292)
Interest (1 per cent)	152	143	150	172	206	279
Balance	(14,294)§	(14,929)	(17,171)	(20,635)	(27,933)	(38,504)

	July (£)	Aug (£)	Sept (£)	Oct (£)	Nov (£)	Dec (£)
Sales	25,000	20,000	10,000	8,000	7,000	6,000
Production (60 per cent)	15,000	12,000	6,000	4,800	4,200	3,600
Expenses	3,292	3,292	3,292	3,292	3,292	3,292
Cash out	18,292	15,292	9,292	8,092	7,492	6,892
Cash in	10,000	18,000	25,000	25,000	20,000	10,000
Cash flow ±	(8,292)	2,708	15,708	16,908	12,508	3,108
Interest (1 per cent)	385	472	449	297	131	7
Balance	(47,181)	(44,945)	(29,686)	(13,075)	(698)	2,403

* October sales
† November sales
‡ December sales

§ Overdraft £15,250 plus interest £152 less £1,108 cash in.

A more realistic balance sheet for the end of the period can now be projected:

Fixed assets			£50,000
Less depreciation			9,000
			41,000
Current assets:			
Stock	£15,000		
Debtors	21,000		
Cash	2,403		
		£38,403	
Current liabilities:			
Creditors (by adjustment to balance)	6,903		
Taxation	12,750		
Overdraft	0		
		19,653	
			18,750
			£59,750
Financed by:			
10,000 ordinary shares of £1 fully paid up			£10,000
Retained profit			49,750
			£59,750

The main features highlighted by the estimated cash-flow exercise are the need for nearly £50,000 in overdraft, and the disturbing fact that the company has a negative cash balance until the last month of the period. What has appeared to be reasonable with simple revenue account and balance sheet projections becomes doubtful as a proposition after deeper analysis. With the company worth under £50,000, it is a much more difficult task to raise funds to finance the year's proposed activities. This example clearly demonstrates the importance of complexity analysis when making decisions, and you will also have noticed how it is possible to extend further into the conjectural areas and construct powerful working tools for subsequent control of operations.

What remains to be done is to choose the actions to be recommended to the organization. In the light of these assessments, original objectives may need to be amended; if this last example had been an actual case, then any proxy objective initially adopted to increase the turnover from £105,000 to £150,000 would now have required rethinking.

The relative cost benefits of alternative actions must now be compared, and also considered in relation to the facilities and people in the case. It is of little use recommending actions that *you* could carry out if they are entirely beyond the capabilities of people in the case. Organizational and procedural analysis is of help here; identifying the problem and locating the source should be conducted against a background of the organization and its current procedures. If the organization is seen to be a complex, interlinked, interacting system whose elements are people, formal and informal structures, tasks and tools, and the system responds to its environment by means of internal and external procedures, then any actions proposed by the analyser stand a better chance of being relevant to the organization and its methods.

This is not to suggest that all proposed changes will be readily acceptable if they are relevant, and you must appreciate that even minor changes will take time to be implemented. Organizational and procedural changes are similar to the effect seen in a large lake of water when several stones of different sizes are dropped in at different points. The resulting ripples spread outwards from those points, eventually covering the whole lake, but the conflicting ripple effect is similar to the organizational change friction experienced in companies where a number of changes have been made. For example, to change field operations by amalgamating an industrial and a consumer sales force and reallocating areas may take over a year to complete, while a relatively minor promotion of, say, a field manager to a brand manager may produce effects throughout the whole system. If a change is made to one element in a system, there will be a greater or lesser impact (directly or indirectly) on every other element in the system.

Considerable practice is essential if one is to become skilled in the techniques of business analysis. It is not a set of skills that can be acquired just by reading about it — you will only become really proficient at it by 'doing' it. Consequently, in the analyses that follow there is a concentration on the application of techniques, although not every possible technique has been used in every case, and you will profit from selecting suitable techniques from one analysis and applying them to another case. Transferring analytical techniques demonstrated in one case to other situations requires considerable practice, and you should always seek guidance from specialist colleagues when you wish to test your grasp of these applied techniques.

In the real world you will normally have specialist advice available, and it is unlikely that you will be required to analyse business situations regularly. Nevertheless a working knowledge of such techniques enables you to understand more clearly what specialist analysers are saying, and, additionally, to know what questions to ask.

Chapters 3 to 6 are laid out to a similar pattern — the case given first in full followed by an analysis using selected appropriate techniques. These analyses serve two purposes, providing a means whereby you can exercise and develop your own analytical skills, and considerable evidence on which you may base your proposed courses of action. The analyses contain questions for you to consider, and these are intended to draw your attention to salient points, facts or statistics in the case or to give you opportunities of applying techniques to the case material. Answers to the questions are given at the end of each chapter, and they often indicate specific areas where proposed actions are required. For example, if you give some thought to Q.3.8 in the Medway Appliances case (Chapter 3), and its answer A.3.8, you will appreciate that the majority of the questions that remain unanswered cover those areas where, in fact, actions must be recommended to the company.

BIBLIOGRAPHY

To provide an appendix that would adequately cover all the techniques that have been employed in this book would require another book of much greater length, if these techniques were to be explained from basic principles. There are dangers in attempting to give the reader short-cut methods to mathematical, statistical and financial numeracy; and to array 'simple' explanations of algebraic formulae, probability inferences and investment analyses is to imply that little effort is necessary to be able to apply them generally. Where such techniques have been used in the book, adequate step-by-step explanations have been given either in the text or in the answers to the self-assessment questions in Chapters 3–6.

For the reader who wishes either to revise or to develop and expand his knowledge of quantitative analysis, the books listed here, together with a brief description of their scope and content, should prove to be of considerable help. Needless to say, the selection of books for this list in no way represents definitive suggestion that they are all necessary or that other books are not as relevant. They have been selected as representative of a cross-section of books used by the author in his own studies of business analysis.

Albanese, R. *Management: Toward Accountability for Performance* (Richard D. Irwin). Although styled as an introductory book on business management, it is comprehensive and surveys a large number of topics important for marketing managers. The text places major emphasis on the manager's accountability for efficient and effective performance. The book is very well organized, very easy to read, and very easy to understand. Each chapter has a set of objectives, together with an outline of the substance; at the end of each chapter comes a list of study objectives, which crystallize the points covered in the chapter. There are also supplements at the end of most chapters; these are designed to illustrate the principles discussed in the chapter and consist mostly of practical case histories.

Battersby, Albert. *Mathematics in Management* (Pelican). The purpose of this book is stated to be an attempt to establish better communication between managers and mathematicians. The mathematical development has been kept to a fairly elementary level and covers network analysis, applications of the equation of a straight line, linear programming, simulation, the use of curved lines, and the use of the computer. All sections have adequate examples, exercises and answers.

Boyce, R. O. *Integrated Managerial Controls* (Longmans). The reader who regards marketing as the total business activity will find this book of immense value, since the author presents the concept of Total Control in a form suitable to the majority of manufacturing companies. The primary object of the work is the indication of the function and importance of computers in the introduction of control systems, together with the design and practical application of any such systems for management. The seven parts of the book comprise management by objectives, control of the financial functions, control in marketing and selling, control of the operating functions, control of investment, data-processing for control, and management controls.

Carlson, Phillip G. *Quantitative Methods for Managers* (Harper & Row). While a very simple book, it is nevertheless extremely useful for the manager who wants to gain a rapid familiarity with quantitative methods in business decision-making. The book offers no panacea for the manager in search of advanced and sophisticated numerate approaches to his problems, but is for the man who wishes to understand the ways in which mathematicians can help him. The situations dealt with comprise a manufacturing quantity lot size, a purchasing quantity lot size, trainee allocation, a transportation problem, product mix, advertising allocation, job sequencing, market training scheduling, servicing, gaming and simulation.

Coutie, G. A., Davies, O. L., Hossell, C. H., Miller, D. W. G. P. and Morrell, A. J. H. *Short-term Forecasting* (Oliver & Boyd). This is the second monograph in the series based on original ICI documents, and covers forecasting methods, seasonal variations, control of forecasts and forecasting errors.

Ellerby, G. *Graphs and Calculus* (Pergamon). Essentially for those people who need a simple introduction to graphs, functions and the calculus. The level is an introductory text for those intending to take an 'O' level type examination in mathematics. It is an altogether easy-to-understand book, and, from the outset, the reader is encouraged to learn the principles. There are copious examples and exercises on straight-line, quadratic, cubic, exponential and logarithmic graphs, rates of change, gradients, differentiation, and integration.

Fitzroy, P. T. *Analytical Methods for Marketing Management* (McGraw-Hill). This is a useful book for a young executive wishing to learn his analytical trade academically. In fact, it was written for undergraduate courses, which emphasize the use of analytical methods in the major decision areas of marketing. The text does assume a knowledge of calculus and basic statistics, although, where possible, the text adopts a geometric exposition. The main subjects dealt with are consumer buying behaviour, market segmentation, organizational buying behaviour, forecasting, advertising strategy, personal selling, pricing, product policy, new product policy, and marketing strategy. The work is ideally suited to the person who wishes to major in marketing research rather than marketing management.

Flegg, G. and Meetham, R. (eds). *An Introduction to Calculus and Algebra*, Volumes 1, 2 and 3, from material prepared by the mathematics staff of the Open University (Open University Press). These three volumes cover the total mathematical field that a business manager is likely to need. In fact, they are probably more extensive than most managers would desire, despite being a condensation of the Open University Foundation in Mathematics and intended for science and technology students as an elementary course. Volume 1 covers sets and mappings, sequences, functions, limits, exponential function, convergence, the definite integral, differentiation and the fundamental theorem of calculus. Volume 2 explores applied calculus, and Volume 3 algebra. Those intending to go deeply into business analysis and to use considerable mathematical application must consider these three volumes as the absolute minimum as a starter.

Green, P. E. and Tull, D. S. *Research for Marketing Decisions* (Prentice-Hall). This may be considered to be a standard book on marketing research; now in its third edition and running to nearly 800 pages, it is a book for the serious student and professional marketing man. There are five main sections: problem formulation, which also reviews the scope of marketing research and the tactics to be adopted, obtaining and organizing respondent data, including sampling, and traditional and Bayesian approaches; analysing associative data with both well known procedures and such newer techniques as multivariate analysis; advanced techniques in analysing associative data — particularly, multiple criterion/multiple predictor association, factor analysis of associative data, distance functions and cluster analysis, and multi-dimensional scaling and conjoint measurement; and selected activities in marketing research. A unique feature is the use of a data bank case study throughout the book, which helps the reader to understand analytical applications by examples.

Greensted, C. S., Jardine, A. K. S. and Macfarlane, J. D. *Essentials of Statistics in Marketing* (Heinemann). This book stays firmly on the practical surface of statistical applications to marketing management situations. It contains sufficient statistical concepts for the business manager to be able to communicate with statisticians, understand the results of statistical analyses and even question doubtful assumptions. The mathematics in the text has been kept as simple as possible, and the topics covered comprise presentation of data, uncertainty and probability, sampling, significance testing of normal and other distributions, conditional probability and Bayesian analysis, index numbers, correlation analysis and trend analysis. This book should be regarded as the very minimum necessary for those students who intend to undertake any business analysis.

Gregg, J. V., Hossell, C. H. and Richardson, J. T. *Mathematical Trend Curves: an Aid to Forecasting* (Oliver & Boyd). One of a series of monographs originally written as ICI reports for distribution within the company to meet a need for simple expositions of modern mathematical techniques and their applications to practical problems. For the business analyst who wishes to apply trend curves to data this book is almost essential. It discusses the choice of a trend curve and slope characteristics of polynomials, exponentials and modified exponentials. For the fitting of trend curves to data there is a simple but fully explained section with adequately illustrated methods.

Haber, Audrey and Runyon, Richard P. *General Statistics* (Addison-Wesley). A more comprehensive and modern treatment of the subject than *Essentials of Statistics in Marketing* (Greensted, op. cit.), with the introduction of what the authors consider new statistical techniques having advantages over former methods. For example, the Sandler A-statistic, which is algebraically equivalent to the Student t-ratio with correlated samples, has been introduced because it drastically reduces the computational procedures required to arrive at a statistical decision. The first fifteen chapters provide a thorough introduction to the fundamentals of descriptive and inferential statistics, and the last three venture into a rather more advanced area, covering such topics as analysis of variance and several of the more widely employed non-parametric tests of significance. The theory of probability is the first of these chapters, but it is treated in a way that is easy to understand and supported with adequate real-life examples.

Keegan, W. J. *Multinational Marketing Management* (Prentice-Hall). This book, which treats marketing on a global scale, is essential for the serious student and practising marketing executive. There are three basic dimensions explored: the traditional consideration of foreign markets and environments, the crossing of national boundaries with marketing mix programmes, and managing marketing programmes in more than one national environment at the same time. It is fully illustrated with actual examples and cases, which are all keyed to the chapter discussion of particular topics.

Leavitt, H. J. and Dill, W. R. *The Organizational World* (Harcourt Brace Jovanovich). This book is about organizations in the contemporary world and the people in those organizations. It is very easy to read and stays fairly 'close to the ground'. It does not deal with organizations by the classical approach, but as consisting of people with tasks, and tools to carry out those tasks, set in structures. For the student and businessman faced with the problem of setting up an organization or reorganizing an existing structure, this book will provide a great deal of food for thought. The authors invite their readers to consider the validity of a basic syllogism as they read and use the book:

1 Complex organizations have a large potential for changing the world.
2 Young people, well educated and well motivated, have a large potential for changing complex organizations.
3 Therefore young people, through organizations, have a large potential for changing the world.

Meek, Ronald L. *Figuring Out Society* (Fontana). The author states that this is a book written by a mathematical simpleton for mathematical simpletons. It assumes no previous mathematical knowledge other than that of the most elementary kind, and it does not make any very substantial advances on the mathematical front as it goes along. The techniques that are presented cover modelling, regression analysis, correlation, elementary sampling theory, marginal analysis, linear programming, stock control, queueing theory, game theory and cost-benefit analysis. These techniques are usually associated with difficult mathematical calculations, but in this book they are explained and illustrated for readers whose main interests are non-mathematical.

Mosteller, F., Rourke, R. E. K. and Thomas, G. B., Jr. *Probability with Statistical Applications* (Addison-Wesley). For those students and businessmen who desire to go further into the mathematics of uncertainty (probability) without the necessity of more than a moderate knowledge of elementary algebra, this book may be regarded as a companion volume to *General Statistics* (Haber, op. cit.). It is suggested that the reader may gain four things from this book: first, an understanding of the kinds of regularity that occur amid random fluctuations; second, experience in associating probabilistic mathematical models with phenomena in the real world, third, skill in using these mathematical models to interpret such phenomena and in predicting, with appropriate measures of uncertainty, the outcomes of related experiences; and fourth, some insight into statistical inference, both classical and Bayesian.

Mulvaney, J. E. and Mann, C. W. *Practical Business Models* (Heinemann). This is essentially a practical man's book on the use of modelling techniques applied to business, with no long list of references nor extensive bibliography. There is very little mathematics and no jargon. It has been based on ten years' experience and covers market models, long-term demand models, planning models, market share, new products, five-year planning, international investment, and how to manage with models. What makes this book so valuable to the businessman and student alike is the way that the authors introduce actual experiences and cases into the text and explain how appropriate models were developed and used.

Nemmers, E. E. and Myers, John. *Business Research, Text and Cases* (McGraw-Hill). This volume is an introductory course in business research and explores marketing, finance and economics. Principles, with examples, are presented in the text, and then sample research studies are exploited as illustrations of good and bad applications of those principles. The book combines all the aspects of business research data sources — though, admittedly, American — and problems, scientific method, and statistical tools, with good and poor examples taken from actual publications.

Richardson, W. H. *Finite Mathematics* (Harper & Row). There are four chapters in this book, which has been well tested in the classroom with large and small groups. The first chapter covers mathematical logic, including truth tables; the second chapter develops the ideas surrounding set theory; the third covers counting and the binomial theorem; and the fourth probability. The book may be regarded as a lightweight introduction to limited areas in mathematics useful for business students. Each chapter is written a little more formally than the preceding one, and the reader who completes this text will be well prepared to investigate further topics in mathematics as applied to business.

Robson, A. P. *Essential Accounting for Managers* (Cassell). This book was written for the non-accountant manager and is the outcome of many years' experience by the author in training centres in the U.K. The approach is direct and free of unnecessary jargon, taking the reader through the successive stages from the analysis of a business situation, through the planning of operations and projects, to a comparison of performance with plan. Remarkably, the whole book may be digested and understood over a few weekends, giving the reader a good grounding in some of the more important areas of the management of the financial aspects of business decisions.

Simon, S. R. *Managing Marketing Profitability* (American Management Assoc.). This work is devoted to profitable marketing, and stems from practical management services carried out in the U.S.A. It treats marketing as a function in a business and looks at the measurement of profit as from the point where the production line ends to the point of final sale and delivery. In this approach the book is therefore limited to what might better be called the 'marketing' approach to profitable selling. Nevertheless it deals more than adequately with the following techniques: assigning direct and indirect costs to functional areas, using rate-of-return as a control device to determine standards of performance, understanding how the needs of a marketing information system differ from custodial accounting principles, relating sales results to profit goals, making astute pricing decisions, and integrating marketing and financial information so as to interpret profit performance.

Stafford, L. W. T. *Business Mathematics* (M & E Handbooks). This must be considered as supplementary to more expansive textbooks and provides a handy digest of the subject in note form. In addition to basic concepts of modern mathematics, it introduces differentiation and integration, the mathematics of finance, inventory control, queueing theory, linear programming, probability and decision-making, regression analysis and sampling. It may be used to help recall the required formulae and method of calculation.

Stockton, J. P. *Introduction to Business and Economic Statistics* (Edward Arnold). For the businessman who intends to be serious about his approach to business statistics, this book is a 'must'. It provides a very full treatment of its subject, and discusses the elementary phases in sufficient detail to serve as an adequate basis for the use of statistical methods in decision-making and business research. After a comprehensive introduction, the subjects discussed, illustrated and amplified with practical examples are the following: collecting and tabulating data, statistical tables, charts, averages, dispersion, skewness, kurtosis, probability, binomial distribution, normal distribution, sampling, tests of significance, statistical quality control, time series, linear secular trend, non-linear trends, seasonal variation, cyclical fluctuations in time series, index numbers, business and economic barometers and forecasting, regression and correlation analysis, linear correlation, and non-linear, multiple and partial correlation. An Instructor's Manual is available to amplify the main text.

Thompson, Sylvanus P. *Calculus Made Easy* (Macmillan). An introduction to calculus, and probably the easiest book on the subject to understand. Only once in its long life, since 1919, has it been enlarged and revised. Although it is intended to take the terrors out of one's attempts to calculate in an advanced manner, it is only of use if one is going to venture fairly deeply into the more complex areas of marketing management.

Van Horne, J. C. *Financial Management and Policy* (Prentice-Hall). The purpose of this book is, first, to develop an understanding of financial theory in an organized manner, so that the reader may evaluate a company's investment, financing and dividend decisions; second, to familiarize the reader with the application of analytical techniques to a wide variety of problems necessitating financial decisions; and, third, to expose the reader to the institutional material necessary for a thorough understanding of the environment in which financial decisions are made. Each chapter has a useful summary at the end, together with problems that have answers in an appendix. This is a book for the marketing man who intends to develop a much more professionally oriented approach to the financial implications underlying all his decisions.

Youse, B. K. and Stalnaker, A. W. *Calculus for Students of Business and Management* (International Textbook Company). The title explains the nature and scope of this book. Only those topics commonly used in the solution of deterministic models are included, and other non-calculus topics, such as linear algebra, difference equations and probability, are not part of the text. The book was written because of the growing demand for education in the fundamentals of calculus in management science and quantitative analysis to be included in the expanding curricula of business schools. It is a useful volume for the student or businessman who does not intend to specialize in quantitative techniques, econometrics or statistics, and will ensure that he is provided with a thorough understanding of rudimentary techniques.

3. Medway Appliances Ltd

This case centres on two main products — domestic cookers and washing machines — and there is a description of how these products have been distributed in the U.K. market, together with price range and some indication of promotional activities. Some attention is paid to the sales organization and to area results, but the crux of the case appears to be whether or not the company should continue to market washing machines. It is also suggested that the range of cookers should be increased, but you might see beneath the surface of the reported meetings considerable personality problems among the members of the management team. An interesting, almost separate problem concerns the opposing interests of companies in the same group trading with each other; Medway is faced with a purchasing conflict over delivery and price of a washing machine major component.

Some of the techniques used in the analysis of this case are management ratio analysis, area profitability comparisons, call frequency comparisons, profit and loss projections and correlation analysis. After you have read the case and made your initial notes and calculations, you should then turn to its analysis and respond as necessary to the questions.

3.1 Data

Medway Appliances Ltd is a subsidiary company of Kent Electrical Ltd, and operates from its headquarters in Chatham, Kent, with sales offices in London, Birmingham and Manchester. Two main products, electric cookers and small washing machines, provide over 90 per cent of the company's turnover. They are developing such other products as space heaters, storage heaters, domestic irons, soldering irons, etc.

Their existing plant at Chatham is laid out for a fairly high throughput of such bulky products as cookers and washing machines, but is not suited, without considerable reorganization, for mass production of the smaller items being considered. Of the products being developed, electric storage heaters could best be fitted into existing facilities, especially as the majority of their production is limited to assembling bought-in parts and components.

The company is managed by four directors — Mark Fyre, Managing Director; Tom Cox, in charge of production; George Challoner, finance; and Fred Tallon, sales. Medway had joined Kent Electric Ltd some years previously, although there was very little interference from the parent company provided adequate profits were made. The years 1965 and 1966 had been particularly difficult, but the parent company appeared to be satisfied that the Medway management had matters under control. The returns for 1967 had been very encouraging, because turnover had increased, surplus labour had been made redundant without union difficulties and costs had been contained so that the largest profit ever had been achieved.

The company had originally been started by Mark Fyre's father at the turn of the century to produce various structural metal shapes. Mark joined the company in 1938 and had been employed in every department until, after his return from military service during World War II, he became assistant to his father. When his father retired in 1963, Mark took over as Managing Director. The company now employed 150—180 people, all at Chatham, with the exception of the field force.

The company was an early entrant into the electric cooker market and had concentrated from the start on a small low-priced cooker for households limited to one or two people. They had hitherto resisted all attempts to extend their range of cookers and were now the leading supplier of a small cooker that retailed for £20—£25. The cookers were marketed for private branding for such concerns as electricity boards and department stores, and, under their own brand, 'Kentfyre'. Their advertising message had not varied for a number of years — 'Kentfyre cookers, for good little cooks'.

In 1946 they started to manufacture washing machines and had patented an 'agitator', a special moulding, which created a high turbulence in the water and increased the cleansing action. Their policy for washing machine marketing had been to aim at the lower end of the market and to supply 'own brand' models through large department stores and other groups. They also sold about 25 per cent of their output under the brand name 'Kentfyre'. Depending on the method of distribution, that is either branded or company-branded, the washing machine retailed at £18—£25.

Turnover had increased each year over the previous four years but there had been fairly extensive capital expenditure, in replacement of equipment and in transport for the wider distribution of the company's products. There had been considerable discussion on the possibilities and merits of opening one or two warehouses in the Midlands and North of England, but they had decided on the 'more flexible course of increasing their transport facilities'.

Late in 1964 it was suggested that they should allow a greater freedom of movement for their supervisory staff and representatives within the Kent Electric group as a whole. While agreeing to this, the company was somewhat disturbed that 'all their key men might leave for better jobs in other parts of the group'. It was this underlying thought that prompted the company to supply all the field force with motor cars. After the valued Cardiff representative left the company in December 1964 for another company in the Kent Electrical group, steps were taken to improve salaries and commissions and cars were bought over the 1965 and 1966 period.

The field sales force covered all electricity showrooms and a large percentage of the electrical appliance outlets. Because many radio and electrical shops did not sell cookers or washing machines, it was difficult to determine the actual number of potential outlets.

Some sales were negotiated with the central purchasing offices of department store groups and, in at least one area the company supplied both cookers and washing machines with the electricity board's own brand name fitted. The company had started its field operations originally in the London area, then expanded to Birmingham and Manchester areas, establishing small sales offices in each of these three cities. The sales offices served as bases for the salesmen, and each office had a shorthand typist to deal with telephone calls and routine work.

The areas were extended to include Bristol, Cardiff and Glasgow, but in 1964 the

Cardiff representative left the company and his area was added to that of the Bristol representative, Charles Tudor. Thus, the areas had not been specifically planned but had developed unevenly over the years. This resulted in somewhat unequal areas, as follows:

London: The area bounded by Southend, Oxford, Southampton, Dover.
Birmingham: North Wales, Midlands, East Anglia.
Manchester: Liverpool, Manchester, Sheffield, Leeds, Hull and Newcastle-on-Tyne.
Bristol: Gloucester, Somerset, Wilts., Devon, Cornwall and South Wales.
Glasgow: Edinburgh, Glasgow, Aberdeen.

Table 3.1 shows the approximate number of outlets in each area.

Table 3.1

	Electricity showrooms	Appliance shops
London	300	4,750
Birmingham	315	3,730
Manchester	300	3,940
Bristol	270	1,900
Glasgow	155	980
	1,340	15,300

All salesmen were paid on a salary plus commission basis — the average salary was about £1,700 and the average commission £500. (See Table 3.8.) There was no determined policy of paying representatives the same basic salary on joining the company and the youngest man, Tom Wedlock, was appointed to the Manchester area in 1966 at £1,500 p.a. On the other hand, when a replacement was required for the Glasgow area, Stuart Jardine was engaged in 1965 at £1,685.

Three areas — Manchester, Birmingham and London — had more than one representative, and the senior men in each area were expected to handle the general office correspondence. Norman Denton looked after the Manchester office, Jim Welsh the London office and Bill Freeman the Birmingham office.

All ten representatives were left much to their own devices in organizing the areas and weekly call summaries were sent to head office for recording. The average number of calls made by each of the representatives each week was thirty. A number of potential accounts were seen only once a year, whereas some good accounts were serviced at least four times a year and more frequently by telephone.

The Manchester representatives had been pressing for an increase in the number of models of cookers, reporting that several large customers would be willing to place orders for further acceptable models in the lower price bracket. There had been discussions between Tallon, Cox and Denton earlier in 1965 and 1966 on the possibility of an inexpensive cooker suitable for both gas and electricity, but, after the considerable resistance to the Cannon dual purpose cooker project by gas and electricity authorities, the idea was dropped.

Jim Welsh and Don Tibbetts in London wanted to drop washing machines altogether. They felt that, although the Medway washer satisfied a segment of the market in the lowest price area, they were wasting time in servicing washing machine customers. They complained that they were unable to explore all potential outlets because of insufficient time and suggested that a fourth salesman should be appointed to the area with the task of opening up new accounts for cookers only.

Several salesmen had raised the question of prices, not because the Kentfyre cooker was too expensive, but because it was apparent that a fairly wide range of prices was being obtained by dealers. Denton, Welsh and Freeman had discussed this quite informally with Mark Fyre at the annual dinner and dance in November 1967, but were simply told by Fyre that the company operated on a straightforward 'profit-on-cost' basis and this produced an adequate return. Suggestions by the three branch managers that the company could probably sell the cooker at a higher price were not taken seriously by their managing director, who was unable to satisfy them on company pricing policy.

They had raised two other matters at that time. One, that there was a definite need for a periodic meeting of all sales personnel and, secondly, that a fresh approach towards publicity was desirable. Fyre promised to look into the possibility of a sales conference despite the fact that none of the men could agree on the objectives of a conference. With regard to their 'modest advertising', as Mark described it, he felt it must be adequate 'because sales are always increasing'.

For many years the company had advertised in four periodicals for the consumer — *Good Housekeeping, Home and Country, Ideal Home* and *House and Garden*. In addition, they took space in the trade periodical *Domestic Equipment Trader*. Mr Tallon did not use the services of an advertising agency but placed his instructions direct with the publications, whose space representatives had been on good terms with Medway for many years. Any new advertisement copy required was prepared by Tallon, and, after approval by the other directors, was given to a design studio in Rochester to complete. The studio also arranged to order any blocks required although the advertisements were fairly simple in approach and new blocks were not often required. Any changes in copy were made by the company to give their advertising, according to Fred Tallon, 'a fresh topical message occasionally'. He also pointed out that, as company sales had increased considerably between 1964 and 1967, the advertising must be paying off. Apart from these general comments, there was no advertising policy laid down and no executive, other than Tallon, specifically charged with the management of the appropriation, which in 1967 was approximately £15,000.

Each year, the company appeared at various exhibitions and had taken space at the previous *Ideal Home* exhibition. Results were not readily attributable to consumer exhibitions and the Board felt that the money could be more usefully spent elsewhere, not necessarily on advertising. No definite decision had been taken on this point.

Recently, the company had been informed by the periodical *House and Garden* that the blocks used in the company's advertisement needed to be renewed. Mr Challoner thought that the periodical should be deleted from the schedule because it was the one slightly odd sized space (11 in x 8 in) compared with the other periodicals the company used and extra block charges always seemed to be cropping up. 'A rationalisation of the media', was what he advocated.

Some informal discussion had taken place between the directors on the possible amount of the advertising expenditure for 1968. A few spaces had already been booked in the same publications, because of early copy dates and, as Mr Tallon reported, the publications had been doing business with the company for years and were 'most accommodating'. However, he thought that the appropriation should be increased to 'have a go in the export field'. If the advertising appropriation were increased and attention turned to export possibilities, then it was thought that the company should look at the possibility of using an advertising agent and engage a junior executive to take some of the load from Fred Tallon.

In 1963, Tom Cox had decided to explore the possibilities of using a plastic agitator in the washing machine instead of the metal one then being used. There were many reasons for this, including certain corrosion problems experienced with the action of detergent, soap and hard water deposits on the metal agitator. It was also considered that the plastic agitator might be cheaper and more attractive to the housewife. Negotiations started with Ashford Mouldings, another member of the Kent Electrical group, but innumerable problems of price were experienced over the next three years.

As a result of a Commercial Instruction from K.E.L. the buyer attempted to change long-standing purchasing habits in 1965, and was successful in changing suppliers and entering into forward order agreements with new suppliers. The effect was an unwelcome increase in cost-of-sales for 1965, with the inevitable effect on company profit. In the buyer's defence it must be pointed out that two of the new suppliers were unable to control costs of raw materials, which were largely obtained from overseas, and these difficulties alone accounted for an increase in cost-of-sales of £25,000. Nevertheless this particular buyer had since left the company and a new man, F. Potts, was appointed in August, 1967. One of his first tasks was to look into the price and delivery position of the polypropylene agitator for the washing machine (see Appendixes I and II).

During 1966 supplies of the plastic agitator had not been delivered according to plan, and frequently Medway Appliances had large stocks of washing machines ready for despatch waiting for agitators. A decision was taken to use the small stock of metal agitators in stock, and arrangements were made for a special order of metal agitators from their previous suppliers to be made in a commendably short time. The Board were satisfied that the increased sales of 80 per cent had justified this course of action. The whole supply position of the polypropylene agitator had now been taken up with the Commercial Director of Kent Electrical.

The Medway Board had been discussing policy matters generally in January 1968, with the objective of planning for future expansion. During the second half of 1967 they had been disappointed to see sales of washing machines falling dramatically, although it was known that total industry sales had been declining steadily since 1963. However, their Birmingham manager, Bill Freeman, had reported in November 1967 that Kentfyre washing machines were being sold in a large discount store in the Midlands. The company had no account with a discount store, and were unable to trace the source of supply to the store. The directors were particularly perturbed at this turn of events, because it was their definite policy not to supply discount houses.

Early sales figures for the first few days in January 1968 indicated that sales of cookers and more especially washing machines were at a much lower level than for the same period in 1967. Furthermore, the Board was not sure how the devaluation of the pound would affect them, both from the point of view of costs of materials and demand for cookers and washing machines. The outlook for 1968 depended to a large extent on what action the Government would take to restore balance to the economy. The squeeze on credit would undoubtedly have a depressing effect on sales; further curtailment of consumer expenditure could be in the form of increased purchase tax or a rise in the initial hire purchase deposits. The Board felt that severe deflationary measures were not likely to increase the popularity of the Government, and, although it had not hesitated to introduce restrictive measures when considered necessary, the Government would be more reluctant to do so as the time for a general election became nearer.

The Medway Board reviewed several possibilities, especially the possible development of an export trade. Fred Tallon was not especially enthusiastic about this particular suggestion, because, as he pointed out, he was nearly sixty years old and did not relish the thought of more travelling. He spent on average one day a week out of the office, usually calling on the large accounts, which were serviced direct from head office. This was thought necessary because a turnover of well over £150,000 was in question. George Challoner also pointed out the greatly increased costs that would be incurred as a result of venturing into the export market, especially the 'inevitable delays in receiving payment'.

The Board were divided on the merits of developing an export trade, mainly because of their lack of experience in exporting but also because they could sell all the cookers they could make at present and there seemed little advantage in exporting just for the sake of it. 'Yet', pointed out Mark Fyre, 'the sales appeared to be on a falling curve.' The matter was held over for a further meeting.

On the possibility of increasing their range of cookers, the directors were concerned at the estimates of Tom Cox, who thought that about £100,000 might be required for investment in additional plant and equipment to increase the range of cookers to half a dozen. This figure was quite separate from the additional labour costs that would be incurred.

Tallon showed his colleagues a marketing report that had been prepared by a young man in his office. This junior executive had investigated the idea of developing a range of five cookers — four additions to the present model and a super model in the high quality bracket containing two ovens, a revolving eye-level grill, a glass door to main oven, oven light, thermostatically controlled simmer hotplate and automatic control devices. Cox condemned this out of hand, saying that at his, Cox's, age he 'could only just cope with the production problems now'. This marketing report also contained a criticism of the brand name Kentfyre, based on a small field research that the young man had carried out personally. Apparently there was practically no brand recognition among the 170-odd interviews he had made over many weeks, and the few housewives who knew of the cooker and the washing machine by this name 'thought it was odd'. There was no mention in the research whether these particular women owned either a Kentfyre cooker or washing machine.

Discussion ranged over the possibility of developing a washing machine with twin-tubs or automatic controls, but it was felt that not only were the production problems too complex but that the liquidation a few years earlier of Rolls Razor followed quickly by that of Duomatic pointed up the dangers to the company of expanding into unknown markets. A suggestion that generated lively discussion was to sell off the washing machine manufacture and concentrate on cookers, although there were thought to be tremendous problems in trying to sell the part of the factory used for washing machine manufacture. It was considered that it would be more

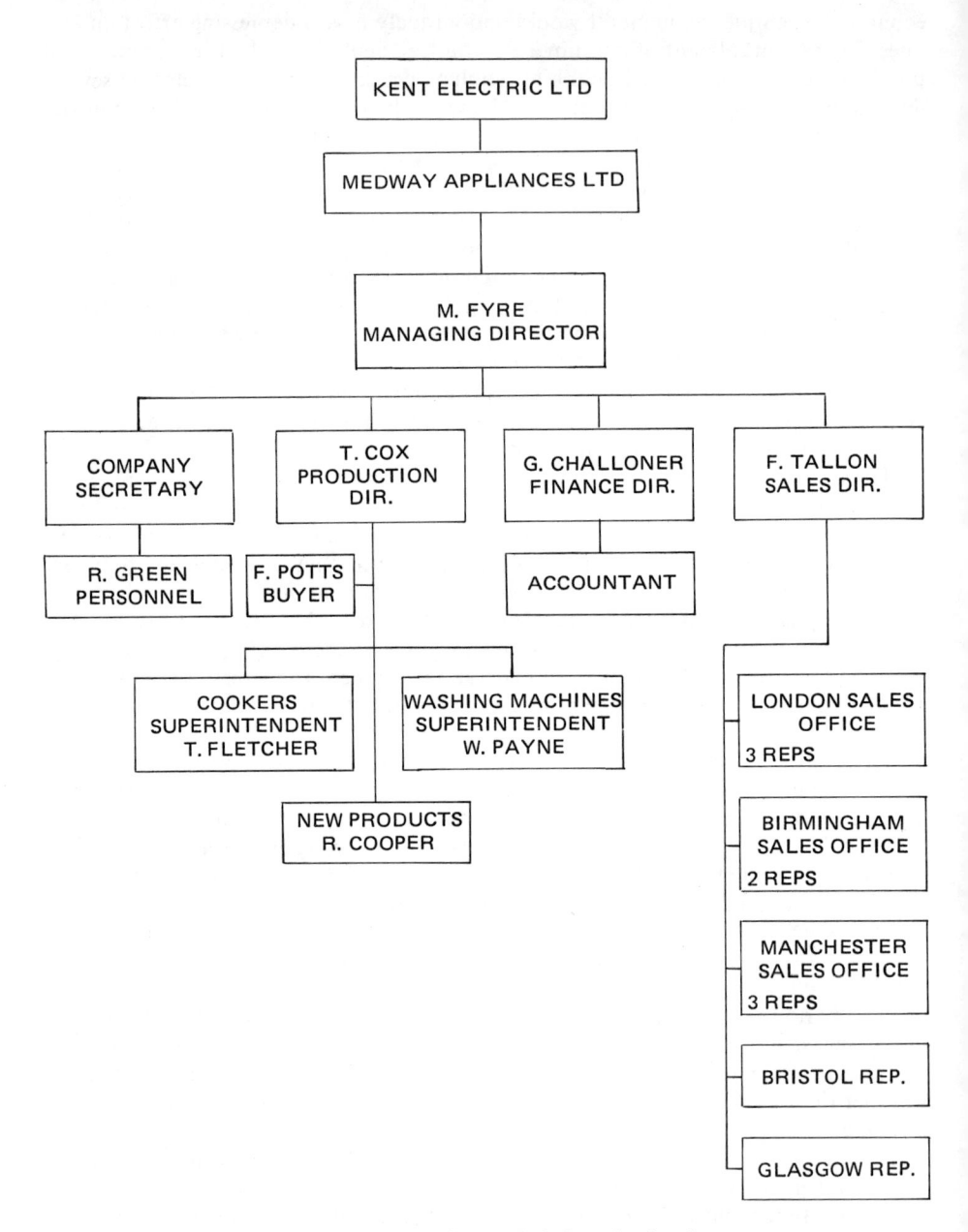

```
                    ┌─────────────────────┐
                    │  KENT ELECTRIC LTD  │
                    └──────────┬──────────┘
                               │
                    ┌──────────┴──────────┐
                    │ MEDWAY APPLIANCES LTD│
                    └──────────┬──────────┘
                               │
                    ┌──────────┴──────────┐
                    │      M. FYRE        │
                    │  MANAGING DIRECTOR  │
                    └──────────┬──────────┘
```

┌──────────────┬──────────────┬──────────────┬──────────────┐
│   COMPANY   │   T. COX   │ G. CHALLONER │ F. TALLON   │
│ SECRETARY   │ PRODUCTION │ FINANCE DIR. │ SALES DIR. │
│   │   DIR.   │   │   │
└──────┬───────┴──────┬───────┴──────┬───────┴──────┬───────┘
       │   │   │   │
┌──────┴───────┐ ┌───┴──────┐ ┌────┴─────┐   │
│   R. GREEN   │ │ F. POTTS │ │ACCOUNTANT│   │
│ PERSONNEL   │ │ BUYER   │ │   │   │
└──────────────┘ └──────────┘ └──────────┘   │

        COOKERS   WASHING MACHINES   LONDON SALES OFFICE — 3 REPS
        SUPERINTENDENT   SUPERINTENDENT   BIRMINGHAM SALES OFFICE — 2 REPS
        T. FLETCHER   W. PAYNE   MANCHESTER SALES OFFICE — 3 REPS
                                                   BRISTOL REP.
        NEW PRODUCTS   GLASGOW REP.
        R. COOPER

Exhibit 3.1   Medway Appliances Ltd, Organization Structure

realistic simply to phase out washing machines and concentrate on cooker production, possibly adding another model.

'Before we add cooker models', said Tallon, 'there is an increasing demand for up to 3 kW storage heaters, which might make a better proposition.'

Tom Cox had to agree that the layout of the factory was such that storage heaters could be made with little reorganization, but he would 'need to go into it in detail especially on the investment needed to give a realistic assessment of production viability'.

Mark Fyre proposed that they should all think about the matters that had been discussed and meet formally in February to agree future policy.

Exhibit 3.1 shows the management organization of Medway Appliances. Profit and loss accounts and balance sheets are supplied for the years 1964—7. Tables 3.2 to 3.7 deal with sales of cookers and washing machines, by Medway and nationally; Table 3.8, already mentioned, deals with salesmen's salaries; and Table 3.9 and Exhibits 3.2 and 3.3 with advertising.

Profit and Loss Accounts 1964—7

	1964 (£000s)	1965 (£000s)	1966 (£000s)	1967 (£000s)
Sales revenue	437	501	556	677
Cost of sales	190	263	261	326
Gross profit	247	238	295	351
Expenses*	196	212	282	290
Net profit before taxation	51	26	13	61
Taxation	25	11	6	26
Profit after taxation	26	15	7	35
Dividend	13	13	—	15
	13	2	7	20
Profit b/f.	38	41	43	50
	51	43	50	70
Transferred to general reserves	10	—	—	10
Retained profit c/f.	41	43	50	60
Some expenses itemized are:				
Manufacturing:				
Wages and salaries	81	97	129	101
Other expenses	20	21	26	25
Administration:				
Salaries	40	41	49	55
Office expenses	12	14	16	19
Other expenses	12	13	25	39

Balance Sheets 1964–7

	1964 (£000s)	1965 (£000s)	1966 (£000s)	1967 (£000s)
Fixed assets:				
Building, plant, equipment at cost	130	166	248	309
Less depreciation	26	45	75	117
	104	121	173	192
Current assets:				
Stock	30	26	55	55
Debtors	48	55	60	103
Advanced payments	3	3	2	2
Cash	99	78	6	–
	180	162	123	160
Total assets employed	284	283	296	352
Financed by:				
Share capital	150	150	150	150
General reserve	48	48	48	58
Retained profits	41	43	50	60
Net worth owners' equity	239	241	248	268
Current liabilities:				
Trade creditors	15	27	38	49
Accum. charges	5	4	4	4
Taxation	25	11	6	26
Bank overdraft	–	–	–	5
	45	42	48	84
	284	283	296	352

Table 3.2 Medway Appliances, Sales of Cookers

	Total	Value
1964	18,070	£361,500
1965	17,640	£400,400
1966	22,355	£417,200
1967	31,400	£563,000

Table 3.3 Medway Appliances, Sales of Washing Machines

	Total	Value
1964	2,680	£40,000
1965	2,920	£49,600
1966	5,280	£104,400
1967	3,850	£77,000

Table 3.4 Industry Deliveries of Electric Cookers in U.K.

1962	490,000
1963	498,000
1964	570,000
1965	535,000
1966	545,000
1967 (9 months)	438,000

Table 3.5 Industry Deliveries of Electric Washing Machines in U.K.

	Total	Value
1962	1,101,600	£46,992,000
1963	1,366,800	£53,832,000
1964	1,195,200	£49,488,000
1965	891,600	£38,604,000
1966	703,200	£31,104,000
1967 (9 months)	503,700	£22,392,000

Table 3.6 Area Sales of Medway Cookers

	1964 No.	£	1965 No.	£	1966 No.	£	1967 No.	£
Manchester	4,638	93,400	4,615	106,450	5,982	110,500	8,072	145,590
London	4,520	91,050	4,165	100,700	5,830	108,000	8,049	144,905
Birmingham	4,102	83,050	4,084	94,350	5,043	100,165	7,104	127,890
Bristol	2,510	50,890	2,290	50,560	2,165	41,010	4,210	76,815
Glasgow	1,813	36,110	1,716	39,600	2,330	42,550	3,064	55,350
	17,583	£354,500	16,870	£391,660	21,350	£402,225	30,499	£550,550
*Head Office	487	7,000	770	8,740	1,005	14,975	901	12,450
	18,070	£361,500	17,640	£400,400	22,355	£417,200	31,400	£563,000

*Includes staff sales and sundry sales at cost to charities etc., but excludes business negotiated in areas direct from Head Office.

Table 3.7 Area Sales of Medway Washing Machines

	1964 No.	£	1965 No.	£	1966 No.	£	1967 No.	£
Manchester	941	14,711	873	16,164	1,585	31,500	1,150	23,050
London	676	10,010	851	14,605	1,329	26,360	960	19,100
Birmingham	444	6,580	563	8,881	1,033	20,400	762	15,250
Bristol	224	3,295	304	4,710	783	15,525	573	11,500
Glasgow	230	3,340	287	4,625	530	10,220	375	7,600
	2,515	37,936	2,878	48,985	5,260	104,005	3,820	76,500
Head Office*	165	2,064	42	615	20	395	30	500
	2,680	£40,000	2,920	£49,600	5,280	£104,400	3,850	£77,000

* Includes staff sales etc., but excludes business negotiated in areas direct from Head Office.

Table 3.8 Salesmen's Salaries and Sales in 1967

		Sales Cookers (£)	Sales Washing m/c (£)	Annual salary (£)
London:	Jim Welsh	64,000	6,000	1,870
	Don Tibbetts	33,000	2,000	1,750
	Gordon Harvey	44,000	1,000	1,675
Manchester:	Norman Denton	53,500	6,500	1,800
	Bill Reynolds	40,000	10,000	1,725
	Tom Wedlock	26,000	4,000	1,575
Birmingham:	Bill Freeman	42,000	8,000	1,775
	Harry Tucker	44,300	3,700	1,650
Bristol:	Charles Tudor	24,000	10,300	1,680
Glasgow:	Stuart Jardine	25,000	5,000	1,725

Note: All salesmen received a straight one per cent commission on all sales made by them.

Table 3.9 Advertising Schedule 1967

CONSUMER PUBLICATIONS
Good Housekeeping (Circ. 167,188)	(M)	6p @ £440	£2,640
Home and Country (Circ. 150,415)	(M)	6p @ £170	£1,020
House and Garden (Circ. over 60,000)	(M)	6p @ £240	£1,440
Ideal Home (Circ. 170,862)	(M)	6p @ £500	£3,000
			£8,100

TRADE PUBLICATIONS
Domestic Equipment Trader (Circ. not known)	12p @ £50	£600
Radio, Television and Electrical Appliance Dealer (Circ. not known)	6p @ £166·25	£998
		£1,598

Consumer advertising	£8,100
Consumer exhibitions	£4,000
Trade advertising	£1,598
Trade exhibitions	£1,000
Production cost	442
	£15,140

	J	F	M	A	M	J	J	A	S	O	N	D
Good Housekeeping		W		C		C		C		C		C
Home and Country	C		W		C		C		C		C	
House and Garden		C	C			W	C			C	C	
Ideal Home	C			W	C			C	C			C
D.E.T.	C	W	C	C	C	C	W	C	C	C	C	C
R.T. & E.A.D.		C		C		C		W		C		C

Exhibit 3.2 Medway Appliances Ltd. Advertising Schedule 1967

	J	F	M	A	M	J
Good Housekeeping		C				
Home and Country			C			
House and Garden				C		
Ideal Home					C	
D.E.T.	C	C	C	C	C	
R.T. & E.A.D.			C		C	

Exhibit 3.3 1968 Bookings C = Cooker;
W = Washing machine

3.11 Appendix I Agitator Mouldings

In February 1963 Ashford Mouldings Ltd of Ashford, a further subsidiary of Kent Electrical Co. Ltd, was invited by Medway Appliances Ltd to quote for the supply of agitator mouldings. They quoted a price of $47\frac{1}{2}$p each, plus tooling cost of £5,000, and a 12-month delivery period for samples and bulk deliveries, 3–4 weeks after approval of samples. They suggested that a double impression tool was desirable, but that if a single impression tool was used, the tooling cost would be lower, though the mouldings would be approximately $62\frac{1}{2}$p each. However, Ashford's estimated that, with a double impression tool, as they gained experience in production, the mouldings' price could be reduced from $47\frac{1}{2}$p to about $42\frac{1}{2}$p each.

In March 1963 the Ashford quotation was accepted and, early in 1964, after the sample mouldings had been approved, deliveries of the bulk supplies started. At this time, Medway paid the tool cost of £5,000.

In April 1965 Ashford Mouldings increased the price from $47\frac{1}{2}$p each to 54p each, because the demand from Medway was below that expected. In June 1965 the price was further increased and Medway agreed to order in lots of 1,000 at a price of 55p each, provided that Ashford Mouldings stored half of each run at Ashford, since there was insufficient storage space at Chatham.

In the second half of 1965 Kent Electrical Ltd began to exert pressure on its subsidiary companies for the establishment of individual unit profit responsibility. This promotion of a more positive policy of cost-effectiveness caused Medway Appliances to adopt a much more critical approach to material and manufacturing costs. Unfortunately they had already run into certain difficulties in their purchasing policies, but in particular, they were concerned at the rising cost of the plastic agitator moulding supplied by Ashford Mouldings Ltd. Medway Appliances decided to look further afield for a moulding source, and one potential supplier, Stone Plastics Ltd of Croydon, was asked to quote. By May 1966 a price of 34p per moulding was estimated with a tooling cost of £2,500.

In November 1966 Stone Plastics submitted a firm quotation of 39p per moulding, with an initial tooling cost of £3,000 to be paid by Medway. However, after discussions between the two companies, it was agreed that the cost of the tooling should be amortized over the first 40,000 mouldings, which would be charged at 46p per moulding. In January 1967 an order was placed by Medway with Stone Plastics.

Later in January 1967 Ashford Mouldings raised the question of a replacement tool being required for the agitator, and were told that the business was being placed elsewhere because Ashford was unable to keep competitive terms. From the discussions at this time Ashford Mouldings were given to understand that the moulding was being obtained for 39p each, including the cost of tooling (the amortization aspect was not disclosed).

A few weeks later Ashford Mouldings raised the matter with the Commercial Director of Kent Electrical Ltd. Later in 1967, after discussions between the two subsidiary companies with Kent Electrical, a meeting was arranged at Ashford in an attempt to clear up the matter. Medway Appliances said that they were carrying out final tests with Stone Plastics, and, when these were satisfactorily completed, all orders would be switched to Stone's. Ashford Mouldings had been asked to table a detailed breakdown of their costing for the moulding, and to itemize the effect the loss of business would have on their profitability. They said that they were unable to supply this information but that $47\frac{1}{2}$p per moulding was the lowest price they could offer. Furthermore, they had no alternative plans for the large vertical press that was being used for the production of the agitator. Medway said that, owing to changes of staff, they were unable to supply copies of all correspondence between themselves and Ashford Mouldings as had been requested by the parent company.

At this stage the prices stated by Ashford's and Stone Plastics were as follows:

Stone Plastics	46p each for the first 40,000
	39p each subsequently
	Tool cost – nil.
Ashford Mouldings	50p each
	Tool cost – already paid.

If orders were not placed with Stone Plastics, there would be cancellation charges and possibly a charge for loss of profit. The reason for Stone's lower price was thought to be that they purchased polypropylene at $26\frac{1}{2}$p a kilo, one penny per kilo cheaper than the price Ashford Mouldings had to pay. In addition, the Stone moulding weighed 625 gm, whereas the Ashford moulding weighed 750 gm. It was known that Stone's possessed a modern horizontal press, compared with Ashford's somewhat old vertical press.

The management of Ashford Mouldings were disturbed at the prospect of losing the Medway business for agitator mouldings, and in January 1968 stated that they would match Stone Plastics' price. They were prepared to supply 40,000 mouldings at 46p each and thereafter at 39p each, and did not consider that the information on costings and profit was necessary.

In February 1968 a meeting was held at Kent Electrical headquarters to arbitrate on the matter and to decide on the future course of action. The main argument was that the loss of business to Ashford's could have a serious impact on Kent Electrical as a whole. As there were no alternative plans for the use of the vertical press, then Ashford's prices and competitive ability would be affected. Approximately 75 per cent of Ashford's output went to other units in the K.E.L. group, and to introduce outside competition on a marginal product was an unwise step. They felt that they had received little cooperation from Medway Appliances in the technical direction, and it was obvious now that Stone Plastics were profiting from the development work at Ashford.

The estimated demand for agitator mouldings had never been maintained by Medway and Ashford's had supplied mouldings during 1966 and 1967 at a barely profitable figure.

Medway Appliances believed that there was no question of introducing an outsider into the operation, because a considerable volume of business was done with Stone Plastics. At the time when negotiations with Stone's had crystallized the price for the moulding at 39p (apart from the cost of the tool), Ashford's wanted 50p each and this 11p difference was a very serious consideration in the costings of a washing machine that was being marketed to the lower segment of the market. Ashford's had been told 12 months previously that it was proposed to change to Stone Plastics for the moulding – that is, Ashford's were kept informed from the outset. Even if the latest Ashford offer had to be accepted, there was still the question of the Stone Plastics' tooling costs and charges for cancellation.

3.12 *Appendix II Kent Electrical Commercial Instruction No. 1 (April 1965) – Trading between Divisions and Companies of K.E.L.*

1 *Principles*
   (a) The prime objective of trading between units of K.E.L. is that they should use and supply materials and products obtainable within the group.
   (b) Each unit is responsible for trading on the most profitable basis, but it should not expand its own profits by resorting to low-price outside supplies at the expense of other K.E.L. divisions or companies able to provide the material or products required at a reasonably competitive price.

2 *Scope*
   (a) These instructions only apply to K.E.L. divisions and subsidiary or sub-subsidiary companies.
   (b) These instructions cover all trading between K.E.L. divisions or companies within the United Kingdom; transactions between United Kingdom units and overseas K.E.L. companies are to be governed by specific arrangements between the parties concerned.

3 *General Rules*
   (a) *Definitions*
   'Manufacturing unit' means the K.E.L. division or company that manufactures the material or products for sale outside K.E.L. or for another K.E.L. division or company.
   'Selling unit' means the K.E.L. division or company that sells the product in the execution of an order from a purchaser outside K.E.L.

(b) The selling unit is responsible for the negotiations with Export Credits Guarantee Department (E.C.G.D.), insurance and financing extended terms of payment. The selling unit must obtain the agreement of the manufacturing unit(s) to any unusual conditions of sale or terms of payment before submission of the offer, and to any modifications that arise before acceptance of the order.

(c) The manufacturing units must bear responsibility for their products in the same way as if they were supplying them directly to the outside purchaser.

4 *Price*

(a) *Selling unit resells products of manufacturing unit*
Where a selling unit resells the products of a manufacturing unit, independently of its own manufactured products, the transaction is to be subject to agreement between the parties concerned.

(b) *Raw materials and incorporated products*
Where a manufacturing unit supplies the raw materials to a selling unit, the price shall be on the most favoured customer basis. Similarly, where the manufacturing unit supplies its products to a selling unit for incorporation in the factory products of the selling unit, the transaction shall be on the most favoured customer basis.

3.2 Analysis

There is a considerable amount of information in this case, and it is advisable to have a general method of investigation — one that can be adopted when there are no salient points requiring immediate attention. The general method suggested is to investigate the various management ratios; great care must be exercised in their use, because they are but means to an end and not ends in themselves. The ratios are based on the information in the profit and loss account and balance sheet. It is perhaps worth emphasizing that the profit and loss account is a statement of the company's financial experience over a period, whereas the balance sheet can be regarded as a financial thermometer — a statement of the company's financial standing at a point in time. Too many deductions from financial ratios must be avoided, since they only give a limited part of the diagnosis and must be interpreted in the light of the size, activity and history of the company.

One of the most commonly used ratios is the profit as a percentage return on the capital employed, although one difficulty is the lack of a generally accepted definition of capital employed. For the purposes of marketing analysis this ratio may be used as a test of the profitability of long-term funds employed in the company, as a test of the effective use of all funds, or even as a test of the profitability of the manufacturing side of the company. The purpose selected will determine how 'capital' is defined. If based on gross capital, then the following are included: share capital, reserves and reserves for taxation, debentures and loans, and current liabilities. If based on net capital employed, then the above less current liabilities are used. There is considerable difference of opinion on the treatment of the following:

1 *Fixed assets*. Whether or not these should be included at their cost or current value.

Medway Appliances Ltd

2 *Depreciation.* Whether or not accumulated depreciation should be deducted from the original cost of the fixed assets.
3 *Non-operating assets.* Whether or not fixed assets in the course of composition should be included in capital.
4 *Intangible assets.* If these appear in the accounts, whether or not they should be included and, if so, how they will be valued.
5 *Investments.* Whether or not these should be included in capital, removed or examined on their own merits and compared with the company's rate of return from their trading.
6 *Cash.* Whether or not cash, especially surplus cash, should be included or excluded from capital.

The general rule to follow is to decide from the start how the various items are going to be defined and then to stick with that practice. For example, because of the several ways in which profit can be defined, the rule generally followed in this book is net profit before taxation.

The calculation of various financial and management ratios for one year is not usually of any great value, for it is the establishment of trends that is important. Comparing ratios and results with external sources is often difficult, because seemingly similar companies in size and type of business can return very different results and ratios. Internal comparisons are very useful, and can be made between different divisions, different products, different factories, different outlets and so on. Relative potential profitability of such proposed courses of action as the expansion of production capacity, or the introduction of a new product, may be assessed by estimating the return on the capital to be employed.

The various management ratios for Medway Appliances are as follows:

Current ratio (or working capital ratio) is
$$\frac{\text{Current assets}}{\text{Current liabilities}}$$

1964	1965	1966	1967
$\frac{180}{45} = 4:1$	$\frac{162}{42} = 3·9:1$	$\frac{123}{48} = 2·6:1$	$\frac{160}{84} = 1·9:1$

This ratio indicates the margin of safety against unforeseen events, but care must be exercised in making judgments on it, because the company's ability to meet its current obligations will depend on the nature of its business, the make-up of the current assets and the ability of the company to obtain further funds. The inclusion of stock — finished goods and work-in-progress — in the assets needs consideration, since the stock may be valued at a figure that may not readily be realized. If the company is experiencing a particularly prosperous period, then this ratio could fall, because increased activity could lead to higher stocks and more debtors but less cash. The trend for Medway is falling, but is still above the ratio 1:1, which is considered adequate.

Liquidity (or acid test) ratio is
$$\frac{\text{Current assets (less stock)}}{\text{Liabilities (less overdraft)}}$$

1964	1965	1966	1967
$\dfrac{150}{45} = 3\cdot3:1$	$\dfrac{136}{42} = 3\cdot2:1$	$\dfrac{68}{48} = 1\cdot4:1$	$\dfrac{105}{79} = 1\cdot3:1$

A ratio of below 1:1 would have denoted some difficulty in the company from the liquidity viewpoint.

Shareholders' interest ratio is

$$\frac{\text{Share capital + reserves + retained profit}}{\text{Total liabilities}}$$

1964	1965	1966	1967
$\dfrac{239}{45} = 5\cdot3:1$	$\dfrac{241}{42} = 5\cdot7:1$	$\dfrac{248}{48} = 5\cdot2:1$	$\dfrac{268}{84} = 3\cdot2:1$

This ratio indicates the respective interest of members and non-members and also the debt capacity of the company. A high gearing of, say, 1:3 would mean that assets are financed mainly by creditors, and the company has a low debt capacity. A low gearing, like that of Medway, indicates the opposite.

Debt ratio is

$$\frac{\text{Total liabilities}}{\text{Total assets}}$$

1964	1965	1966	1967
$\dfrac{45}{284} = 1:6\cdot3$	$\dfrac{42}{283} = 1:6\cdot7$	$\dfrac{48}{296} = 1:6\cdot2$	$\dfrac{84}{352} = 1:4\cdot2$

This ratio shows the extent to which assets are financed from creditors rather than from capital and reserves. The lower the proportion of debt financed by creditors, the better from the creditors' viewpoint and the more able the company to absorb losses from unexpected events.

With debtors' ratio, the amount owing from debtors in the balance sheet will be that at a certain time when balances were struck. Nevertheless this figure can be used as a rough guide to the collection period permitted by the company, that is, the number of weeks that credit is given to their customers.

$$\frac{\text{Debtors} \times 52}{\text{Sales}} = \text{number of weeks' credit given}$$

1964	1965	1966	1967
$\dfrac{48 \times 52}{437} = 5\cdot7$	$\dfrac{55 \times 52}{501} = 5\cdot7$	$\dfrac{60 \times 52}{556} = 5\cdot6$	$\dfrac{103 \times 52}{677} = 7\cdot9$

If the number of days in the collection period is required, 365 is substituted for 52. It is apparent that Medway has given more credit to customers in 1967 than in previous years, or, to put it another way, 11 per cent of sales were outstanding from debtors in 1964 to 1966 but the percentage had risen to 15 per cent in 1967.

Medway Appliances Ltd

Creditors' ratio is

$$\frac{\text{Creditors} \times 52}{\text{Purchases}}$$

This ratio is calculated in a similar manner to the ratio for debtors except that total purchases of materials is used. The resultant figure is the number of weeks' credit taken by the company, or, if 12 is substituted for 52, the number of months'. It is not possible to calculate the period of credit usually taken by Medway, because there is no separate figure given for materials purchases. However, here is where the value of trend analysis is seen. From the accounts we see that the cost of sales is £190,000, £263,000, £261,000 and £326,000 for the four years. If it is assumed that the materials proportion of these figures is, say, 40 per cent, then we can conjecture that materials costs for the four years were £76,000, £105,200, £104,400 and £130,400, and calculate a creditors' ratio for each year, as follows:

1964	1965	1966	1967
$\frac{15 \times 52}{76} = 10$	$\frac{27 \times 52}{105} = 13$	$\frac{38 \times 52}{104} = 19$	$\frac{49 \times 52}{130} = 20$

This is a somewhat striking revelation. If 40 per cent of the cost of sales is for materials, then the company is taking 20 weeks to pay its invoices.

We interpose the first of our self-examination questions here. Answers are given at the end of the chapter.

Q.3.1 Is the company maintaining too high a stock level in your estimation?
Q.3.2 What has been the company's profit on capital employed over the past four years and what conclusions might be drawn from the ratios?

We can now compare the company's share of the total market for cookers with the reservation that Medway's cookers are of the very small type. Their average price, extracted from Table 3.2 for each year, is £20.00 (1964), £22.70 (1965), £18.66 (1966), and £17.93 (1967). Table 3.10 shows the cookers' share of the market.

Table 3.10

Percentage of market volume of cookers

1964	3·17
1965	3·30
1966	4·10
1967	5·38

Notice that Medway's sales of cookers declined between 1964 and 1965 by 2·38 per cent, yet industry sales declined by 6·14 per cent. Furthermore Medway's sales in 1966 and 1967 increased by 26·73 per cent and 40·46 per cent respectively, while total industry sales increased by only 1·87 per cent and 7·16 per cent for the same two years. The difference between Medway's range of cookers and those of the rest of the industry is that Medway produce only a very small cooker, which is a very small segment of the market. If it is conjectured that industry sales of cookers generally follow a normal distribution, then Medway's share of the small cooker market might be rather high. If there is little competition in this segment, Medway may well possess something of the order of 80 per cent of the segment. For the moment this percentage share is not important. What is important is that, while their share of the total market is small, their share of the particular segment may be so high that they cannot readily increase sales without enormous input of promotion.

The company's operations in the washing machine market are not very significant. See Table 3.11.

Table 3.11
Percentage of industry sale of washing machines

1964	0·22
1965	0·33
1966	0·75
1967	0·57

Comparing Tables 3.6, 3.7 and 3.8, we can determine the amount of business obtained in each area by Tallon (Table 3.12).

Table 3.12

	Tables 3.6, 3.7 Company (£)	Table 3.8 Salesmen (£)	Tallon's sales (£)	(per cent)
London	164,005	150,000	14,005	9
Manchester	168,640	140,000	28,640	17
Birmingham	143,140	98,000	45,140	32
Bristol	88,315	34,300	54,015	61
Glasgow	62,950	30,000	32,950	52
Head Office	12,950			
	£640,000	£452,300	£174,750	27 per cent

From Table 3.12 it is evident that the Birmingham, Bristol and Glasgow areas contain a great number of house accounts — probably too many for adequate servicing.

The profitability of the areas can be estimated by means of the information in the profit and loss account and Table 3.8, and one or two assumptions. Assume that travelling expenses for each salesman are £1,500 a year, and annual office expenses for each of the three £3,000 — this to include the salary of the girls there. Now we can allocate items directly to areas as follows:

Salesmen's salaries	£17,225
Salesmen's commission (1 per cent)	4,523
Salesmen's expenses	15,000
Office expenses	9,000
	£45,748

The remainder of the indirect expenses have to be allocated proportionately to the areas. They are the following:

Medway Appliances Ltd

Manufacturing expenses	£126,000
Balance of salaries	33,252
Balance of office expenses	10,000
Balance of 'other' expenses	24,000
Balance of total expenses	51,000
	£244,252
Manufacturing cost of sales	48·15 per cent

Q.3.3 How would you allocate these expenses to the areas?

3.21 *Profitability of Areas*

London

Sales		£150,000
Cost of sales 48·15 per cent		72,225
		77,775
Salaries	£5,295	
Commission	1,500	
Travel expenses	4,500	
Office expenses	3,000	
Other expenses		
$\dfrac{£244,252 \times 150,000}{£640,000}$	57,247	
		71,542
Area profit:		£6,233 = 4·16 per cent

Manchester

Sales		£140,000
Cost of sales 48·15 per cent		67,410
		72,590
Salaries	5,100	
Commission	1,400	
Travel expenses	4,500	
Office expenses	3,000	
Other expenses		
$\dfrac{£244,252 \times 140,000}{£640,000}$	53,430	
		67,430
Area profit:		£5,160 = 3·69 per cent

Birmingham

Sales		£98,000
Cost of sales 48·15 per cent		47,187
		50,813
Salaries	3,425	
Commission	980	
Travel expenses	3,000	
Offices expenses	3,000	
Other expenses		
$\dfrac{£244,252 \times 98,000}{£640,000}$	37,401	
		47,806
Area profit:		£3,007 = 3·07 per cent

Bristol
Sales £34,300
Cost of sales 48·15 per cent 16,515
17,785

Salaries 1,680
Commission 343
Travel expenses 1,500
Other expenses
$$\frac{£244,252 \times 34,300}{£640,000}$$ 13,090
16,613

Area profit: £1,172 = 3·42 per cent

Glasgow
Sales £30,000
Cost of sales 48·15 per cent 14,445
15,555

Salaries 1,725
Commission 300
Travel expenses 1,500
Other expenses
$$\frac{£244,252 \times 30,000}{£640,000}$$ 11,449
14,974

Area profit: £581 = 1·94 per cent

Head Office and Mr Tallon
Sales £187,700
Cost of sales 48·15 per cent 90,378
97,322

Proportion of expenses
$$\frac{£244,252 \times 187,700}{£640,000}$$ 71,635

Profit: £25,687 = 13·69 per cent

Table 3.13 shows these data in summary form.

Table 3.13

Area	Sales (£)	Mfg cost (£)	Expenses (£)	Profit (£)	As per cent
London	150,000	72,225	71,542	6,233	4·16
Manchester	140,000	67,410	67,430	5,160	3·69
Birmingham	98,000	47,187	47,806	3,007	3·07
Bristol	34,300	16,515	16,613	1,172	3·42
Glasgow	30,000	14,445	14,974	581	1·94
Tallon and H.O.	187,700	90,378	71,635	25,687	13·69
	£640,000	£308,160	£290,000	£41,840	6·54

Q.3.4 The total profit in this summary is £41,840 yet the profit in the P & L account is £61,000. Why is there a difference of £19,160?

Even allowing for the fact that the profitability of the areas has been done fairly crudely because of lack of information, the area profits are rather low, and it is only because of the turnover provided by the 'house accounts' covered by Tallon that substantial profit is made. The company's history of profit on sales is as follows:

1964	1965	1966	1967
11·67 per cent	5·19 per cent	2·34 per cent	9·01 per cent

Action needs to be taken to raise profit levels to, say, 10 per cent of sales. First, we can consider the present sales per outlet (Table 3.14).

Table 3.14

	Outlets	Total sales (£)	Sales per outlet (£)
London	5,050	164,005	32·48
Manchester	4,240	168,640	39·77
Birmingham	4,045	143,140	35·39
Bristol	2,170	88,315	40·70
Glasgow	1,135	62,950	55·46

It is interesting to note that the Glasgow area with the lowest total sales has the highest sales per outlet, although too much should not be read into these figures.

Q.3.5 Could the reason for this high sales-per-outlet figure in Glasgow be that the outlets are better serviced?

The salesmen make an average of thirty calls a week. If we assume that they have a total of three weeks' vacation a year, then the ten men will be able to make 10 x 30 x 49 = 14,700 calls a year.

Of the 16,640 accounts, some are visited once a year and some are seen 'at least four times a year'. As there is little information available on the annual sales per account, we can only conjecture as to the likely call rates. Assuming that all electricity showrooms are visited four times a year, this requires,

$$1,340 \times 4 = 5,360 \text{ calls a year, leaving}$$
$$14,700 - 5,360 = 9,340 \text{ calls.}$$

If we assume that 20 per cent of appliance shops are visited four times a year, this requires,

$$15,300 \times 20 \text{ per cent} \times 4 = 12,240 \text{ calls a year.}$$

As there are only 9,340 calls available for these 12,240, we can assume that there is some other basis for customer servicing.

Q.3.6 What possible conclusions can you draw from this apparent shortfall of salesmen's calls? If you can make any tentative judgments, what action would you recommend or what further investigation would you suggest?

3.22 Problem of Washing Machines

There is considerable interest in phasing out washing machines and concentrating on cookers, perhaps with an extended range. If the company stops washing machine manufacture for the next year, it is unlikely that it will be able to replace the lost revenue with profitable sales of new products immediately.

Q.3.7 What are the implications of the company ceasing to market washing machines but still wishing to maintain annual growth?

A final point to consider is the problem of the plastics agitator. The decision will most likely hinge on the interpretation of 1(b) in Appendix II, '... should not expand its own profits by resorting to low-price outside supplies, at the expense of other K.E.L. divisions or companies able to provide the material or products required at a reasonably competitive price'.

If you decide to phase out washing machine manufacture, this Ashford v. Stone controversy becomes an academic exercise. If you decide that the mouldings are required, it is necessary to calculate what the cost of withdrawing from Stone Plastics' negotiations will amount to, and what loss of profit will be caused to Medway by staying with Ashford Mouldings.

3.23 *Advertising*

Advertising needs to have a 'professional touch' and perhaps two decisions might be offered: first, the appointment of an advertising manager and then the appointment of an advertising agency. The appropriation could be in the region of £20,000 to £30,000 – this to include the salary of the advertising manager. One of the important things that needs to be done in this direction is the establishing of advertising objectives.

Q.3.8 Are there any possible remaining problems on which decisions might have to be taken?

3.3 Report

A report on Medway Appliances might be constructed along the following lines:

Aim. To continue to develop in the U.K. domestic market, *or* to continue to develop in the U.K. domestic durables market, *or* to develop in the U.K. and overseas markets for durable consumer goods. (There are many other aims you may prefer to adopt.)

Purpose. To provide a minimum agreed return on investment to the parent group. (You may perceive several reasons for this, which would underline the fact that there are always at least two reasons why we do anything – a good reason and the *real* reason.)

Objectives. Examples that might be adopted are the following:
  1 To introduce five new electric cookers into the company's product range by the end of one year.
  2 To phase out washing machines over the next two years.
  3 To increase the range of washing machines to four types over the next two years.
  4 To achieve a net profit before tax of at least 12 per cent of sales during the next year.

5 To eliminate house accounts and reallocate all accounts to the sales force within six months.

These examples of objectives are diverse enough for you to understand that not only are some of them completely incompatible but that the majority of objectives can only be adopted after the actions proposed to achieve them have been assessed. Supposing that, as a result of your reading of the case and your understanding of the opinions and abilities of the people in the case, you were convinced that Medway should phase out washing machines. This could be adopted as an objective, but the resulting loss of turnover (see Q.3.7 and A.3.7) by not selling washing machines implies, by calculation, that sales of cookers would have to be increased by something in the order of 40 per cent if the company is to maintain its turnover and results. The objective should not be adopted before the action has been assessed in this way. Consider the sequential linking discussed in Chapter 1. Phasing out washing machines, the consequent loss of turnover and the release of executive and other management and sales time might be linked with an extension of the range of cookers such that new cooker revenue would gradually replace and eventually greatly exceed the lost washing machine turnover. This could be assessed quantitatively, and a decision then recommended whether or not to select this particular course of action.

You will probably understand now why the temptation to provide you with complete reports on these cases has been resisted. There can be no one best set of objectives and actions, and to give you even a suggested report might tend to restrict your own ideas. To recommend phasing out washing machines to Medway executives can have as much merit as recommending that they expand their range of machines.

It is in this direction possibly more than any other where the use and value of case work is apparent. It is the practicability and reasonableness of your proposals supported by adequate argument, quantified as far as possible, that becomes the major consideration. In real life a company may achieve equal financial success and employee satisfaction by the selection and adoption of one from two or more quite different plans; in case analysis diametrically opposed reports can also command equal respect.

ANSWERS TO QUESTIONS

A.3.1 Opening and closing stock valuations are sometimes omitted from a company's summary accounts but can usually be calculated. Consider the profit and loss accounts and balance sheets. Between 1965 and 1966 stock as shown in the balance sheets increased from £26,000 to £55,000, that is, by £29,000. Sales in 1966 were £556,000, and cost of these sales £261,000. The calculation is,

Sales		£556,000
Opening stock	£26,000	
Manufactured	£x	
	£x + 26,000	
Cost of sales	£261,000	
Closing stock	£55,000	

Therefore, $x = £261,000 + £55,000 - £26,000 = £290,000$

Notice in the profit and loss accounts that certain of the expenses have been itemized; in particular, some of the manufacturing expenses are deducted after the 'cost of sales'. With the information we have extracted above we can now redraft the account for 1966, as follows:

Sales (£000s)		556
Opening stock	26	
Manufacturing	290	
Manufacturing expenses	155	
	471	
Closing stock	55	
Cost of sales		416
		140
Less expenses (282−155)		127
Net profit before taxation		13

This is the more usual method of setting out the account. You may care to prepare the account for 1967.

The stockturn ratio can be calculated when the opening and closing stock figures are known:

$$\text{Average stock} = \frac{\text{Opening + closing stock}}{2}$$

Therefore average stock in 1967 was (55,000 + 55,000)/2 which is £55,000. This is 8·12 per cent of sales, or, as a reciprocal, sales are 12·31 times the average stock held. This can be considered to be a very modest stockholding.

A.3.2 Profit on capital employed for the four years:

1964	1965	1966	1967
21·34 per cent	10·79 per cent	5·24 per cent	22·76 per cent

A.3.3 Of the expenses to be allocated to the areas, manufacturing expenses can be apportioned according to sales turnover because it relates directly to turnover. Salaries, office, 'other' and the balance of total expenses should be allocated according to the activities they cover. For example, salaries of staff who are not engaged in calling on customers will be mainly for the administration of the company and might possibly be allocated according to the volume of work engendered by those customers. This we do not know, although we do know the numbers of outlets and the turnover on each area. The relevant percentages of totals are given in Table 3.15.

Table 3.15

Area	Outlets	Per cent	Turnover (£)	Per cent
London	5,050	30	164,005	26
Birmingham	4,045	24	143,140	22
Manchester	4,240	25	168,640	26
Bristol	2,170	13	88,315	14
Glasgow	1,135	7	62,950	10
Head office	–	2	12,950	2
	16,640	100*	£640,000	100

* Note that the percentages do not sum to 100 because of rounding.

These calculations do not include the effort of Tallon in the areas as a separate amount. It can be assumed that the orders and work resulting from his efforts will need a similar proportionate amount of administration, and instead of using the area totals from Table 3.8, as we have done already, we can recalculate with the totals taken from Tables 3.6 and 3.7 which include Tallon's efforts.

London

	Sales	£164,005
	Less cost of sales 48·15 per cent	78,968
		85,037
Salaries	5,295	
Commission	1,500*	
Travel	4,500	
Office	3,000	
Apportioned	62,591	
		76,886
		£8,151 = 4·97 per cent

* Note that only the salesmen's commission has been deducted. Any other commissions paid to Tallon and others are assumed to be in the expenses apportioned according to turnover.

Manchester

	Sales	£168,640
	Less cost of sales 48·15 per cent	81,200
		87,440
Salaries	5,100	
Commission	1,400	
Travel	4,500	
Office	3,000	
Apportioned	64,360	
		78,360
		£9,080 = 5·38 per cent

Birmingham

	Sales	£143,140
	Less cost of sales 48·15 per cent	68,922
		74,218
Salaries	3,425	
Commission	980	
Travel	3,000	
Office	3,000	
Apportioned	54,628	
		65,033
		£9,185 = 6·42 per cent

Bristol

	Sales	£88,315
	Less cost of sales 48·15 per cent	42,524
		45,791
Salaries	1,680	
Commission	343	
Travel	1,500	
Apportioned	33,705	
		37,228
		£8,563 = 9·7 per cent

Glasgow

	Sales	£62,950
	Less cost of sales 48·15 per cent	30,310
		32,640
Salaries	1,725	
Commission	300	
Travel	1,500	
Apportioned	24,025	
		27,550
		£5,090 = 8·09 per cent

Head Office

Sales	£12,950
Less cost of sales 48·15 per cent	6,235
	6,715
Apportioned expenses	4,943
	£1,772 = 13·68 per cent

A.3.4 £37,000 of other goods have not been used in the calculation. As all the expenses have been allocated (£290,000) then £37,000 less 48·15 per cent manufacturing cost is profit:

$$48\cdot15 \text{ per cent} = \frac{\begin{array}{r}£37,000\\17,816\end{array}}{£19,184}$$

This is approximately equal to the £19,160 difference (the variation is due to rounding of figures).

A.3.5 The sales-per-outlet figures include sales obtained by Tallon. If we calculate the sales per outlet obtained by the salesmen, we have the data shown in Table 3.16.

Table 3.16

	Outlets	Total sales (£)	Sales per outlet (£)
London	5,050	150,000	29·70
Manchester	4,240	140,000	33·02
Birmingham	4,045	98,000	24·23
Bristol	2,170	34,300	15·81
Glasgow	1,135	30,000	26·43

This table gives quite a different picture from previous calculations. There is no correlation whatsoever between the two sets of sales per outlet:

X	Y	
32·48	29·70	$\Sigma X = 203\cdot80$
39·77	33·02	$\Sigma X^2 = 8,621\cdot35$
35·39	24·23	$\Sigma Y_2 = 129\cdot19$
40·70	15·81	$\Sigma Y^2 = 3,508\cdot00$
55·46	26·43	$\Sigma XY = 5,244\cdot65$

$$R = \frac{n\Sigma XY - \Sigma X \Sigma Y}{\sqrt{[n\Sigma X^2 - (\Sigma X)^2][n\Sigma Y^2 - (\Sigma Y)^2]}}$$

$$= \frac{-105 \cdot 67}{(39 \cdot 65)(29 \cdot 15)}$$

$$= -0 \cdot 09$$

Sales estimates can be calculated on the basis of either Manchester sales per outlet (£33.02) being the highest or Glasgow sales per outlet (£55.46) in the previous calculation. See Table 3.17.

Table 3.17

	Outlets	Sales/Outlet (£)	Sales 1967 (£)	Sales estimate (£)
Manchester	4,240	33·02	140,000	140,000
London	5,050	33·02	150,000	166,750
Birmingham	4,045	33·02	98,000	133,560
Bristol	2,170	33·02	34,300	71,650
Glasgow	1,135	33·02	30,000	37,470
				£549,430
Glasgow	1,135	55·46	62,950	62,950
London	5,050	55·46	164,005	280,070
Manchester	4,240	55·46	168,640	235,150
Birmingham	4,045	55·46	143,140	224,330
Bristol	2,170	55·46	88,315	120,340
				£922,840

A more accurate approach would be to consider cookers and washing machines separately as pieces and as value per outlet in 1967 (Table 3.18).

Table 3.18

		Cookers per outlet		Washing machines per outlet	
		pieces	value (£)	pieces	value (£)
London	5,050	1·6	28·80	0·19	3·78
Manchester	4,240	1·9	34·27	0·27	5·41
Birmingham	4,045	1·8	32·40	0·19	3·38
Bristol	2,170	1·9	34·67	0·26	5·22
Glasgow	1,135	2·7	48·77	0·33	6·70

These figures have been analysed from Tables 3.6 and 3.7, and therefore include Tallon's efforts in the areas. It is not possible to extend this analysis usefully any further — for instance, to individual salesmen's performances (Table 3.8) — because we are not sure how many outlets each man has to look after. In passing, an interesting point is the comparatively high sales per outlet of cookers and washing machines in Scotland.

A.3.6 Assume that calls are made by salesmen four times a year on 75 per cent of electricity showrooms and three times a year on, say, 20 per cent of other outlets:

London (3 men)
3 x 30 x 49 = 4,410 calls

    75 per cent x   300 x 4 =   900
    20 per cent x 4,750 x 3 = 2,850
                                   3,750

Manchester (3 men)
3 x 30 x 49 = 4,410 calls

    75 per cent x   300 x 4 =   900
    20 per cent x 3,940 x 3 = 2,364
                                   3,264

Birmingham (2 men)
2 x 30 x 49 = 2,940 calls

    75 per cent x   315 x 4 =   945
    20 per cent x 3,730 x 3 = 2,238
                                   3,183

Bristol (1 man)
30 x 49 = 1,470 calls

    75 per cent x   270 x 4 =   810
    20 per cent x 1,900 x 3 = 1,140
                                   1,950

Glasgow (1 man)
30 x 49 = 1,470 calls

    75 per cent x   155 x 4 =   465
    20 per cent x   980 x 3 =   588
                                   1,053

From this can be seen that Birmingham and Bristol would not have sufficient representative servicing to cover the estimated calls. Further investigation is essential to determine exactly how many buying points there are in the areas, what is the likely business from them, and how many times a year it is necessary to visit them.

A.3.7 If the company does not sell washing machines in the next year it will lose £77,000 turnover (if we base our argument on the 1967 figure – it could be a lot higher if we consider the 1966 experience of sales). If the company intends to increase its revenue by, say, 20 per cent in the next year, sales must be increased by £135,400 to £812,400. The current sales of cookers is £563,000, which implies that the company would need to increase sales of cookers by £812,400–£563,000 = £249,400. Now the average price of cookers is £20, requiring that 249,400/20 = 12,470 extra cookers have to be sold to make up the loss of sale of washing machines and to allow for the increased turnover. This is an increase of 40 per cent.

In view of the possible saturation of the company's market segment for small cookers, it may be impossible to achieve an increase of the order of 40 per cent in the U.K., and the company may have to consider selected export markets.

A.3.8 Some questions that remain unanswered are the following:

How should salesmen's calls be organized?
What extra cooker models should be introduced to extend the company's range?
Is the price of the present cooker too low?
Should there be more frequent and formal meetings of the sales force and, if so, how often and where should they be held?
What are the most likely periodicals in which to advertise?
What is the best way to introduce designated successors to Cox and Tallon?
Should Tallon's accounts be distributed to the sales force and, if so, how should it be done and how will commission arrangements be affected?
What sales turnover should be aimed for in 1968, and over which products should it be divided?
What might be the implications in the statement in the case that 'early sales figures for the first few days in January 1968 indicated that sales of cookers and more especially washing machines were at a much lower level than for the same period in 1967'?

4. Soloran Ltd

It is rather easy to overlook the deeply imbedded problems in the Soloran case, and a fairly deep analysis is necessary to reveal the implications of any marketing decisions that might be taken. The main thing you should learn from a careful study of Soloran is that marketing men must learn to count the cost of all their decisions. Between a current revenue (profit and loss) account and one projected for 12 months ahead lie many patches of difficult and troubled financial waters, which have to be negotiated.

4.1 Data

Soloran Ltd originated as a small company in 1936, when it was set up by Dr John Bragg, who had obtained his doctorate in science at a Swiss university. The company produced a range of fruit juice squashes and jams, and their products always enjoyed a high reputation for the degree of concentration of fruit and for the fact that only sugar and a minimum of preservative were added. Their products have never contained any artificial sweeteners, and this policy had serious consequences for the company during the war years of 1939 to 1945, when sugar was rationed in the U.K., and, subsequently, the policy had a restricting influence up until 1953, when sugar ceased to be rationed.

It had been the aim of Dr Bragg to keep the company fairly small but to produce a good wholesome product. He was not interested in developing the company into a mass-production unit competing with the large fruit juice and squash bottlers, but concentrated on producing a high-class product at their sole factory in the heart of Cumberland, England. The factory is a modern single-storey building at Kirkland, Frizington, overlooking the attractive Ennerdale lake. The plant is well laid out, and has been developed on its original site in an area that is predominantly residential. As there are no other factories or commercial undertakings much nearer than Whitehaven, and because of the excellent labour relations, there are no industrial problems and the fifty-odd employees enjoy comparatively high wages and work in ideal surroundings.

Dr John Bragg had developed during 1925—36 in Villach, Austria, his birthplace, a system of extracting juice from fruit such as oranges, grapefruit and lemons, and had patented the process, which was then widely known in the industry as the 'Jaybee' process. Subsequently, alternative juice extraction methods were developed by competitors and the Jaybee process was largely superseded. Nevertheless the company's objective for quality fruit squashes was maintained, and they had resolutely refused to use synthetized flavours in any of their manufactures. A contributory factor to the quality of their products is the water supply in the Frizington area, which helped to make Soloran squashes 'tastefully fruitier' (to quote their publicity slogan).

While the factory, which was largely a bottling plant, was not extended to cope with the demand for Soloran squashes, to go some way to meet demand concentrates were supplied to other bottlers of squash and carbonated drinks throughout the U.K. Since then the turnover of concentrates had increased to become one and a third times the turnover of squashes in 1966 and in 1967, and in 1968, nearly twice that of squashes.

The orange, lemon and grapefruit squashes were distributed mainly through wine and spirits wholesalers, grocery wholesalers and wholesale chemists. But since 1958 large retail outlets had also been supplied, as had a few of the larger cooperative society outlets.

In 1962 the company concentrated its preserves manufacture in two types of marmalade, one a coarse cut peel and the other a finely shredded peel, and a blackberry jam made from the local Cumberland fruit. Each was packed in 1-lb glass jars.

From 1953 to 1963 growth was continuous, though modest, with one representative covering the north of England and another based in the London area, with the remainder of the country, including Northern Ireland and the Channel Islands, covered by twelve commission agents. It was during this period that the company introduced preserves into its range, marketed under a 'Cumberland' trademark, but sales were never spectacular; after limiting the range to the types already mentioned, sales were marginally profitable at a turnover of around £10,000 a year.

Dr Bragg died in October 1965 after a long illness, and his widow sold her majority shareholding to a cousin, Mr Alexander Curlew, who then took over the company as its chief executive. Curlew was then 48 years old, with long experience in the insurance industry, and, although he had never reached high executive office, was a successful branch manager of his company's Leeds office. He had invested a small legacy wisely and had sufficient capital when the opportunity arose to acquire the shares of Bragg's widow, resign from the branch manager's post and take over Soloran Ltd.

In 1966 Curlew had two other directors on the board with him: one was Harry Frederick, production director, aged 45, who had joined the company in 1954 as production supervisor; and the other was the sales director, Sam Manston, aged 42, who had joined the company in 1960 after many years with a medium-sized chocolate and confectionery manufacturer in the North Midlands, where he had been sales office manager with responsibility for home and export sales administration. These three directors and the management structure are shown in Exhibit 4.1.

There are now eight full-time representatives selling squashes and preserves, one full-time man selling concentrates to bottlers in the south of England (approximately south of a line drawn across the country through North Birmingham). There are fourteen commission agents, ten selling squashes and preserves, and four selling concentrates.

The areas for squashes, preserves and Vitoran are as follows:

1 E.C., W.C., W.1, W.2 districts of London.
2 S.E. London districts south of Thames; Surrey.
3 S.W. London districts south of Thames; Surrey
4 N., E. London districts, part of Hertfordshire; Essex.

5 W., N.W., S.W. London districts north of Thames.
6 Derbyshire, Nottinghamshire, Leicestershire, Staffordshire, Shropshire, Warwickshire, Lincolnshire, and Rutlandshire.
7 Cumberland, Westmorland, Northumberland, Durham, North Riding of Yorkshire.
8 Lancashire, Cheshire and North Wales.
9 Sussex, Hampshire, Dorset.
10 Devon, Cornwall.
11 Bristol, Gloucestershire, Herefordshire, Wiltshire, Somerset.
12 Wales (except North Wales).
13 Norfolk, Suffolk, Cambridgeshire.
14 Northamptonshire, Huntingdonshire, Bedfordshire, Buckinghamshire, Berkshire, Oxfordshire.
15 East and West Ridings of Yorkshire.
16 Scotland.
17 Northern Ireland.
18 Channel Islands.

Full-time representatives are employed in areas 1 to 8; commission agents are employed in areas 9 to 18. The county names refer to the old counties, before the reorganization of 1973.

The areas for concentrates are the following:

Southern England	All south of a line through north of Birmingham.
Northern England	All north of a line through Birmingham.
Scotland	
Northern Ireland	
Channel Islands	

A full-time representative is employed for Southern England to sell concentrates. The other four areas are serviced by agents.

A small office is maintained in London S.E.1, as a base for Adams, the full-time Southern England representative selling concentrates, and as a headquarters for the export business, which is managed by the South East London and Kent representative, Mr Barlow.

In May 1967 Soloran introduced a new product to their range in 'Vitoran', an orange drink concentrate with added vitamins. It contained a stated amount of vitamin C per fluid ounce, and a prescribed amount of Vitoran was recommended to be taken diluted with water three times a day. It was packed in half-sized bottles, two dozen to a case. As production was limited, it was decided to restrict Vitoran to the area adjacent to the plant, that is, Area 7, the then Cumberland, Westmorland, Northumberland, Durham and the North Riding of Yorkshire. Sales, though not tremendous, were around 1,600 dozen bottles in the last eight months of 1967 and 2,400 dozen in 1968. Production of Vitoran in 1968 was approximately 50 per cent of the desired Vitoran capacity.

Keith Rigby, aged 33, the assistant sales manager, was previously the South East

London and Kent representative, and had been promoted to Head Office in September 1967. He maintained contact with some key accounts, carried out routine sales office duties and made occasional field visits as instructed by Sam Manston. Rigby had obtained a good Higher National Certificate in Business Studies, and had taken his Diploma in Marketing in May 1968, gaining a distinction in the case-study paper in Part III. He then had discussions with the Department of Marketing at a Northern University with a view to reading for a degree in marketing. The company were not too sure whether they would be prepared to release him, or, if they did, how they could employ him and make use of his knowledge when he returned to the company. The matter was not resolved by December 1969, although Rigby had been told by Manston to raise it again in the New Year.

Up to 1965 there had been only two full-time representatives — Rigby in London and Adams, who was then selling concentrates throughout the whole of the U.K. Some of the agents who were then working for the company were invited to become full-time representatives, and a complete reorganization of areas was made. At the same time, it was decided to increase the number of large retail outlets and all salesmen (full-time representatives and agents) were instructed to obtain one retail distributor for every 10,000 of the population per area. They were left to their own devices in the location of the retail outlets.

Representatives operated an eight-weekly call schedule on all accounts in their area, and were expected to make calls on prospects when possible. A daily report of calls was made, with quantity of each product ordered and discounts allowed. Each call was classified according to type of outlet, e.g. cooperative society, wholesaler (by trade), independent grocer, retail wine merchant and so on. Space was provided on the form to list the prospects visited.

No analysis was made of these reports, although Rigby made a practice of extracting any that were interesting or abnormal, and passing a photostat to Manston. The agents were not required to make reports, but posted orders either from a company order book or the customers' own orders.

Quotas had been established for the areas in which the full-time representatives were operating but, as several of the salesmen were comparatively newly appointed to the full-time staff, the quotas were as yet used only as a basis for the calculation of commission. These quotas for 1968 are shown in Table 4.1.

Table 4.1

Area	Annual quota (£)
1	8,000
2	10,000
3	9,000
4	5,000
5	4,000
6	5,000
7	7,000
8	8,000
Southern England	68,000

An attempt was made to forecast squash sales each year from the previous year's results. About 15 per cent increase per year was thought reasonable, but this varied, depending on the weather during the previous year. Thus, if squash sales were, say, £105,000 in 1967, then it was expected to obtain £120,000 sales in 1968. In the event 1968 had a very poor summer, with much rain, and sales fell well below forecast. It was hoped to achieve between £140,000 and £150,000 sales of squashes in 1969. Similar reasoning lay behind estimates of sales of concentrates, although a somewhat more ambitious forecast had been accepted for 1969, when the company hoped to achieve sales of £215,000.

Monthly statements showed unit and sterling sales for each product during the previous month, cumulative sales for each product, and corresponding sales for the same period in the previous year. Monthly production figures were also given, together with the outstanding order position and a brief analysis of variances. Over the past several months the preparation of these statistical returns had become burdensome, and it was agreed to accept quarterly returns for the time being.

All production was packed in glass bottles, jars and containers, because plastic bottles were unsuitable for liquids with a high fruit juice concentrate content. Maximum capacity on a single shift working is 700-dozen bottles of squashes and/or Vitoran a day and 50-dozen jars of preserves. As the production of concentrates was so simple, no real measurement of capacity had been made, and it was confidently thought that concentrates turnover could be increased to £350,000 a year without overstraining production facilities. In 1967 and 1968 overtime had been worked for a short period to cope with the demand for preserves. Space was available in the plant for another WACO mixing, filling and labelling machine — at a cost of £5,000 — which would produce another 60-dozen jars a day; but it was also possible to increase output by working overtime or by introducing a two-shift system, although no preliminary approach had been made to the union concerned.

At a Board meeting early in December 1968 the directors considered giving the staff a Christmas bonus, although this had not been done previously, but decided against it. Representatives occasionally received a small bonus in addition to their normal commission but this was only in recognition of special services rendered to the company. The directors thought that the representatives on the whole were paid rather well. They received a car and were paid a salary, expenses were paid as incurred and a commission of 1 per cent was paid against invoice on all sales in excess of quotas.

Agents received no salary or expenses but received a commission on all sales. This was $7\frac{1}{2}$ per cent on sales at full list price; 5 per cent on sales where minimum or medium discount was given; $2\frac{1}{2}$ per cent on sales where maximum discount was given. The price list and discounts for squashes, preserves and Vitoran are as follows:

PRICES AND DISCOUNTS

Delivery carriage paid on all orders of £5 and over.

Orange, lemon and grapefruit squashes — 1-doz. 26-oz bottles to a case

Recommended resale price	$17\frac{1}{2}$p per bottle
List price	£1·$67\frac{1}{2}$ per dozen

Discounts (per cent)

Multiple retail organizations (minimum 6 cases)	$7\frac{1}{2}$
Wholesalers (min. 12 cases)	$12\frac{1}{2}$
Selected wholesalers, large multiples (min. 24 cases)	$17\frac{1}{2}$

Quantity Allowances (not additional but alternative to the ordinary discounts) may be given at salesmen's discretion, as follows:

6 to 11 cases	$2\frac{1}{2}$p per case
12 to 23 cases	4p per case
24 to 35 cases	5p per case
36 to 49 cases	6p per case
50 to 99 cases	$7\frac{1}{2}$p per case
100 to 149 cases	9p per case
150 to 199 cases	10p per case
200 and over	11p per case

Vitoran
2-doz. 13-oz bottles to a case

Recommended resale price	$12\frac{1}{2}$p per bottle
List price	£1.25 per dozen

Similar discounts and quantity allowances are applied and customers may make up orders for squashes and Vitoran to qualify for discounts.

Preserves —
Marmalade, Cumberland Berry
2-doz. 1-lb jars to a case

Recommended resale price	$7\frac{1}{2}$p per jar
List price	75p per dozen

Discounts (per cent)

Multiple retail organizations (min. 6 cases)	10
Wholesalers (min. 12 cases)	$12\frac{1}{2}$

Concentrates of various formulations

List price to bottlers £4·$62\frac{1}{2}$ to £4·90 per gallon in non-returnable glass containers.

Quantity discounts available on quotation.

Within a 100 miles radius of Whitehaven all deliveries were made by the company's own transport. Deliveries to areas beyond this limit were usually made by rail or road transport, although sometimes large volume orders were delivered direct as far as Bristol, Birmingham and London.

The company used the services of depots in Birmingham, Manchester, Glasgow, Cardiff, Hemel Hempstead and Maidstone, which were owned by transport contractors who delivered orders within a prescribed area of each depot and, in addition, carried stocks of bottled squashes and preserves. Each contractor, except Glasgow, collected bulk loads from the Soloran plant in Kirkland to replenish stocks, while the Glasgow depot was supplied by the company's own transport.

Depots did not hold stocks of concentrates because a different formulation of concentrate was supplied to each bottler. Mr Rigby was responsible for stock deliveries to the depots, while the representative or agent in the area concerned maintained a supervisory function over the depot, also arranging for despatch of stock against orders, requisitioning for replenishment of stock and keeping the stock records.

Distribution costs per unit (1 case of 1 dozen squash, or 1 case of 2 dozen Vitoran or preserves), were as follows:

By company's own transport	$7\frac{1}{2}$p per case
By rail	$17\frac{1}{2}$p per case
Ex-depot (including bulk delivery to the depot)	14p per case

For costing purposes, transport charges were calculated on the ratio of sales in different areas. Half the sales were delivered from Kirkland, a third were ex-depot and the remainder were delivered by rail. Therefore, the transport costs were calculated as follows:

$$
\begin{array}{lll}
3 \text{ cases (ex-Kirkland)} @ 7\frac{1}{2}p & = 22\frac{1}{2}p \\
2 \text{ cases (ex-depot)} @ 14p & = 28p \\
1 \text{ case (by rail)} @ 17\frac{1}{2}p & = 17\frac{1}{2}p \\
\hline
& 68p
\end{array}
$$

The average cost of delivery was therefore approximately 11p per case, irrespective of contents.

At a Board meeting on 2 January 1969, Mr Curlew raised the subject of publicity. Of the £20,000 spent in 1968, £10,000 had been spent on point-of-sale material, price lists and sales literature. Four-inch double column display advertisements had been placed in the *Sunday Express, Homes and Gardens, Vogue, Harper's Bazaar, Ideal Home* and occasionally in substantial provincial papers such as the *Yorkshire Post*. From February to August posters had been displayed for one month at the railway stations of Kings Cross, Birmingham, Liverpool, Manchester, Newcastle-on-Tyne and Glasgow. As the length of hiring was short, the company had to accept whatever sites were available, but always tried to obtain sites near train arrival boards. For a three-month period during the summer 500 panels were taken on London Underground trains. All advertising was placed through a small advertising agent in Carlisle.

Mr Manston said that £20,000 was insignificant to create brand awareness for squash. He gave details of the sums spent by some of their competitors (Table 4.2).

Table 4.2

Company	12 months' expenditure as at Dec. 1968 (£)
Schweppes	450,000
Tree Top	300,000
Coca Cola	150,000
Quosh	120,000
Pepsi Cola	100,000
Robinson's	100,000
Suncrush	100,000
Hunt's Soft Drinks	75,000
Britvic	50,000
Sunfresh	50,000
Rose's Lime Juice	30,000

He said that the figures in Table 4.2 were published in the monthly trade press, and emphasized that although not all the sums related to squash advertising — Schweppes, for example, advertised mainly soft drink additions such as bitter lemon and tonic water — they were all competing in the soft drinks market, and Soloran must regard all drink manufacturers as potential competitors. On the other hand, he pointed out the tremendous weight of advertising for the squash products of Tree Top, Quosh, Suncrush and Sunfresh, which added up to well over half a million pounds. He also gave details of the sums spent on advertising jams, honey and marmalade. Robertson's spent £300,000, Gale's Honey £110,000, Chivers' £60,000, and Hartley's £50,000 — a total of well over £500,000 for these five alone. The other two directors were obviously impressed by these figures, and were in no doubt as to the size of the publicity task that confronted the company.

'However', said Manston, 'there is another matter which I would like to raise before we proceed. For several weeks now I have been concerned about my own future. I have been approached by my old company, who have offered me a position which I find difficult to decline. I've talked this over with my wife and we have considered it from all angles, especially from the children's viewpoint. As you know, they are at a crucial age in their education. Naturally, I have also given a lot of thought to Soloran and my loyalties here. I would like to accept the offer, although I have not given a definite answer yet. I have until Friday to say 'yes'. I would like to accept the offer and hope that I can start with them on April 1st.'

This news was greeted with shocked silence by the other two. Then Curlew said, 'Sam, I think I can understand your position. We don't want to stand in your way but, I think it would be better for all concerned if you leave as soon as possible. Staying on here until the end of March would help neither of us.'

After further, minor, discussions, the meeting ended without any other business being raised. Sam Manston cleared up his outstanding items and left his office for the last time on 12 January 1969. Curlew and Frederick had several discussions about the situation and decided to appoint a marketing manager as successor to Manston as quickly as possible.

Exhibit 4.1 shows the existing management organization, and Tables 4.3 to 4.7 sales turnover and breakdowns. The data section concludes with profit and loss accounts (pp. 94—98) and balance sheets for 1967 and 1968.

Table 4.3   Sales Turnover of Soloran Ltd for Years 1966, 1967 and 1968

	1966	£000s 1967	1968
Squashes	160	157	110
Preserves	8	10	8
Concentrates	210	205	196
Export (squashes)	12	10	12
Vitoran	—	2	3
	390	384	329

4.2 Analysis

The management of Soloran have decided to appoint a marketing manager to replace Sam Manston as quickly as possible. There is a number of ways in which this new manager can look at the operation of the company.

Q.4.1   If you were appointed to the position of marketing manager to Soloran Ltd, where would you start making decisions?

There are only two years' financial figures in the case, so it is not possible to draw any firm conclusions. The basic ratios for these two years are shown in Table 4.8. (p. 98).

Table 4.4 Unit Sales* Soloran Ltd.

	1967			1968		
Area	Squashes	Preserves	Vitoran	Squashes	Preserves	Vitoran
1	14,600	1,570		11,200	1,720	
2	15,100	620		14,050	510	
3	10,300	470		8,250	440	
4	9,700	380		5,300	320	
5	6,400	460		4,200	450	
6	7,800	650		5,600	520	
7	7,200	450	820	6,300	390	1,210
8	15,000	780		11,200	510	
9	3,000	260		1,400	180	
10	2,600	340		1,300	270	
11	3,300	220		2,100	130	
12	2,400	140		750	80	
13	2,800	430		2,100	220	
14	5,100	580		3,400	370	
15	7,000	830		4,800	480	
16	2,200	120		1,400	80	
17	1,100	50		850	10	
18	1,600	–		1,350	–	

*A unit is a case of 1-doz. bottles, squashes, 2-doz. preserves or 2-doz. Vitoran.

Table 4.5 Sales per Product Group per Area

	1967				1968			
Area	Squashes	Preserves	Conc.	Vitoran	Squashes	Preserves	Conc.	Vitoran
1	£21,450	£1,885			£15,200	£2,033		
2	21,300	750			19,050	610		
3	14,100	560			12,050	530		
4	13,000	455			8,100	385		
5	9,100	540			6,150	540		
6	11,000	780			8,200	625		
7	10,000	540		£2,000	9,100	470		£3,000
8	21,400	930			16,100	620		
9	4,400	310			2,050	220		
10	3,700	400			1,850	325		
11	5,350	260			3,000	155		
12	3,300	175			1,050	95		
13	4,200	520			3,000	265		
14	7,400	695			5,000	445		
15	10,500	990			7,000	575		
16	3,000	145			2,050	95		
17	1,600	65			1,200	12		
18	2,200	–			1,850	–		
S.E.			£88,000				£84,000	
N.E.			58,600				56,100	
Scotland			14,500				13,900	
N.I.			14,900				14,200	
C.I.			29,000				27,800	
	£167,000	£10,000	£205,000	£2,000	£122,000	£8,000	£196,000	£3,000

Soloran Ltd

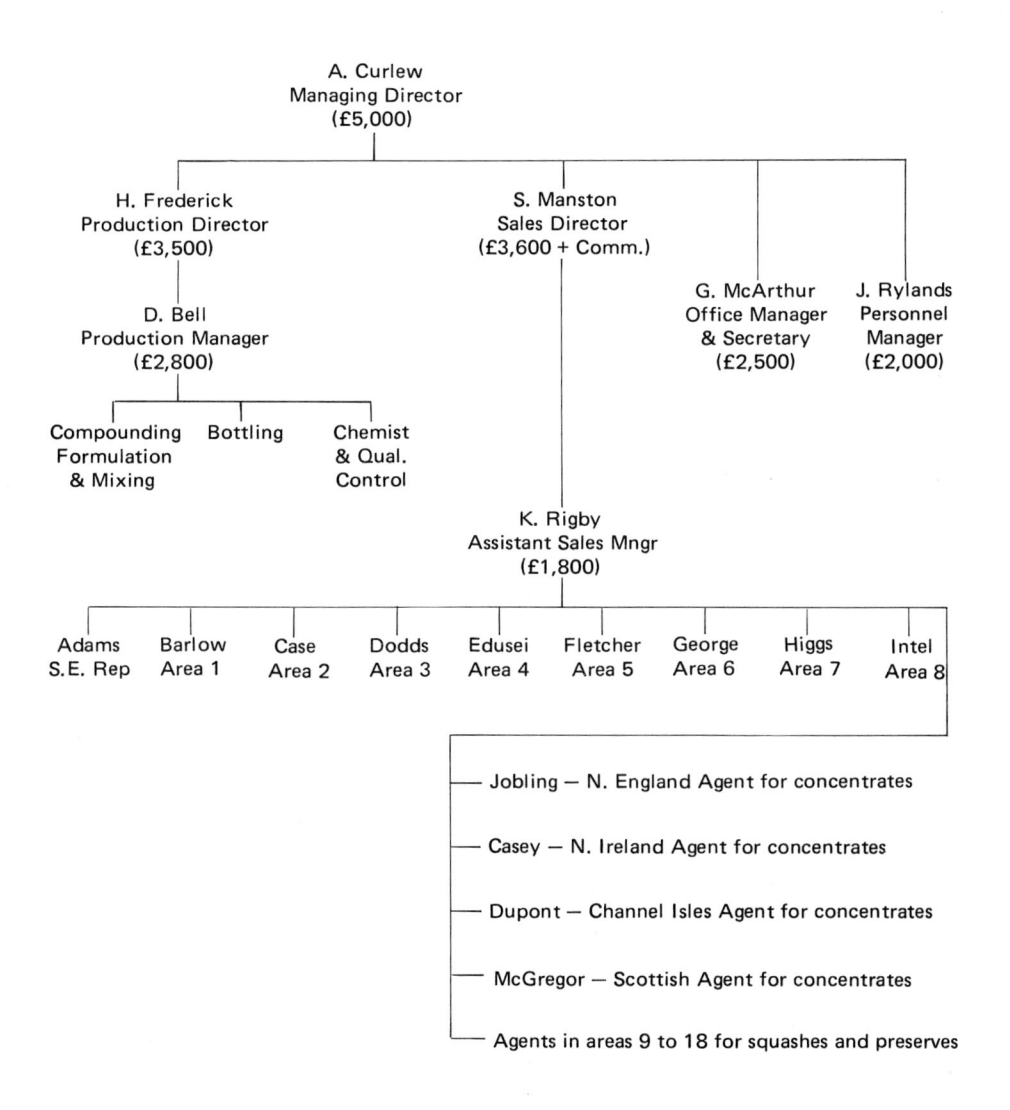

```
                      A. Curlew
                   Managing Director
                      (£5,000)
                          |
    ┌─────────────────────┼─────────────────────────────────┐
H. Frederick          S. Manston                                         
Production Director   Sales Director                                      
(£3,500)              (£3,600 + Comm.)                                    
    |                     |                    G. McArthur      J. Rylands
D. Bell                   |                    Office Manager   Personnel
Production Manager        |                    & Secretary      Manager
(£2,800)                  |                    (£2,500)         (£2,000)
    |
┌───┼────────┬──────────┐
Compounding  Bottling   Chemist
Formulation             & Qual.
& Mixing                Control

                          |
                      K. Rigby
                  Assistant Sales Mngr
                      (£1,800)
                          |
┌──────┬──────┬──────┬──────┬──────┬──────┬──────┬──────┐
Adams  Barlow Case   Dodds  Edusei Fletcher George Higgs  Intel
S.E. Rep Area 1 Area 2 Area 3 Area 4 Area 5 Area 6 Area 7 Area 8
```

    Jobling — N. England Agent for concentrates

    Casey — N. Ireland Agent for concentrates

    Dupont — Channel Isles Agent for concentrates

    McGregor — Scottish Agent for concentrates

    Agents in areas 9 to 18 for squashes and preserves

Exhibit 4.1   Company Organization and Salaries as at 1 January 1969

Table 4.6 Monthly Breakdown of Sales of Soloran Squashes, Vitoran and Concentrates for 1968 in Sterling

Areas	J	F	M	A	M	J	J	A	S	O	N	D
1	900	1,100	1,200	1,250	1,400	1,550	1,600	1,500	1,200	1,100	1,200	1,200
2	1,200	1,400	1,200	1,250	1,950	2,050	2,850	2,500	1,600	1,000	850	1,200
3	800	850	1,000	1,050	1,200	1,400	1,550	1,400	1,100	700	600	400
4	400	460	500	630	750	780	850	700	630	1,000	900	500
5	400	450	470	530	600	750	770	600	500	300	400	380
6	400	500	500	700	800	900	850	650	600	1,000	950	350
7	800	900	950	1,050	1,250	1,300	1,500	1,400	1,050	750	400	750
8	1,000	1,150	1,200	1,200	1,450	1,600	1,650	1,550	1,200	1,050	1,500	1,550
	5,900	6,810	7,020	7,660	9,400	10,330	11,620	10,300	7,880	6,900	6,800	6,330
9	40	80	85	120	250	350	400	320	220	80	70	35
10	30	80	95	110	225	355	370	250	150	75	60	50
11	60	120	125	180	350	470	650	400	300	125	120	100
12	25	40	45	60	120	150	110	125	125	70	90	90
13	55	125	130	175	330	490	660	380	340	85	130	100
14	100	200	200	350	550	850	950	800	450	250	200	100
15	140	250	310	420	840	1,120	1,450	1,100	1,000	200	100	70
16	35	75	80	135	230	370	450	300	190	85	65	35
17	30	45	50	45	90	200	250	150	80	70	90	100
18	25	85	100	105	235	365	375	245	140	65	60	50
	540	1,100	1,220	1,700	3,220	4,720	5,665	4,070	2,995	1,105	985	730
	6,440	7,910	8,240	9,360	12,620	15,050	17,285	14,370	10,875	8,005	7,785	7,060
Sc.	280	560	580	850	1,600	2,100	2,900	2,400	1,400	650	310	270
N.I.	300	550	560	770	1,550	2,000	3,200	2,500	820	760	600	590
C.I.	550	1,100	1,200	1,500	3,200	4,000	5,600	4,200	3,000	2,450	600	400
S.E.	3,650	3,250	5,500	7,000	8,500	14,000	10,500	5,250	4,800	6,550	7,000	8,000
N.E.	1,000	1,900	2,000	3,300	5,800	7,780	8,850	7,750	6,800	5,400	3,520	2,000

Soloran Ltd

Table 4.7 Breakdown of Concentrates

	1966 (£)	1967 (£)	1968 (£)
Southern England	87,500	88,000	84,000
Northern England	57,000	58,600	56,100
Channel Islands	38,500	29,000*	27,800
Scotland	12,500	14,500	13,900
Northern Ireland	14,500	14,900	14,200
	£210,000	£205,000	£196,000

* A French concentrate manufacturer captured a large slice of this market in 1967.

PROFIT AND LOSS ACCOUNTS

	1967 (£)		1968 (£)	
Sales		384,000		329,000
Increase in stocks		+2,000		+26,000
Value of production		386,000		355,000
Materials	108,500		101,500	
Direct labour	106,000		96,000	
Factory overhead	23,500		20,150	
		238,000		217,650
Manufacturing profit		148,000		137,350
Sales manager and staff	6,000		6,000	
Salesmen and agents	24,000		26,500	
General administration	14,000		15,000	
Distribution costs	15,000		13,800	
Advertising	20,000		20,000	
Depreciation	8,500		7,500	
Financing	3,500		3,500	
Office expenses	7,000		6,000	
		98,000		98,300
Net profit		50,000		39,050
Taxation		23,800		18,500
		26,200		20,550
Dividend		10,000		10,000
		16,200		10,550
Profit B/F		73,425		89,625
Retained profit		£89,625		£100,175

SOLORAN LTD SUMMARY BALANCE SHEETS

	1967 (£)	1968 (£)
Fixed assets:		
Buildings	40,000	40,000
Plant etc.	20,000	25,000
Vehicles	11,000	15,000
	71,000	80,000
Depreciation	15,500	23,000
(*continued on p. 98*)	55,500	57,000

SUMMARY BALANCE SHEETS *continued*

	1967		1968	
Current assets:				
Stock	12,000 (£)		38,000 (£)	
Debtors	118,000		105,600	
Cash	125		1,000	
	130,125		144,600	
Less current liabilities:				
Creditors	21,000		20,000	
Taxation	23,800		18,500	
Overdraft	1,200		12,925	
	46,000		51,425	
		84,125		93,175
		£139,625		£150,175
Financed by:				
50,000 shares @ £1,00		50,000		50,000
Retained profit		89,625		100,175
		£139,625		£150,175

Table 4.8

	1967 (per cent)	1968 (per cent)
Return on investment	35·8	26·0
Sales/funds	275	219
Profit/sales	13	11·7

Even from this scant evidence, the company is not exactly expanding at a great rate, although we must be very careful not to draw too many conclusions from just two years' results.

Q.4.2 Armed with this information on the company's operations for the last two years, where do you consider it is advisable to look next?

From Table 4.4 we can estimate the dozens of squashes and fruit juices sold in 1968. Note, however, that a unit of squash is a case containing one dozen while a unit of 'Vitoran' is a case containing two dozen. In 1968 therefore,

85,550 dozen units of squashes make	1,026,600 bottles
1,210 dozen units of 'Vitoran' make	29,040 bottles
	1,055,640

Q.4.3 Is there any way of determining at what level of capacity the factory is working?

From your consideration of the level of capacity at which the factory is operating you will appreciate that production can be increased considerably without overstraining resources. You will also understand that it is possible to reach a sales figure of about twice that of 1968 — that is, around £650,000.

Between 1967 and 1968 areas 1 to 18 all lost sales, but, owing to the different discounts that were given, some areas experienced a greater loss than their declining unit sales might indicate. For example, in the areas shown in Table 4.9, turnover for squashes declined by a greater percentage than their sales volume.

Table 4.9

Decrease between 1967 and 1968

	Unit sales	Per cent	Turnover	Per cent
Area 1	−3,400	−23	−£6,250	−29
Area 2	−1,050	−7	−£2,250	−11
Area 11	−1,200	−36	−£2,350	−44
Area 13	−700	−25	−£1,200	−29
Area 15	−2,200	−31	−£3,500	−33
Area 17	−250	−23	−£400	−25

This would seem to indicate that there was some price cutting by means of increased discounts being offered in an attempt to obtain more sales, yet the resulting turnover has actually been less. It is interesting to note that the squashes sales volume and sales turnover both declined overall by 27 per cent.

If the total revenue for squashes is divided by the total number of units of squashes sold in each of the two years, we can determine the average unit price. Dividing £167,000 by 117,200 gives £1.425 per unit for 1967; and £122,000 over 85,550 gives £1.426 per unit for 1968.

If this operation is carried out for all areas (by using the data from Tables 4.4 and 4.5), a number of interesting facts emerge. Areas 1 and 2 have both reduced the average price of squashes between 1967 and 1968 — area 1 from £1.47 to £1.36 and area 2 from £1.41 to £1.36 — and both have sold considerably less. Area 11 dropped the price from an average of £1.62 a unit to £1.43, which is a reduction of nearly 12 per cent, yet sales fell in volume, as we have seen, by 36 per cent. As no areas experienced an increase in sales over the previous year, we might be led to assume that there was some other influence in the market causing this rather than attribute it to problems in areas.

Q.4.4 Are we told, or is there any way of determining, the average commission earned by the agents?

The full-time representatives are engaged in areas 1 to 8, and one is selling concentrates in the south-east. We are given the area quotas in the case (Table 4.1) and can therefore calculate the commission they receive (Table 4.10).

From the profit and loss account (p. 97) we know that a total of £26,500 was paid to salesmen and agents in 1968, so we can make the following calculation:

Total payments to salesmen, agents		£26,500
Agents commission (*see* Table 4.12)	£7,112	
Full-time men's commission	628	
		7,740
		£18,760

100   Business Analysis for Marketing Managers

Table 4.10

Area	Squashes (£)	Preserves (£)	Total (£)	Quota (£)	Excess (£)	1 per cent Commission (£)
1	15,200	2,033	17,233	8,000	9,233	92·33
2	19,050	610	19,660	10,000	9,660	96·60
3	12,050	530	12,580	9,000	3,580	35·80
4	8,100	385	8,485	5,000	3,485	34·85
5	6,150	540	6,690	4,000	2,690	26·90
6	8,200	625	8,825	5,000	3,825	38·25
7	12,100*	470	12,570	7,000	5,570	55·70
8	16,100	620	16,720	8,000	8,720	87·20
S.E.	84,000**		84,000	68,000	16,000	160·00
					£627·63, but say	£628·00

* Includes £3,000 of Vitoran.
** Concentrates.

The figure of £18,760 (*see* p. 99) accounts for the salaries and expenses of the full-time salesmen, but a number of assumptions need to be made if we are to take this analysis any further, because we are not told what these sums amount to for each man. An inspection of the area totals in Table 4.5 indicates that the south-east man selling concentrates and the salesmen in areas 1 and 2 might all be higher paid men than those in the other areas simply because their annual turnovers are so much higher. In our conjecture we cannot suppose salaries to be in the same proportion to turnover, because the south-east man's salary would be out of all reason, as his turnover is £84,000. Nevertheless it would be reasonable to expect this man to receive a higher salary than any of the other men. Let us assume that he receives £3,000 and that the men in the better areas, 1, 2, 3, 7 and 8, receive between £2,000 and £2,500. What is left could be allocated according to the men's turnover. While this may not be exactly correct, it will enable us to proceed with a conjectural analysis of what the area profitabilities are. See Table 4.11.

Table 4.11

Area	Estimated salary and expenses of full-time men
1	£2,500
2	2,500
3	2,000
4	1,500*
5	1,200*
6	1,560*
7	2,000
8	2,500
S.E.	3,000
	£18,760

* Salaries allocated approximately in proportion to area turnover.

We can now estimate the costs directly attributable to each area by combining the information we have analysed into Table 4.12.

Table 4.12

Area	Estimated salary and expenses (£)	Commission (£)	Total area direct costs (£)
1	2,500	92	2,592
2	2,500	97	2,597
3	2,000	36	2,036
4	1,500	35	1,535
5	1,200	27	1,227
6	1,560	38	1,598
7	2,000	56	2,056
8	2,500	87	2,587
9		114	114
10		109	109
11		158	158
12		57	57
13		163	163
14		272	272
15		379	379
16		107	107
17		60	60
18		93	93
S.E.	3,000	160	3,160
Scotland		695	695
N.I.		710	710
C.I.		1,390	1,390
N.E.		2,805	2,805
			£26,500

Q.4.5 What other expenses are there to consider and how might these be allocated to the areas?

Various estimates may be made of the cost of manufacture, but, in the absence of any other information, the figures for 1968 have been used as a basis; £217,650 as a percentage of the value of production (£355,000) is 61·31 per cent. There is no particular merit in using such a figure, and 62 per cent could have just as easily been used in the calculation. Tables 4.13 to 4.16 show how net profit per area may be worked out.

There is considerable imbalance in Tables 4.13 to 4.16 among the sales figures, between the south-east man selling concentrates and the rest of the full-time salesmen, and between the full-time men and the agents. If we calculate the monthly turnover as a percentage of annual total turnover for areas of full-time men and areas where there are agents, we have the pattern shown in Table 4.17 (p. 103).

Table 4.13   Areas 1 to 6

Area	1	2	3	4	5	6
Sales	£17,233	£19,660	£12,580	£8,485	£6,690	£8,825
Mfg cost	10,566	12,054	7,713	5,202	4,102	5,411
	6,667	7,606	4,867	3,283	2,588	3,414
Direct costs	2,592	2,597	2,036	1,535	1,227	1,598
	4,075	5,009	2,831	1,748	1,361	1,816
£52,000 by turnover	2,723	3,106	1,988	1,341	1,057	1,394
	1,352	1,903	843	407	304	422
£5,579 by unit sales	771	869	519	336	278	365
Net profit	£581	£1,034	£324	£71	£26	£57
	3%	5%	3%	0·84%	0·39%	0·65%

Table 4.14   Areas 7 to 12

Area	7	8	9	10	11	12
Sales	£12,570	£16,720	£2,270	£2,175	£3,155	£1,145
Mfg cost	7,707	10,251	1,392	1,333	1,934	702
	4,863	6,469	878	842	1,221	443
Direct costs	2,056	2,587	114	109	158	57
	2,807	3,882	764	733	1,063	386
£52,000 by turnover	1,986	2,642	359	344	498	181
	821	1,240	405	389	565	205
£5,579 by unit sales	472	699	94	94	133	50
Net profit	£349	£541	£311	£295	£432	£155
	3%	3%	14%	14%	14%	14%

Table 4.15   Areas 13 to 18

Area	13	14	15	16	17	18
Sales	£3,265	£5,445	£7,575	£2,145	£1,212	£1,850
Mfg cost	2,002	3,338	4,644	1,315	743	1,134
	1,263	2,107	2,931	830	469	716
Direct costs	163	272	379	107	60	93
	1,100	1,835	2,552	723	409	623
£52,000 by turnover	516	860	1,197	339	191	292
	584	975	1,355	384	218	331
£5,579 by unit sales	139	225	315	88	51	81
Net profit	£445	£750	£1,040	£296	£167	£250
	14%	14%	14%	14%	14%	14%

Soloran Ltd

Table 4.16 Geographical Areas

Area	S.E.	N.E.	Scot.	N.I.	C.I.
Sales	£84,000	£56,100	£13,900	£14,200	£27,800
Mfg cost	51,500	34,395	8,522	8,706	17,044
	32,500	21,705	5,378	5,494	10,756
Direct costs	3,160	2,805	695	710	1,390
	29,340	18,900	4,683	4,784	9,366
£52,000 by turnover	13,272	8,864	2,196	2,243	4,392
	16,068	10,036	2,487	2,541	4,974
£8,221 by unit sales	3,523	2,353	583	596	1,166
Net profit	£12,545	£7,683	£1,904	£1,945	£3,808
	15%	14%	14%	14%	14%

Table 4.17

Annual total of areas 1 to 8 where full-time men selling consumer products: £96,950

Monthly turnover of areas 1 to 8 as a percentage of £96,950

Jan.	6·1
Feb.	7·0
Mar.	7·2
Apr.	7·9
May	9·7
June	10·7
July	12·0
Aug.	10·6
Sep.	8·1
Oct.	7·1
Nov.	7·0
Dec.	6·5

Annual total of S.E. area where full-time man selling concentrates: £84,000

Monthly turnover of area as a percentage of £84,000

Jan.	4·4
Feb.	3·9
Mar.	6·6
Apr.	8·3
May	10·1
June	16·7
July	12·5
Aug.	6·3
Sep.	5·7
Oct.	7·8
Nov.	8·3
Dec.	9·5

Annual total of areas 9 to 18 where agents selling consumer products: £28,050

Monthly turnover of areas 9 to 18 as a percentage of £28,050

Jan.	1·9
Feb.	3·9
Mar.	4·4
Apr.	6·1
May	11·5
June	16·8
July	20·2
Aug.	14·5
Sep.	10·7
Oct.	3·9
Nov.	3·5
Dec.	2·6

Annual total of N.E., Scot., N.I. and C.I. areas where agents selling concentrates: £112,000

Monthly turnover of areas as a percentage of £112,000

Jan.	1·9
Feb.	3·7
Mar.	3·9
Apr.	5·7
May	10·9
June	14·2
July	18·4
Aug.	15·0
Sep.	10·7
Oct.	8·3
Nov.	4·5
Dec.	2·9

From Table 4.17 it is clear that the full-time men have different sales patterns from those of the agents. By dividing the year into two main parts — the five peak months May to September and the seven off-season months — we can arrange the pattern as in Table 4.18.

Table 4.18

	Five peak months (£)	(per cent)	Seven off-season months (£)	(per cent)	Total (£)
Squashes:					
Full-time men	49,530	51	47,420	49	96,950
Agents	20,670	74	7,380	26	28,050
Concentrates:					
Full-time man	43,050	51	40,950	49	84,000
Agents	77,450	69	34,550	31	112,000
	£190,700	59	£130,300	41	£321,000

Q.4.6 The total shown in Table 4.18, £321,000, is different from that given in the profit and loss account for 1968. How can the difference be accounted for?

There are two ways in which these analysed figures can be used to prepare an estimate of sales for the next year. If it is assumed that the agents selling squashes are only pushing sales during the peak period, in which they achieve 74 per cent of their total year's turnover, then we can argue that a similar pressure exerted during the other seven months will achieve higher sales. At present the agents are obtaining 26 per cent of their sales in these seven off-season months; and this can be calculated to equal 50 per cent of their annual total. Thus, if £20,670 is to represent 50 per cent (and not 74 per cent), the total these agents should be capable of is approximately £41,340.

A second approach to estimating sales is to assume that the full-time men could achieve greater sales during the peak season to the extent that their efforts would achieve around 70-odd per cent of their annual total during the peak five months.

We have already analysed the full-time men's squashes sales as monthly percentages of totals — January 6·0 per cent, February 7·0 per cent and March 7·2 per cent, for example — and illustrated the fact that the agents' monthly percentage sales are well below these — January 1·9 per cent, February 3·9 per cent and March 4·4 per cent. Therefore these monthly figures for the agents could be increased proportionately.

Q.4.7 Using the analysis thus far, can you prepare a sales estimate for 1969 with the sales figures adjusted as you consider necessary, and taking into consideration that not only does the company expect to increase sales by 15 per cent each year but that 1968 was a poor year because of the weather?

It is now necessary to go through the case thoroughly and decide which products are to be promoted in the next year and which areas need special promotions. A useful method is to prepare a projected profit and loss account to highlight the areas where marketing controls can be exerted. The sales estimate finally agreed

Soloran Ltd

must obviously be the result of discussion and argument, but, for the purpose of this analysis, let us assume that our sales target is to be £400,000.

Consider the following projected revenue account:

Sales estimate		£400,000
Decrease in stocks, say,		21,000
		379,000
Materials (say 28 per cent of net sales)	£106,120	
Labour (say 27 per cent of net sales)	102,330	
Overheads (say 6 per cent of net sales)	22,740	
		231,190
Gross profit		147,810
Less expenses (say 25 per cent of sales)		100,000
Net profit		47,810
Taxation (say 47½ per cent)		22,710
		25,100
Profit brought forward		100,175
		£125,275

You will appreciate that whereas the revenue (profit and loss) account is a record of a period's operations, usually a year, the balance sheet is a financial statement of the company's position at a point in time. Nevertheless, we can make use of this by estimating what the balance sheet might look like at the end of the period covered by our projected revenue account.

Take a projected balance sheet as at end of 1969 as follows:

Financing will be by the total of shares plus the retained profit—50,000 £1 shares			£50,000
Retained profit (from revenue account)			125,275
			£175,275
Fixed assets, say, remain the same as in 1968 for this calculation			80,000
Less depreciation of, say, £5,000 (which must be added to that already recorded)			28,000
Written down value of fixed assets:			52,000
Current assets:			
Stock (£38,000 closing stock in previous balance sheet less the £21,000 reduction proposed)	17,000		
Debtors (say 25 per cent of sales)	100,000		
Cash (calculated at end)			
		£ (a)	
Current liabilities:			
Creditors (say 20 per cent of materials)	21,224		
Taxation (as in P & L a/c)	22,710		
Overdraft (calculated at end, if required)			
		£ (b)	
			£ (c)
			£175,275

Balance sheets may be set out horizontally, with assets on the left and liabilities on the right, or vertically. The financing of the company (in this example £175,275) must equal the sum of the fixed assets plus the difference between the current assets and current liabilities. In the example partly completed (c) is an amount which, when added to the written-down value of fixed assets, equals £175,275. Thus (c) = £175,275 − £52,000 = £123,275.

We know that current assets (a), minus current liabilities (b), equals (c), £123,275; therefore we have to insert either cash or overdraft to make the account balance. The amount to be entered to achieve the balance is cash of £50,209, making the current assets £167,189; deducting the total of current liabilities, £43,934, we have £123,275, the required figure.

> *Q.4.8 Using the same percentages for materials, labour, overheads, expenses, debtors, creditors and taxation, prepare a projected revenue account for the period but with no increase or decrease in stocks and draw up a projected balance sheet.*

You should be able to see the projected revenue account as a useful marketing aid in directing attention to those vital areas that have to be controlled. In the example discussed, where the cash position is shown to be £50,209, if stocks were allowed to increase and debtors (caused by increased sales on credit) were also allowed to increase, together by an amount exceeding £50,209, then there would be a figure required for overdraft and there would be no cash. If you intend to use the revenue account in this way and, in this case, reduce the stocks by £21,000, you will understand that procedures will need to be instituted in the sales operation of the company to ensure that stocks are gradually reduced over a period. We are not told if this figure for stock represents finished stock or raw materials, although it will probably be a combination of the two and a further investigation would be necessary before decisions could be made.

In Chapter 2 we discussed a method of looking at debtors and creditors in terms of weeks outstanding shown in the balance sheet. For 1968 the figure of £105,600 represents 17 weeks of sales outstanding, and for 1967 debtors of £118,000 represent 16 weeks of sales outstanding. Unless there is information to the contrary (there is little on this point in the case), you must be guided by these figures and introduce this length of credit into your considerations. Whether or not it is agreed that it is too long a time to leave accounts outstanding is another matter. If you decide that accounts must be cleared in a shorter period of time than is the mode at present, then, not only must the necessary instructions be issued, but you must be quite clear as to how such instructions have to be carried out. For example, if you decided that your creditors were too long outstanding and you wished to obtain the advantages of earlier settlement terms, then, providing the cash was available, you could discharge your creditors simply by having cheques sent to them. The matter regarding debtors is not as simple. You cannot, by a stroke of the pen, discharge your debtors: you cannot issue instructions to the effect that, henceforward, all accounts will be payable within a stated period of time and expect to see results. Collection of accounts outstanding is a very arduous business, taxing the ingenuity of even the best people in credit management. Therefore, if you consider that it will be good marketing policy to reduce the length of credit given to the company's accounts, you must also consider, first, whether this will adversely affect the sales and, second, how long before your decision will become effective.

To appreciate the effect of credit given to customers on marketing policy it is desirable to look closer at what happens during the year as a result of a sales forecast having been adopted. In this case we have seen that factory capacity can be expanded to about double the present output and, if extra shifts are worked and new bottling equipment introduced, production can rise to permit sales estimates well in excess of £500,000 to be made.

For our purposes let us assume that we have estimated sales for the next year at £400,000, and ignore increase or reduction in stock, so that it will remain at the present valuation of £38,000. The cost of production can be assumed to be 61 per cent of sales and distribution to remain at 4 per cent.

A point to note in passing is that arguments can frequently occur, especially when cases are being discussed in syndicates, about the level of percentage, amount of expenses or some other quantifiable matter. For example, you might take issue with the suggestion here that distribution costs should be retained at 4 per cent. No amount of argument can alter the fact that we do not know what cost might be over next year, and to insert too high an amount is as unwise as ignoring the problem altogether. The best course is to insert a figure, knowing that it may be suspect and have to be reviewed, and use it as a sort of 'bench mark'. After the analysis refinements can be made to allow for lower or higher amounts in the calculations, and two possible levels of results computed — the most pessimistic and the most optimistic — with actual results being monitored and compared with these two types of estimates.

The profit and loss account for 1968 indicates the other expenses that have to be considered. Sales manager and staff salaries might be increased from £6,000 to £8,000, general administration from £15,000 to £16,000, advertising to £24,000, and office expenses to £6,600 to round off the total expenses to £100,000, as we shall see shortly.

The amount for salesmen and agents — £26,500 — is, as we have discovered, made up of £18,760 salary to full-time men and £7,740 commission. What we do not know is how the estimated £400,000 for 1969 will be achieved between the full-time men and the agents. Here is where much argument can be generated without much progress being made. We can show that the split between the full-time and part-time men in 1968 was approximately 57 per cent (£189,000) to 43 per cent (£140,000); we could make efforts to ensure that in 1969 the split was nearer 50/50, but could assume a 60/40 split.

As the agents receive a much higher commission rate than the full-time men, who have in addition to achieve a quota before commission is paid, it is important to establish a 'bench mark' from which to work. We have elected to set the salesmen's salaries and expenses at a figure of £20,000, and take the figure of £7,740 we have analysed for commission as a percentage of £329,000 — 2·35 per cent — and use it as a basis for all commission paid in 1969, on the assumption that matters will not greatly change in twelve months. Thus 2·35 per cent of the estimated £400,000 is £9,400, from which it will be understood why office expenses were set at £6,600 to make the total add up to £100,000.

The next consideration is the pattern of sales likely in 1969, and, in the absence of any special promotions to alter this pattern, it may be assumed that it will remain as in 1968. This can be calculated (Table 4.19) with the help of the totals of figures in Table 4.6.

Table 4.19

Month	Sales (£)	Percentage of Total	As percentage of £400,000 (£)
January	12,220	4	16,000
February	15,270	5	20,000
March	18,080	6	24,000
April	22,780	7	28,000
May	33,270	10	40,000
June	44,930	14	56,000
July	48,335	15	60,000
August	36,470	11	44,000
September	27,695	9	36,000
October	23,815	7	28,000
November	19,815	6	24,000
December	18,320	6	24,000

The percentages have been rounded, because there is no sense in calculating predictions to various decimal places when it is general patterns we are trying to devise.

Before preparing our month by month forecast, we have to consider how the manufacturing costs and expenses will be incurred. It is likely that production will be conducted in line with sales because of the perishable nature of the product, although with goods such as the electrical products in Medway Appliances, production might be maintained at a fairly steady level throughout the year. This is a problem that will have to be considered separately for each case.

The cost of production can be calculated for each month as 61 per cent of the sales value. Distribution costs will also be incurred each month in direct proportion to sales, and can be calculated at 4 per cent of the current month's sales value.

Commission is paid one month after the sales are made, so that 2·35 per cent of the previous month's sales value will be entered each month. The expenses for sales manager and staff, salesmen's salaries and expenses, general administration and office expenses amount to £50,600, and can be assumed to be incurred in regular outgoings each month. One twelfth of the sum, £4,217, can be considered as outgoing each month.

Advertising is subject to a policy decision. For this calculation we assume that the £24,000 is spent in equal amounts each month from April to September inclusive.

Cash coming in takes about 16 weeks, as we have calculated, and if we assume that the incoming cash is equal to sales four months before, we have taken this lag into consideration. Thus, for January 1969, incoming cash will be September's sales of £27,695, February's incoming cash will be October's sales of £23,815, and so on — the monthly totals found in Table 4.6.

At the end of 1968 there was a cash balance of £1,000 and also an overdraft of £12,925. The £1,000 balance must be carried into January. Interest to be paid on the overdraft can be at the rate of, say, 12 per cent, 1 per cent of the sum outstanding the previous month to be charged each month.

Soloran Ltd

A cash-flow statement combining all these items can now be prepared, as follows:

Month	Jan. (£)	Feb. (£)	Mar. (£)	Apr. (£)	May (£)	June (£)
Sales	16,000	20,000	24,000	28,000	40,000	56,000
Cash in	27,695	23,815	19,815	18,320	16,000	20,000
Cash out:						
Mfg 61 per cent	9,760	12,200	14,640	17,080	24,400	34,160
Dist. 4 per cent	640	800	960	1,120	1,600	2,240
Expenses	4,217	4,217	4,217	4,217	4,217	4,217
Comm. 2·35 per cent	431	376	470	564	658	940
Advtsg	–	–	–	4,000	4,000	4,000
	15,048	17,593	20,287	26,981	34,875	45,557
Cash flow + or (–)	12,647	6,222	(472)	(8,661)	(18,875)	(25,557)
Cash B/F	1,000	3,518	6,786	6,314	(2,347)	(21,245)
O/D repaid	10,000	2,925	–	–	–	–
Interest	129	29	–	–	23	212
Cash bal. + or (–):	3,518	6,786	6,314	(2,347)	(21,245)	(47,014)

	July (£)	Aug. (£)	Sept. (£)	Oct. (£)	Nov. (£)	Dec. (£)
Sales	60,000	44,000	36,000	28,000	24,000	24,000
Cash in	24,000	28,000	40,000	56,000	60,000	44,000
Cash out:						
Mfg 61 per cent	36,600	26,840	21,960	17,080	14,640	14,640
Dist. 4 per cent	2,400	1,760	1,440	1,120	960	960
Expenses	4,217	4,217	4,217	4,217	4,217	4,217
Comm. 2·35 per cent	1,316	1,410	1,034	846	658	564
Advtsg	4,000	4,000	4,000	–	–	–
	48,533	38,227	32,651	23,263	20,475	20,381
Cash flow + or (–)	(24,533)	(10,227)	7,349	32,737	39,525	23,619
Cash B/F	(47,014)	(72,017)	(82,964)	(76,445)	(44,472)	(5,392)
O/D repaid	–	–	–	32,737	39,525	–
Interest	470	720	830	764	445	54
Cash bal. + or (–)	(72,017)	(82,964)	(76,445)	(44,472)	(5,392)	18,173

The real impact of increasing the sales to £400,000 is now seen as a problem of organizing the funding of the operation. Cash flow goes negative in March by £472 and does not go positive until September with £7,349; the overdraft of £12,925 is soon cleared up, by February, but financial help is required by April, with an overdraft of £2,347, which rises to £82,964 at the height of the season in August and only becomes cash in hand in December.

As we have already pointed out, it is possible to argue with a number of these assumptions: production levels, cash collection, distribution costs, commission arrangements and so on. The real lesson to be learned from the situation is that no marketing man should make decisions unless he understands the implications of those decisions. Simply to prepare a projected profit and loss account for the period under consideration is like nominating the island one wishes to arrive at in a year's time. What the marketing man must be aware of is the state of the water between the islands. While he would not necessarily be required to prepare cash-flow statements for any proposals he intends to undertake, he must work closely with the accountants and financial managers to ensure that he appreciates the full impact of his proposals.

> *Q.4.9 Assuming that it is still intended to aim for a sales turnover of £400,000, what might be done if the cash-flow statement prepared is accepted as a reasonably accurate portrayal of what might happen?*

4.3 Report

A report on Soloran Ltd might include the following:

Aim. Possibly to expand in the soft drinks industry, although there is sufficient evidence to suggest that expansion might be in another direction.

Purpose. The 'reasons why' for the company's current operations are fairly obvious, although it is worth while if you have an opportunity of discussing it in a group to conjecture about the purpose behind Mr Curlew's move from insurance to soft drinks.

Likely objectives and actions are discussed and assessed fully in the analysis. Specific objectives need to be given to the representatives, the agents, or to both, and we have already calculated the various costs and benefits of altering the distribution system. The implications of greatly increasing the company's turnover for the next year have also been fully explored.

ANSWERS TO QUESTIONS

A.4.1 Obviously there is no one right way to tackle the company's problems, but it is probably right to say that you should definitely not start by making decisions. First you should obtain all the facts relating to your approach to the company; however, although this is easy to say, it is not always easy to do. Frequently we do not understand the language of the people with whom we have to work, and, in consequence, fail to recognize problems. Therefore, you might start by making sure you understand the way in which the company operates and the 'language' it uses. When you are in a position to proceed further, you should endeavour to locate the causes of the problems you may have detected. However, it is useful to tackle this by accepting that problems can only be located in two main areas: in the work situation and in people. The work situation can be further subdivided into machinery, plant and equipment, and the methods or procedures used; and people can be divided into groups and individuals. The first real decisions that have to be made, then, are the locations of the problems that you discover; and remember that different managers will see the same problems as being located in entirely different places. For example, falling sales of squashes could be seen by different managers as a problem located in the product (the work-place), the way in which the product is distributed (methods of operation), the ineffectiveness of the sales manager (individual), or in the poor performance of the sales force (the group).

A.4.2 Possibly you could use some of the management ratio calculations discussed in Chapter 2 although with this case you have only two years' financial and statistical information. Whichever way you decide to investigate, you should consider both internal and external possibilities. While it is not normally expected that one would need to look much beyond the limits of the actual case study for information, there would be no great difficulty in determining the population for the areas listed on pp. 87, 88, and calculating a 'sales per thousand' for all the areas to see which is the 'best'.

A.4.3 We know already that approximately 1,055,640 bottles were sold in 1968, and in the case read that 'maximum capacity on a single shift working is 700-dozen bottles of squashes and/or Vitoran a day'. Therefore,

700 x 12 x 5 (days) x 50 (weeks) = 2,100,000 bottles a year.

Consequently the factory was working at about 50 per cent of bottling capacity. Sales of concentrates in 1968 were £196,000, and it is stated that these could rise to about £215,000, which indicates that they were at about 90 per cent of capacity of concentrates production in 1968.

A.4.4 'Prices and Discounts' (p. 90) lists three discounts that can be given to buyers (7½, 12½ or 17½ per cent), depending on the nature of their business and the volume they place with Soloran. Agents received no salary but received a commission of 7½ per cent on sales at full list price, 5 per cent commission on sales where 'minimum or medium' discount is given, and 2½ per cent on sales where maximum discount is given. Full list price for squashes is £1.675 a unit, minimum discount is 7½ per cent, medium discount is 12½ per cent, and maximum discount 17½ per cent. The three discounted prices are as follows:

	£1.675		£1.675		£1.675
Less 7½ per cent	0.125	Less 12½ per cent	0.209	Less 17½ per cent	0.293
	£1.550		£1.466		£1.382

We have already computed the average price at £1.425; therefore it is apparent that 12½ per cent discount has been given, which means that the agents are most likely working on an average of 5 per cent commission.

A.4.5 The profit and loss account indicates the other expenses that have to be considered, and they can be allocated to areas in a number of ways. We have calculated them (Table 4.20) as allocated direct to areas, allocated by sales turnover and by units sold.

Expenses allocated direct to areas and in proportion to turnover are straightforward, but those to be allocated according to unit sales are not so easy, because there is no information on units of concentrates sales. One way is to apportion £13,800 first to concentrates and non-concentrates sales — £196,000 and £133,000. Dividing £13,800 in this proportion allows £8,221 to be allocated to areas selling concentrates and £5,579 to be allocated to areas selling non-concentrates. Thus £8,221 will be allocated according to turnover, as there is no information on sales volume and £5,579 will be allocated according to unit sales.

Table 4.20

	Direct (£)	By turnover (£)	By units sold (£)
Sales manager and staff		6,000	
Salesmen and agents	26,500		
Administration		15,000	
Distribution			13,800
Advertising		20,000	
Depreciation		7,500	
Financing		3,500	
Office expenses	6,000		
	£32,500	£52,000	£13,800

A.4.6 The total of £329,000 in the profit and loss account includes £8,000 for preserves, which is also shown in Table 4.5.

A.4.7 Any number of sales estimates may be prepared from the question posed and the information available. Tables 4.21 and 4.22 show two, but they are not put forward as the only two possible.

Table 4.21

Areas	1968 sales (£)	Adjustment of agents (£)	15 per cent added (£)
1–8	96,950		111,493
9–18	28,050	41,340*	47,541
S.E.	84,000		96,600
N.I. Scot. C.I. N.E.	112,000	154,900**	178,135
Preserves	8,000		9,200
	£329,000		£442,969

* £20,670 total for five peak months assumed to be 50 per cent of annual total.
** £77,450 total for five peak months assumed to be 50 per cent of annual total.

Table 4.22

Areas	1968 sales (£)	Adjustment of full-time men (£)	15 per cent added (£)
1–8	96,950	182,385*	209,743
9–18	28,050		32,258
S.E.	84,000	132,100**	151,915
N.I. Scot. C.I. N.E.	112,000		128,800
Preserves	8,000		9,200
	£329,000		£531,916

* £47,420 total of seven off-season months assumed to be 26 per cent of annual total.
** £40,950 total of seven off-season months assumed to be 31 per cent of annual total.

In Tables 4.21 and 4.22 the total estimated for concentrates sales is in excess of the £215,000 estimated in the case, and therefore needs to be reduced accordingly.

A.4.8 A projected account for £400,000 is as follows:

Sales estimate for 1969		£400,000
Cost of materials (say 28 per cent)	£112,000	
Labour (say 27 per cent)	108,000	
Overheads (say 6 per cent)	24,000	
		244,000
Gross profit		156,000
Less expenses (depreciation figures £5,000, financing figures £3,500)		108,500
		47,500
Taxation (say $47\frac{1}{2}$ per cent)		22,560
		24,940
Profit brought forward		100,175
Retained profit		£125,115

A balance sheet as at the end of this period is as follows:

Fixed assets			£80,000
Depreciation (£23,000 + £5,000)			28,000
			52,000
Current assets:			
Stock	38,000		
Debtors	100,000		
Cash (calculated)	34,115		
		172,115	
Current liabilities:			
Creditors, 20 per cent	22,400		
Taxation	26,600		
		49,000	
			123,115
			£175,115
Financed by:			
50,000 £1 shares			50,000
Retained profit			125,115
			£175,115

A.4.9 While it must be assumed that the Board will be able to organize the funding of the operation, it might be possible to reduce the number of weeks during which monies are outstanding. However, if an instruction is issued immediately, it would be several months before any improvement might be achieved. Other outlets might be developed, especially the cash-and-carry outlets, where merchandise is paid for very quickly. A review of all the company's customers should be made to see whether the long credit taken is general or restricted to certain accounts. It might be worth considering a new price schedule that gives much more attractive terms to those accounts paying quickly. If settlement terms are to be amended, it is important to estimate with the salesmen the degree to which existing business might be affected.

5. Owen and Davies

While this is a short case, it nevertheless contains some deceptively difficult problems. The text indicates that the advice of a marketing consultant is being sought, and you should view the case from that particular role. There are problems concerning the product, pricing structure, the method of distribution, the type of promotion and the different service requirements of the two products.

5.1 Data

Harry Owen walked into the bar of the Crown Hotel, Bangor, North Wales, and ordered a large Scotch. While standing, thoughtfully sipping his drink, he hardly noticed the only other customer in the bar, who stood at the other end, drink in hand, looking wistfully out of the window across the straits to Anglesey. Suddenly Owen recognized the other man and exclaimed, 'Hullo John. I didn't notice you there. How's tricks?'

John Davies, a burly middle-aged man, lived in nearby Bethesda and had been employed at the local plant at Beaumaris by one of the large U.K. electrical manufacturers. He started, turned, and walked up to Harry Owen and said, 'About as frustrating as they could be. They're closing down Beaumaris and I've got three months' notice.'

'They're what?' exploded Owen, looking amazed.

'S'true', said Davies, 'bit of a shock for everyone. Things have been difficult for the past year or so but no one thought that they'd close the whole plant down. Most we thought would happen would be some redundancies.'

'Sorry. I didn't mean it quite like that John', replied Owen quickly, 'I mean – uh – you – er – well, I'm damned.'

Davies frowned and a puzzled look spread over his face as Harry Owen took a gulp from his glass and then said, 'Exactly the same has happened to me John – 'cept I've got cash in lieu of. I'm free except for the few small matters like the problems of feeding the family, paying the mortgage, and one or two other trifles in a few months' time.'

'Well – that's astounding', returned John, 'I thought you were well placed with your company.'

'I am – uh – or rather – I was', explained Harry, 'but we've been taken over and it's a question of which man has the longer service who is kept on. The chap who is taking over from me has been with this outfit all his life.'

Harry Owen was about the same age as John Davies. They had been to the same school, but John had left to go straight into industry and then took a sandwich course to get a Higher National Diploma in electrical engineering. Harry had read chemistry at Nottingham University and gained a first-class honours degree. For some time he had thought of going on to do a Ph.D., but decided to go into industry instead. For some years he had been employed in the food industry and, up to the present time, had been with a medium-sized company in Bangor. He and John Davies met quite often at various social and business functions in the area, and although they were not what could be called constant friends, they each had a very high regard for the other. Harry asked the barman for further drinks and then asked John, 'What are you going to do now then?'

The barman handed over the drinks and John took his, thanked Harry, and then said hesitatingly, 'I'll tell you what I'd really like to do. I have – uh – I've been working on an idea – nothing to do with the company, mind you – but I'd like to start on my own. I've a little money and I'm sure that I could raise some. Would you like to hear about the idea and give me your opinion?' Harry agreed and they moved to a couple of seats at the side of the lounge. John started to explain.

'With the terrific increase in leisure time – sorry', he laughed, 'I didn't mean to be funny about our present position, but people at all levels have more and more time on their hands and they are not always satisfied to be watching the goggle-box. There is a definite trend towards do-it-yourself leisure activities. I'm particularly interested in music-making activities, or, more accurately, an instrument for music-making – an electronic organ.'

He opened his briefcase and took out a folder and then handed Harry an illustration (see Exhibit 5.1).

'This is it', he said. 'I repeat – this has nothing to do with my company and I've been working on this in my own time at home. There's a lot more music tuition in

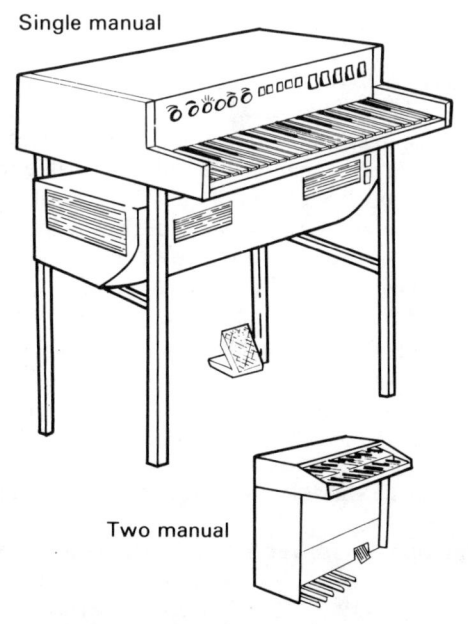

Exhibit 5.1 Davies' electronic organs

schools, and pop music is one of the leading pastimes for the teenage market. I've developed an instrument that can be used for all types of music and can be used in the home or in a public hall. It's not a toy but a proper musical instrument that can be played by professionals as well as amateurs. It's easy to play, and very much easier to play than a piano because you can get a great deal more effects electronically. Do you remember those cinema organs?'

'Just about', said Harry, smiling, 'the organist used to sit in the organ and come up through the floor.'

'Well, I'm not suggesting that this is anything like being in that class, but it can give a few of the same effects — it can sound like a cinema organ or a church organ.'

'You've got two types?' asked Harry.

'No. It's the same organ. The one organ can be played to sound like a church organ or a cinema organ depending how you set the switches. I'm not first in the field, mind you, but I think that this instrument has many advantages over others I've seen. During the last ten years or so there has been a great increase in music-making — even the piano is beginning to sell again. With the surge forward of miniaturization in electronics the size and cost of electronic organs has been cut tremendously. The Americans have a lead in their construction, but the Japanese are also in the field, and I think the time is ripe now for a really good British-made instrument.' He took another paper from his case headed 'Electronic Organ', and handed it to Harry. 'Here's a description of it', he said, 'perhaps you'd like to scan through it.' Harry took the paper from John and read as follows:

> The electronic organ has a keyboard and amplifier and is housed in a cabinet with four legs. The keyboard has forty-nine keys, which, with three pitch switches, provide the equivalent of seventy-three keys. Compared with an ordinary piano with eighty-eight keys the electronic organ is very light and compact, and is approximately 105 cm wide (3 ft 6 in.) and 60 cm deep (24 in.). Music power output is 15 watts. The electronic circuitry has provided five basic tones and a tremolo, which, together with the three pitch switches and the foot-operated swell pedal, enables a wide range of effects to be obtained. Two special features are the special control that enables full tonal value to be played in a comparatively small room without loss of quality — in effect, a full organ sound in miniature — and five basic rhythms, which are normally only found on organs of much greater cost. Chords can be played over the whole range of the keyboard, which can be divided when required into two at middle C, so that different pitch switches can be applied to the lower and upper parts of the keyboard to obtain effects that are normally only obtainable with a two-manual organ. There are input and output sockets to allow recordings to be made direct from the organ to tape and also to play a pre-recorded piece of music through the amplifier while the operator is, in effect, accompanying it. The amplifier is set below the keyboard assembly with the sound directed towards the player — although it would be possible to make the assembly with the sound coming from the sides.

'This is really fascinating, John', said Harry, looking up. 'Have you actually made a prototype?'

'Oh yes', replied John, 'I play it too. It's in a rather crude cabinet at present though.'

'What's the smaller drawing here?' asked Harry, pointing to the lower illustration in Exhibit 5.1.

'That's a two-manual organ, which I haven't actually made yet, but which will be just as straightforward. It would have about 20 watts power compared with 15 with the single manual and have a lot more features. A bit more costly of course — say another £50.'

'What are these stick-like things — oh, I suppose they are foot pedals, are they?' Harry looked interested, pointing again to the lower illustration.

'Yes. Those are thirteen pedal notes. And the larger pedal on both illustrations is the foot swell pedal. That lets you increase or fade away the sound.'

'Have you costed the production fairly carefully?' put in Harry.

'I've costed the single-manual both with and without the automatic rhythms, but have only estimated the two-manual organ at about fifty quid extra. I can keep costs down because I make use of standard mass-produced components. I'll let you have a look at the figures, if you're really interested. You could certainly let me have an unbiased opinion.'

'What about the market for them?' added Harry.

'Well, there are two main sectors in this particular area of keyboard instruments — the piano and the organ. In recent years the electronic organ seems to have been making a separate sector for itself. Sales of pianos are — oh — I'm not quite sure — in the region of about 10,000 a year in the U.K. I think; they cost about £275 upwards, although I'm not too sure about this figure. With inflation, they're probably well above this now. In the States sales of electronic organs have been rocketing over the past few years and sales of organs are about 70 per cent of piano sales . . .'

'Sales of electronic organs are 70 per cent of piano sales?' interjected Harry.

'No. Sales of *all* organs are 70 per cent. In general they have larger homes in the States — larger rooms — and seem to be able to stuff the odd console organ in a corner of the living room. Anyway, I reckon that the total market in the U.K. must be at least fifty per cent of piano sales, which means that about 5,000 electronic organs should be sold each year.'

John Davies went on to explain that there had been a great increase in competitive activities between electronic-organ manufacturers over the past few years. There were about ten U.S. manufacturers operating in the U.K. and about half a dozen British manufacturers. American companies selling in the U.K. usually had their instruments assembled in the U.K. and sold through sole-appointed concessionaries. They had concentrated on the console organ, and, by scaling down the cabinet size and features, were able to offer a very attractive 'package' to would-be purchasers. This included free home trials, special tuition, a self-tutor, an album of specially arranged music for the keyboard, full instructions with full service guaranteed, and a rhythm record or cassette tape with pre-recorded rhythms to supply a full band accompaniment for popular music. U.K. and European manufacturers were unable to compete with the American console organ, but had been particularly successful in the development and sales of electronic keyboards and organs for dance bands, public entertainment and home use. Most manufacturers made considerable use of demonstrations to promote sales and often a professional player would be used to illustrate the possibilities of the instrument. Such demonstrations were conducted on a shared basis, with several dealers in an area

Business Analysis for Marketing Managers

Table 5.1 Manufacturers of Electronic Organs

Manufacturer	Keyboard without amplifier	Keyboard with amplifier (£)
Baldwin, U.S.A.		450
S.S. Bird, U.K.		400
Compton, U.K.		500
Eksonic, Italy	250	
Farfisa, Italy	260	
Hammond, U.S.A.		265 up
Harmonics, U.K.		150
Hohner, Germany	120–250	
Jennings, U.K.	100–175	300
Livingstone Burge, U.S.A.		450
Lowrey, U.S.A.		275
Magnovox, U.S.A.		350
Miller, U.K.		325
Parie, Holland		475
Philips, U.K.		200
Thomas, U.S.A.		240
Vox, U.K.	175–300	
Watkins, U.S.A.	265	
Wurlitzer, U.S.A.		450
Yamaha, Japan		350

Table 5.2 Dealer Stocks of Electronic Organs

Fifty musical dealers were visited in London, the Midlands and the North of England to determine which organs were stocked or sold by them.

Type of instrument	No. of dealers stocking
Keyboard only:	
Farfisa	29
Hohner	20
Vox	11
Eksonic	9
Watkins	9
Keyboard and amplifier:	
Harmonics	28
Thomas	26
Lowrey	24
Hammond	23
Bird	18
Miller	10
Yamaha	10
Philips	10
Jennings	9
Magnovox	9
Baldwin	8
Compton	4
Burge	3
Parie	1
Wurlitzer	1

benefiting from the one demonstration. There were few, if any, musical instrument wholesalers in the U.K., although several wholesalers held stocks of musical accessories. Sales of organs were made through dealers, who were normally appointed on a selective basis, but, with the better known U.S. organ-manufacturers, they were appointed on an exclusive basis and given areas that became their exclusive responsibility.

As John finished speaking, he handed Harry two further papers with information concerning brand shares of organs sold in the U.K. (Tables 5.1 and 5.2).

'This is most impressive, John', emphasized Harry. 'I like this whole scheme very much. Yes, most impressive. Would you believe me if I told you that I, too, had been working on something to start on, on my own? Not that it's like your idea but . . .' he paused, slowly shaking his head. 'Isn't it strange that we should meet like this? Both of us in similar circumstances with our companies, or, rather, late companies, and both of us with ideas for setting up in business on our own.'

'You mean — you've an idea for developing a musical instrument?' John asked incredulously.

'No', said Harry quickly, 'My idea is very different, but I must say I am beginning to prefer *your* scheme to mine!' He pulled out a folder from his case and started to explain to John the idea he hoped to develop. 'It's very simple really but I think it has terrific potential — er — or at least I thought it did until I heard your plans. You're dealing with a leisure market and, I agree with you, there's much more leisure time at all levels now than ever there was. I was thinking of going into the fruit juice market — a specialized fruit juice blended from the juices of orange, grapefruit, lemon and pineapple with added vitamins. They are blended in such a way that no one flavour is predominant. It has a very special, peculiarly pleasant taste. Not too sweet and not too tart. Here again, this has nothing to do with my company, and it is the result of a personal negotiation I've had with a North American outfit who introduced a similar juice on to their market about ten years ago. I have the offer of importing this concentrate direct from the Canadian suppliers as sole concessionaire in the U.K. Landed at London it's just over £14 a container. The container has 25 litres of concentrate and a small sachet of additive.'

'But, aren't there enough fruit juices on the market already?' interrupted John.

'Yes, but this is not simply a fruit juice sold like any other drink. The intention is to supply it through milk distributors as a refreshing drink for breakfast, and also as an occasional drink during the day. With a sweetener instead of sugar it is ideal as a slimmer's drink — and you know how important the slimming fad is these days. I wouldn't be bottling it, simply franchising it through milk distributors. They would dilute it, bottle and chill it, and send it out with their roundsmen. Millions of bottles of it are being delivered with the milk in Canada and the U.S.A.' He handed John two papers. 'Here is the information on the product and a breakdown of costs. You'll see that I've not included the cost of sugar or sugar substitute, but it still means that a bottle of the drink can be delivered to the door at a very attractive cost.'

John started to read the two following papers:

FRUIT JUICE CONCENTRATE

Ingredients of finished product
Water, sugar (or sweetener), concentrated fruit juices, citric acid, sodium citrate, ascorbic acid, brominated vegetable oil, acacia, provitamin A.

Vitamin content
Vitamin C: 25 mg per 100 cc of finished product.
Provitamin A: 1,050 I.U. per 100 cc of finished product.

Packaging
Supplied to bottlers in 25-litre containers, together with a sealed plastic container of additive to be mixed in according to instructions before bottling. Total weight of container 30 kg. To be stored at 8°C.

1 – 25-litre container of concentrate
1 – container of additive
400 litres of water
48 kg sugar (or equivalent sweetener)

Put water into a container at temperature of 6°–8°C, agitate and add slowly fruit juice concentrate and then sugar or sugar substitute. Continue slow agitation for at least fifteen minutes. Five minutes before bottling, add contents of plastic container (the additive) and bottle immediately. Lower temperature of bottled product immediately to 2°C and chill for a minimum period of twelve hours.

FRUIT JUICE COSTING

Cost per 25-litre non-returnable container C.I.F. London, including British dock dues, wharfage, etc.	£14·23
Transport from dock to dairy, estimated	0·20
	14·43
Profit to company, say, 25 per cent	4·81
	£19·24

With 48 kg of sugar the yield is approximately 900 $\frac{1}{2}$-litre or 1,600 $\frac{1}{2}$-pint bottles. If sugar substitute is used, slightly less number of bottles will result.

Estimated costs per $\frac{1}{2}$-litre bottle (based on 900 bottles)

Bottle	£0·005
Labour	0·00025
Overheads, say,	0·0003
Admin., say,	0·00025
	0·0058
Ingredients £19.24/900	0·0213
	£0·0271 per $\frac{1}{2}$-litre bottle

To this must be added the cost of sugar, or sweetener, a percentage for advertising, and commission to roundsmen.

Estimated costs per ½-pint bottle (based on 1,600 bottles)

Bottle	£0·005
Labour	0·00025
Overheads, say,	0·0003
Admin., say,	0·00025
	0·0058
Ingredients £19.24/1,600	0·012
	£0·0178 per ½-pint bottle

Plus cost of sugar, or sweetener, advertising, and commission.

As he started to read the information on fruit juice and the costing of the operation, John said, 'Harry, you may as well look at the costing for the organ', and handed Harry a paper.

'I've also looked into some advertising costs', he added, and gave Harry Owen the information in Tables 5.3 and 5.4.

Table 5.3 Electronic Organ Costing

Based on an output of ten organs a week with myself and four girls, and assuming that the girls receive £20 a week. With three more girls output could be increased to twenty organs a week.

	Single-manual organ	
	Without automatic rhythm (£)	With automatic rhythm (£)
Materials	35	100
Labour	14	16
Overheads and sundries	5	5
Transport, packing	3	3
Administration	1	1
	58	125
Company profit at 50 per cent	29	62
	£87	£187

Table 5.4 Advertising Costs

Publication	Frequency	Whole page (£)
Music and Musicians	Monthly	75
Musical Opinion	Monthly	25
Crescendo International	Monthly	65
Music Teacher (6,318 circ.)	Monthly	33
Record Retailer (7,061 circ.)	Weekly	140
Piano World (2,964 circ.)	Monthly	40

'I think that I should make 50 per cent profit on each organ, don't you?' asked John Davies.

'Well it depends on the turnover you're hoping for', replied Harry; 'you've still to include the cost of advertising, commission to the sales agents, dealers' profit, and so on. You'll sell to dealers of course. They'll need to have demonstrators — still I suppose they'll have those anyway for pianos. How many will you be able to produce in a year?'

'Steady on', laughed John, 'I've only just produced the prototype.'

Harry looked intently at John and said in slow and measured tones, 'I much prefer your scheme now to mine. I'm quite prepared to put my capital behind your venture.'

John Davies pursed his lips, rubbed his chin and gave a long, low 'hm'. He said with a slight smile over his face, 'Harry, I honestly prefer your scheme. It has all the makings of a successful operation. It's in the food line and isn't so dependent on people's income. I like the idea of the slimming angle too. What capital I have I'm prepared to put with yours to back the breakfast fruit juice franchising to milk distributors.'

The two men could understand that probably neither of them had sufficient capital to back his own scheme, even if they obtained help from other sources. Together they stood a good chance of making a success of one of the ventures, but not of the two. The problem was, which of the two ventures offered the better opportunity and how could they arrive at a decision?

'Let's have one for the road', sighed John, 'sleep on it and meet again in a day or so.'

A few days later the two men met again in slightly different circumstances but both entirely convinced that they should pool their resources and start in business together. They had each discussed the proposals with their families and gained their support. Harry Owen said that he had about £4,250, but that he would need about £50 a week to maintain a minimum standard of living. John Davies said that he had about £4,150 and would need a similar sum for his basic requirements each week.

'This means', said Harry, 'that we have about £8,500, and if we see Dai Jones at the National Westminster, he may be prepared to support us with a loan against our house properties or something like that. It means that we can think in terms of having about — uh — what would you think, £10,000?'

'Well, I would think so', agreed John. 'Another thing I've been thinking of is someone to help us with the marketing. After all, neither of us has any real experience in that direction.'

'Be nice if we could find someone who'd be prepared to come in on the ground floor and put up some capital', mused Harry, 'although we still have to agree which of the two ventures seems the better bet.'

'Yes, we can't ask anyone to join us until we've made up our minds what we are going to do. After all, we can't ask a bloke to join us in a venture to sell organs or fruit drinks', said John, laughing.

'I'll tell you what', suggested Harry, 'let's put our problem to a marketing consultant and ask his advice. At least he should be able to give us sound reasons for both of the propositions and then we can perhaps decide which we'll do. Who knows, if things go well, we might even be able to develop both propositions in time.'

'Fair enough', replied John, looking at his watch. 'We can just about sort something out today.'

5.2 Analysis

One or two figures need correcting in the case. In Table 5.3, the costing for the electronic organ, Davies shows the company making a profit of 50 per cent. This is really only $33\frac{1}{3}$ per cent, because he has confused profit on sales with profit as a percentage of cost: 29 of 58 = 50 per cent and 62 of 125 = 50 per cent.

It is difficult to compare the costing of fruit juice with that of the organ to assess the relative merits of the two products. The costing for fruit juice omits the cost of sugar or sweetener, the cost of promotion, and the commission to be paid to milk roundsmen. The costing for the organ includes an item for labour — £14 for the non-rhythm organ and £16 for the organ with rhythm. This is based on production of ten organs a week, with girls' wages of £80 (4 x £20), and £60 a week for Davies. Therefore, the £140 total gives £14 per organ. The extra labour for the organ with rhythm is probably one more girl at £20 a week. However, if you consider the fruit juice costing, you will see that there is no figure for Owen's weekly wage. Later we shall need to revise these costings so as to be able to compare the two propositions.

5.21 *Fruit Juice*

The two men have decided to put their ideas before a marketing consultant, who will need to prepare marketing plans and suggestions for each product and let the men decide on their course of action. There is no particular point of entry in this case, so let us look at the potential market for the fruit juice breakfast drink. In the U.K. there are approximately 18 million households that could form the basic market. Just what percentage of this figure is the potential for the proposed company is a difficult question. Start with the suggestion that 5 per cent of this market buys one bottle of fruit juice a week:

$$18 \text{ m} \times 52 \times 0.05 = 46{,}800{,}000 \text{ bottles a year!}$$

That is undoubtedly a high figure, so let us assume that 5 per cent of this market will buy a bottle just once during the year: 18 m x 0.05 = 900,000 bottles. This seems to be a much more reasonable figure and, incidentally, fits in neatly if we decide to recommend $\frac{1}{2}$-litre bottles, since one 25-litre container makes up 900 of them. This would mean that 1,000 containers a year would be required — about twenty a week. If $\frac{1}{2}$-pint bottles are adopted, the number of containers of concentrate would be 900,000/1,600 = 563 containers.

> *Q.5.1* *If 5 per cent of the U.K. market bought a bottle six times a year, how many 25-litre containers would be required if the bottles were (a) $\frac{1}{2}$-pint, (b) $\frac{1}{2}$-litre?*

In view of the limited amount of cash the two men may have at their disposal it is important to keep this in mind when considering the level at which we discuss their operations. We could not, for example, consider their taking over a factory valued at £250,000 when they have only a total of around £10,000 with which to launch their operation.

Look at the suggestion made that 5 per cent of the market would take six bottles in a year and consider, first, $\frac{1}{2}$-pint bottles with 3,375 25-litre containers being required in a year. Owen and Harris would probably need to import in consignments of about three months' supplies — say 845 containers. From the fruit juice costing we know the cost of the container landed in London is £14.23, which means that 845 containers will cost £12,024, and, assuming that Owen and Davies would have to pay their invoices 90 days after delivery of goods (or even after despatch of goods), they will need to have a very large sum three months after starting in business.

Naturally we can argue that it is not necessary to import 845 containers all at once, and that they should gradually work up to a manageable level. Nevertheless it is useful to determine the amount of cash required to finance their operations. Perhaps 100 containers might be a reasonable initial order, and, later on in this analysis, we can look at this more closely. In passing, you will appreciate that, with $\frac{1}{2}$-litre bottles, considerably more containers would be needed, so this is a point to keep in mind. We should now construct a price schedule and consider the likely profit from the fruit juice operation. One of the points not covered in the case is the inclusion of sugar or sweetener. In 1972 sugar prices were already beginning to increase, and when analysing cases where external influences may change, it is essential to establish a base or 'bench mark' from which to work. In 1971 the following prices obtained:

56 lb of sugar	£2·38
56 x 0·4536 = 25·4 kg	
25·4 kg of sugar therefore cost	2·38
Therefore 48 kg of sugar will cost	2·38 x 48/25·4
	= £4·50

A price for the fruit juice in alternative bottle sizes can now be constructed:

Table 5.5

	$\frac{1}{2}$-pint	$\frac{1}{2}$-litre
Bottle	0·005*	0·005*
Labour	0·00025*	0·00025
Overheads	0·0003*	0·0003*
Administration	0·00025*	0·00025*
	0·0058	0·0058
Ingredients £19.24/1,600	0·012	
Ingredients £19.24/900		0·0214
Sugar £4.50/1,600	0·0028	
Sugar £4.50/900		0·005
	£0·0206	£0·0322

*Estimated costs.

In addition to this suggested basic price must be added the profit for the dairy, advertising costs, and commission to the milk roundsmen.

Q.5.2 What profit would Owen and Davies be making on this basis?

In the absence of other information on costs we must proceed with our conjectural analysis and pose the question as to what might be a reasonable price to charge the consumer for a ½-pint bottle and a ½-litre bottle of fruit juice? With the costings suggested, perhaps 4p. for the ½-pint and 5p for the ½-litre might suffice though this would mean 1.94p (4 − 2·06) for the former and 1·78p (5 − 3·22) for the latter to cover all other expenses. This can be considered slightly differently as 48·5 per cent for expenses for the ½-pint and 35·6 per cent for expenses of the ½-litre size.

We must look at these possible expenses a little more closely. An important consideration is at what percentage profit and at what level of turnover is the milk distributor likely to agree that this is a worth-while proposition to adopt? If Owen and Davies can make an attractive proposition, it is more likely to receive favourable consideration by the distributors. A price structure based on the 4p and 5p suggestions can therefore be explored.

If the ½-litre bottle is sold at 5p, then 1·78p is left to cover all other expenses and distributor profit. If the distributor wants 25 per cent profit, which is 1·25p, this leaves 0·53p. Supposing the milk roundsman is paid 10 per cent commission on sales — 0·5p a bottle — this leaves 0·03p for advertising. However, 0·03p is only 0·6 per cent (0·03 of 5). Note that these percentages agree with the estimate previously made — they add to 35·6 per cent.

If the milk distributor's profit is reduced to, say, 20 per cent and the roundsman's commission to, say, 7½ per cent, there will be 8·1 per cent for advertising. Here is the possible price structure for ½-litre bottle selling at 5p.

Cost of production	£0·0322
Milk distributor, 20 per cent	0·01
Advertising, say, 8·1 per cent	0·00405
Milk roundsman, say 7½ per cent	0·00375
	£0·05

Q.5.3 Applying these percentages to the ½-pint bottle costing, can you prepare a price structure for it?

You will now have appreciated some of the problems of constructing a price on estimates and conjectures. We might even consider different price levels to determine the different profits and commissions possible. For example, a resale price of 6p for a ½-litre bottle might mean a price structure as under:

Cost of production	£0·0322
Roundsman, 7½ per cent commission	0·0045
Advertising, 10 per cent	0·006
Milk distributor	0·0173 = 28·8 per cent profit
	£0·06

One question not covered is, Who actually does the advertising? If Owen and Davies do it, the amount, which will come from their 25 per cent profit, will be certain to be limited, and directed to milk distributors.

Q.5.4 Do you think that we have covered most of the major items in the costing for the fruit juice?

Assume that an initial order for, say, 500 containers is placed by the company.

126   Business Analysis for Marketing Managers

This will require a consideration eventually of 500 × £14·43 = £7,215. If this quantity is sold in the three months, 273 of the containers (average 21 a week for 13 weeks) will cover their basic £50 a week each, and 227 (500 − 273) will provide the profit. At £4·81 profit per container (£19·24 − £14·43) this will be £1,091·87 total profit. Their total turnover would be 500 × £19·24 = £9,620, and therefore their profit would be 11·35 per cent.

Q.5.5 *If they sell 500 every quarter, what will be their total profit and percentage profit for the year, assuming costs and prices maintained?*

5.22 The Organ

We can now look at the costing and price structure for electronic organs. First, recalculating Table 5.3 and removing the weekly labour cost included for Davies, we get a costing for organs based on a production of ten per week (Table 5.6).

Table 5.6

	Without rhythm (£)	With rhythm (£)
Materials	350	1,000
Labour, 4 girls @ £20	80	80
Overheads etc.	50	50
Transport, packing	30	30
Administration	10	10
	£520	£1,170

An important question to be answered is whether the labour that Davies puts into production is vital and whether an allowance must be made in the above costing. It is assumed that Davies included an amount that would cover his personal requirements rather than an amount reflecting the actual technical work he provided. If the selling of organs were successful, both Davies and Owen would be busy in the management of the company and the expert labour now provided by Davies would have to be bought from someone else. For this reason it might be advisable to include an amount to cover this specialized labour − perhaps £50 a week is a good 'bench mark' from which to start. This would increase the cost for ten organs to £570 and £1,220 a week.

A major consideration is the amount to add for company profit. It is hardly acceptable to work with percentages here and add a percentage comparable with that of fruit juice, since there is a wide difference in turnover of stock. If the suggestion in the case is used and 50 per cent added, this means that the organs could sell at £85.50 (£57 + £28·50) and £183 (£122 + £61).

It is supposed that the company will sell organs to selected dealers and, before attempting to calculate a resale price, we should determine how many they would need to sell in, say, a week in order to break even each week. Starting with the non-rhythm organ and assuming that they make ten a week, then, with the £50 a week each they take out for personal needs, the cash outflow is £670 a week. If they produce the organ and sell it at £85·50, they would need to sell eight a week to break even (670/85·50 = 7·8). If they produce the with-rhythm model, their cash outflow would be £1,320 a week because of the extra £650 for materials, and, at a selling price of £183 they would have to sell eight a week to break even (£1,320/183 = 7·2).

Another breakeven figure can be calculated by assuming that they only produce sufficient to meet orders, and by taking all the costs that can be regarded as fixed or rigid, as follows: labour 4 x £20, overheads £50, administration £10, and the two partners £100. This totals £240 a week. Let us consider first the non-rhythm organ with materials plus transport and packing £38 (£35 + £3). If these are sold at £85·50, there is a contribution of £47·50 from which the breakeven figure of just over 5 can be calculated (£240/£47·50 = 5·05). However, this is an unsatisfactory method, because it does not take into account the raw materials and components that will have to be stocked, and works from the basis that no organs are ever carried in stock. Let us consider a modest production run of ten organs a week and restrict our calculations to the non-rhythm organ. The production costs are as follows:

Materials based on 10 a week	£350
Girls' labour	80
Davies' replacement labour	50
Overheads	50
Administration	10
Owen's and Davies' weekly take-out	100
	£640

On the basis of a four-weekly cash budget, £640 a week is £2,560 every four weeks, and we can now prepare a cash flow statement (Table 5.7) assuming that no sales are made in the first month and modest sales start in the second month to reach maximum in about six months. Dealers are assumed to take two months' credit.

Table 5.7 highlights the dangers inherent in the marketing of electronic organs. You will probably agree that the table includes a level of sales that is very optimistic indeed, and, if sales are at a much lower rate through the first year, the negative balance that has to be carried is far beyond the capability of Owen and Davies' present financial resources. The cash flow for the with-rhythm is even more striking, because the cash outflow for materials is at a rate of £5,160 every four weeks.

At £85.50 the breakeven figure is about eight a week. If we wish to determine the price for various breakeven points, the formula is,

$$\frac{670}{x} = \text{breakeven point}$$

where x = the price: 670/85.50 = 7·84. Thus, if the formula is rearranged, the price for various levels of breakeven can be determined:

A breakeven of 7 per week: x = 670/7 = £95·71.
A breakeven of 6 per week: x = 670/6 = £111·67.
A breakeven of 5 per week: x = 670/5 = £134.

Table 5.7 Electronic Organ Cash-flow Statement

		Month 1	Month 2	Month 3	Month 4	Month 5	Month 6
Unit sales		—	4	8	20	40	40
Revenue	£				342	684	1,710
Cash out:							
Production	£	2,560	2,560	2,560	2,560	2,560	2,560
Transport	£	—	12	24	60	120	120
Int. 12 per cent p.a.	£	—	26	52	78	102	122
Cash + or (−)	£	(2,560)	(2,598)	(2,636)	(2,356)	(2,098)	(1,092)
Balance	£	(2,560)	(5,158)	(7,794)	(10,150)	(12,248)	(13,340)

		Month 7	Month 8	Month 9	Month 10	Month 11	Month 12
Unit sales		40	40	60	40	40	40
Revenue	£	3,420	3,420	3,420	3,420	5,130	3,420
Cash out:							
Production	£	2,560	2,560	2,560	2,560	2,560	2,560
Transport	£	120	120	180	120	120	120
Int. 12 per cent p.a.	£	133	127	121	116	109	86
Cash + or (−)	£	607	613	559	624	2,341	654
Balance	£	(12,733)	(12,120)	(11,561)	(10,937)	(8,596)	(7,942)

A breakeven of 4 per week: $x = 670/4 = £167·50$
A breakeven of 3 per week: $x = 670/3 = £223·33$.

While these breakeven figures are given for one week, this same relation holds for the whole year. Thus, if a price of £134 is selected, then the breakeven figure is five a week or 50 per cent of the year's production — assuming that production is at a steady level.

It will be useful to determine the sensitivity of price, and one way in which this may be done is to list the dealers stocking particular brands according to the prices of those brands (Table 5.8). This information can be obtained from Tables 5.1 and 5.2.

Table 5.8

	Number of dealers stocking	Price (£)
Harmonics	28	150
Thomas	26	240
Lowrey	24	275
Hammond	23	265
Bird	18	400
Miller	10	325
Yamaha	10	350
Philips	10	200
Jennings	9	300
Magnavox	9	350
Baldwin	8	450
Compton	4	500
Burge	3	450
Parie	1	475
Wurlitzer	1	450

From this information we can now determine the degree of correlation, as follows:

X	Y
28	1·5
26	2·4
24	2·8
23	2·7
18	4·0
10	3·3
10	3·5
10	2·0
9	3·0
9	3·5
8	4·5
4	5·0
3	4·5
1	4·8
1	4·5

From which,

$\Sigma X = 184$
$\Sigma X^2 = 3,442$
$\Sigma Y = 52$
$\Sigma Y^2 = 196·32$
$\Sigma XY = 531$

$$R = \frac{n\Sigma XY - \Sigma X \Sigma Y}{\sqrt{[n\Sigma X^2 - (\Sigma X)^2][n\Sigma Y^2 - (\Sigma Y)^2]}}$$

$R = -0·77$

The coefficient of determination (R^2) is thus equal to 59 per cent. This relatively high degree of inverse correlation leads us to the conclusion that the lower the price the more likely dealers are willing to stock it.

You will recall that, if a breakeven figure of 50 per cent is required (five a week), then the basic price is £134. If dealers wish to receive $33\frac{1}{3}$ per cent profit, the selling price to the public must be £134 + 50 per cent = £201.

Q.5.6 To break even at the same rate with the 'with rhythm' organ and to give the dealers the same rate of discount, at what price should it be sold by Owen and Davies?

An electronic organ needs demonstrating, and it is unlikely to find wholesalers willing to stock it. Therefore, it is essential to distribute it through dealers, and it is desirable to lay down certain minimum criteria for dealers selected to sell the instrument. They should already be selling musical instruments, and, preferably, electronic organs. A member of their staff able to demonstrate the organ should normally be in attendance at the outlet. Adequate servicing facilities should be readily available, and, naturally, the dealers selected should possess premises with adequate space for displaying and demonstrating organs.

Initially it will be wise to restrict the distribution to the area within fairly easy access of the place of manufacture, and, as it is desirable to maintain the production of organs at a fairly high constant level, an estimate should be made of the number likely to be sold in the first, second and third years as a total and per dealer. At a production level of ten a week, or 500 a year, fifty dealers appointed to carry the product would need to sell ten a year — not an unduly large number. However, such dealers would expect to have support in terms of advertising and dealer aids. From Table 5.4 it will be seen that to insert a whole page in 50 per cent of the issues of all available publications to the trade would cost some £5,000, although it is not suggested that this is necessarily the best way, or even a recommended way, of advertising this organ. The constraints of keeping the final price as low as possible yet high enough to achieve a sensible breakeven point are in conflict, and a lot of thought will be required before the exact price can be set.

Perhaps further thought can be given to such specialized market segments as churches, public halls, hospitals, institutions, colleges, and so on. It may be unwise however, to consider going to these direct, and bypassing the dealer.

Initially sales will have to be obtained by Owen and Davies themselves, and it may be possible to appoint one or two agents as business increases. Settlement terms should be attractive enough to ensure that payment is made early by dealers. If neither of the two men play the organ skilfully enough, they must ensure that dealers so appointed possess such skill. It might be necessary for them to appoint their own demonstrator, who would then be able to advise on dealers' abilities.

A number of publicity objectives appear possible. The organ should be established as an authentic musical instrument and not as a play toy. Its advantages are that it is easier to play than a piano and possesses a wide range of tonal qualities, its size and weight make it ideal for the modern home, electricity energy consumption is negligible, and it can be easily carried in a comparatively small car.

Q.5.7 What suggestions might be offered to the two men for the launch of the organ?

5.23 Further Considerations

If it is decided to market the breakfast fruit juice concentrate, then there are fewer problems than with the organ, especially as far as cash flow is concerned. Perhaps the best way to launch the product is to offer the milk distributors a 'package deal'. Owen and Davies should be prepared to establish and develop the idea of a breakfast fruit juice drink being delivered at the same time as the milk by the milk roundsman. First, this has to be directed to selected distributors, and, second, it will be aimed at the general customers of that distributor.

Q.5.8 What suggestions might be offered for the launch of the breakfast fruit drink?

While there is not so much of a cash-flow problem with the fruit juice drink, it is as well to reconsider it. Apart from the salary that Owen and Davies require, it can safely be assumed that they will need to employ at least one girl either full- or part-time to carry out the office duties. Just what salary she will need is impossible to say, but if it is assumed to be at a level of £20 a week, then adjustments can be made for differing levels, and also when others are employed. By making arbitrary estimates of salaries, wages and other expenses, a projected profit and loss account can be made and, with an estimate of sales for a year, a cash-flow statement prepared.

Cost of girls, full- or part-time, say	£2,000
Travelling expenses	250
Postage and telephone	100
Sundries, say	500
Advertising in first year	1,000
	£3,850

The following is the projected profit and loss account:

Sales of 2,000 containers, at £19.24		£38,480
Less cost at £14.43		28,860
		9,620
Less expenses:		
Owen and Davies' salaries, 52 × £100	£5,200	
General expenses listed above	3,850	
		£9,050
Net profit		£570

It must be emphasized that these figures are not necessarily correct but are given to illustrate the method used. You will probably need to insert new figures and then recalculate your own cash flow-chart (Table 5.9). Before this can be

Table 5.9 Fruit Juice Cash-flow Statement

		Jan.	Feb.	Mar.	Apl.	May	June
Unit sales		50	80	100	120	150	160
Revenue	£	–	962	1,539	1,924	2,309	2,886
Cash out:							
Expenses	£	754	754	754	754	754	754
Materials	£	–	–	7,215	–	–	7,215
Int. 12 per cent p.a.	£	–	8	6	70	59	44
Total out	£	754	762	7,975	824	813	8,013
Cash + or (–)	£	(754)	200	(6,436)	1,100	1,496	(5,127)
Balance	£	(754)	(554)	(6,990)	(5,890)	(4,394)	(9,521)

		July	Aug.	Sep.	Oct.	Nov.	Dec.
Unit sales		180	170	160	150	150	150
Revenue	£	3,078	3,463	3,271	3,078	2,886	2,886
Cash out:							
Expenses	£	754	754	754	754	754	754
Materials	£	–	–	–	7,215	–	–
Int. 12 per cent p.a.	£	95	73	47	22	71	50
Total out	£	849	827	801	7,991	825	804
Cash + or (–)	£	2,229	2,636	2,470	(4,913)	2,061	2,082
Balance	£	(7,292)	(4,656)	(2,186)	(7,099)	(5,038)	(2,956)

done, an estimate of sales of containers through the year is needed, and, here again, this following estimate may not agree with your own ideas:

J	F	M	A	M	J	J	A	S	O	N	D
50	80	100	120	150	160	180	170	160	150	150	150

The expenses listed above, £9,050, are apportioned in twelve equal amounts of £754 a month. Additionally, we assume that an initial order for 500 containers is placed and three further deliveries are made — in April, August and December — payment being made two months after delivery. It is also assumed that the milk distributors will pay one month after they have taken delivery of the containers.

Q.5.9 Using this information from Table 5.9 can you prepare a new projected profit and loss account for the year's operation?

On the sales pattern and expenses level we have chosen you will appreciate that cash flow is a major item in the company's operation, as there is always a negative balance amounting to their total available capital by June (the month is not necessarily June, but it is the sixth month of their operation). Perhaps the price of £19.24 is too low and 2,000 containers a year may not be a high enough turnover to absorb the regular expenses. You may care to recalculate at a level of, say, 4,000 containers a year and a price of slightly in excess of £20 each. Finally in contrast, we offer the following suggested projected profit and loss account for the electronic organ operation — the 'without rhythm' model — at a price of £134 to the dealer:

Estimated sales revenue, 450 at £134		£60,300
Materials, 500 at £35	£17,500	
Labour: 1 man 52 × £50	2,600	
4 girls 52 × £80	4,160	
Overheads, say 52 weeks at £50	2,600	
	26,860	
Less closing stock of materials	1,750	
		25,110
Gross profit		35,190
Less expenses:		
Owen and Davies' salaries, 52 × £100	5,200	
Administration, 52 × £10	520	
Transportation, 450 × £3	1,350	
Advertising, say	5,000	
Travelling expenses, say	1,000	
Postage, telephone, say	1,500	
Financing, say	1,000	
Sundries, contingencies, say	2,000	
		17,570
Net profit		£17,620

5.3 Report

A report on the choice for Owen and Davies might include the following:

Aim. This will depend on the actions you recommend, and there are almost as many arguments for adopting one product as for the other. It is also conceivable to recommend neither product.

Purpose. There is an indication in the text that the purpose underlying the Owen and Davies' venture is that they wish to be in business on their own rather than be employed by a large organization. An external consultant would be wise to take this into consideration when reviewing possible recommendations. There is also a danger that the two men may be so enthusiastic about their prospective business activities that they fail to recognize certain financial dangers inherent in the proposed operations.

The text makes it clear that Owen and Davies are only able to adopt one of the two possible products, and therefore a decision for one or the other has to be made before any objective can be adopted. The possible actions are assessed in the analysis and it is left to you to decide which of the two products should be recommended. You may be interested to learn that when this case was set for the final examination for the Diploma in Marketing in 1972, of the 2,000-odd scripts submitted by candidates, there was an almost fifty-fifty split between the organs and the breakfast drink.

ANSWERS TO QUESTIONS

A.5.1 If 5 per cent of the U.K. market bought a ½-pint bottle six times a year, the number of containers that would be required would be 562·5 × 6 = 3,375 containers. The figure for ½-litre bottles would be 1,000 × 6 = 6,000 containers.

A.5.2 The price structure for the ½-pint and the ½-litre does not really affect the profit that Owen and Davies might make, because the price structure is for the resale price by the milk distributor. However, in this structure the container is costed at £19.24, which would mean that the company O. & D.) would make 25 per cent (£4.81 as a percentage of £19.24).

A.5.3 Price structure for ½-pint bottle selling at 4p:

Cost of production	£0·0206
Milk distributor, 20 per cent	0·008
Advertising, 8·1 per cent	0·00324
Milk roundsman, 7·5 per cent	0·003
	£0·03484

This is, of course, considerably less than the selling price of 4p. The reason is that we have compared two price structures using identical percentage on costs of 35·6 per cent, but this only relates to the ½-litre bottle. The ½-pint bottle has 48·5 per cent to cover expenses. A suggested price structure for ½-pint bottle selling at 4p is the following:

Cost of production	£0·0206
Roundsman, say 7·5 per cent	0·003
Advertising, say 10 per cent	0·004
Milk distributor, 31 per cent	0·0124
	£0·04

A.5.4 One of the major items, which has not been included in the costings, is the payment to Owen and Davies. Each has said that he needs £50 a week. If we assume that the company makes a profit of £4.81 (= 25 per cent), and that the two men are paid out of profits, then they will have to sell containers at a rate of 21 a week (£100 divided by £4.81 = 20·79) to pay for their basic £50 each.

A.5.5 The text, and this question, has been discussing gross profit and not net profit. If they sell 500 containers a quarter, then the calculation is as follows:

2,000 at £19.24	£38,480
2,000 at £14.43	28,860
	9,620
52 weeks at £100	5,200
	£4,420 = 11·49 per cent

A.5.6 The price charged by the dealers to the public will not affect the breakeven figure for sales of Owen and Davies, since this breakeven figure is based on their prices to the dealers. The costing for the 'with rhythm' organ is £1,170 + £50 to cover the specialized labour = £1,220. Adding the weekly amount the two men require, this becomes £1,320. The breakeven figure is found by dividing this by the price; the price is found by dividing the same figure, £1,320, by the breakeven figure:

$$\frac{1,320}{5} = £264$$

If the dealer operates on a 33⅓ per cent profit on sales, then, adding 50 per cent, we have £396 to the public. This figure does not affect the breakeven figure for Owen and Davies.

A.5.7 There are many possible answers to the problem of launching the organ. Perhaps the launch should be confined to their more immediate areas (around Lancashire and Yorkshire) for the first few months or so. Musical trade press correspondents could be invited to a press reception and a demonstration given with a well known professional player illustrating the range and flexibility of the organ. This might be repeated in several large towns, with local selected dealers being invited to attend. As the initial marketing of the organ would be restricted geographically, it would be unwise to use national media or to advertise widely.

A.5.8 Perhaps the best way to launch the breakfast drink is to offer the milk distributor a 'package deal'. Owen and Davies should be prepared to introduce the idea of delivering a fruit juice drink with the milk to the milk roundsman and his customers once the milk distributor has decided to proceed with the operation. The initial task will be to convince milk distributors that there is worth-while profit in the scheme, and to sign them up for a trial period of, say, six months. Owen and Davies might introduce the scheme first to the milk roundsmen by arranging to have enclosed in the men's wage packets a teaser campaign over a period of about three weeks announcing that '*Jrink* (whatever name is chosen) is coming', and finally that '*Jrink* is here' — when samples should be given to the milkmen. A similar teaser campaign might be aimed at the public, and the best way of getting them to try it is to distribute samples. Owen and Davies would need to supply samples in their 'package deal', as it is unlikely that the dairy would wish to be bothered making them up. When samples are left at houses, order forms for deliveries should also be left, perhaps in the form of a 'collar' that slips over the neck of the milk bottle. Posters will be required for the sides of the milk floats, and perhaps self-liquidating offers made, such as drinking cups. Free lapel badges, balloons and similar small items of interest to children can be included in the promotional package.

A.5.9 A projected profit and loss account for the fruit juice operation over a year, using the figures in the cash flow calculation, might be the following:

Sales for the year, 1,620 at £19.24		£31,169
Purchases	£28,860	
Less closing stock 380 at £14.43	5,483	
		23,377
Gross profit		7,792
Less expenses:		
12 × £754	9,048	
Financing (from cash flow)	545	
		9,593
		£(1,801)

6. Upton, Vance and Wells Ltd

This is a complex case, with opportunities of applying a limited number of quantitative techniques to its analysis. A behavioural situation arises fairly quickly, as the sales director leaves the company and Mike Parsons, a new man from outside the company, is appointed sales manager, with most of the responsibilities but not all the authority of the departed director. If you deal with the case from the position of Parsons, you will find that the constraint is significant, since some of the company's problems are fundamental and require board decisions.

6.1 Data

Upton, Vance and Wells Ltd is a medium-sized company manufacturing a wide range of portable buildings. They have production facilities in the U.K. at Stevenage, Herts.; Romford, Essex; and Gravesend, Kent. The five directors are John Upton, aged 44, managing; Charles Vance, 40, finance; Ted Young, 61, sales; Bill Talbot, 45, production; and the Secretary, Martin Wells, aged 51. The organization chart is shown in Exhibit 6.1.

The company was started in 1927 by Upton's father, who died in 1965. In consequence, John had taken over the task of chairman and managing director somewhat earlier than had been expected. Before then he had been in charge of production at the three factories, and, on his assuming the role of chief executive, Bill Talbot, who was then the production manager at Stevenage, was made production director.

Vance's father had joined Upton senior a couple of years after Upton had started the business, and Martin Wells' uncle had joined the other two just before World War II. It was the war that had given U.V.W. the opportunity of developing and expanding its portable buildings operations, and, by 1942, they were engaged almost entirely on contract work for several government departments. All kinds of portable structures were contracted for, both manufacture and, where necessary, erection. They had made observation huts, barracks, site sheds, airfield stores, offices, farm buildings and even field hospital units. Their expertise had developed immeasurably during this period, enabling them to produce structures with a high strength-to-weight ratio that were easily and quickly erected, were weatherproof in widely differing climatic conditions and were simple to maintain. In recent years improved glazing of greenhouses, the introduction of various plastics sections and components, ventilation improvements and other advanced production techniques had put U.V.W. products among the leaders in their field.

Wood constructions are produced at Stevenage, where there is a 20-acre site with

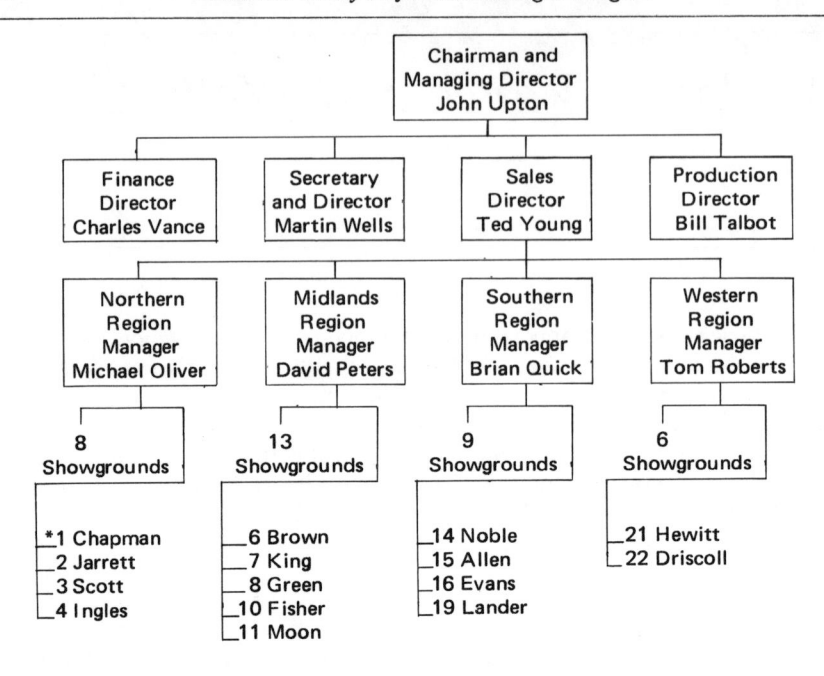

```
                    ┌─────────────────────┐
                    │ Chairman and        │
                    │ Managing Director   │
                    │ John Upton          │
                    └─────────────────────┘
                              │
   ┌──────────────┬───────────┴────────┬──────────────┐
┌──────────┐ ┌──────────────┐  ┌──────────┐   ┌──────────────┐
│ Finance  │ │ Secretary    │  │ Sales    │   │ Production   │
│ Director │ │ and Director │  │ Director │   │ Director     │
│ Charles  │ │ Martin Wells │  │ Ted Young│   │ Bill Talbot  │
│ Vance    │ │              │  │          │   │              │
└──────────┘ └──────────────┘  └──────────┘   └──────────────┘
```

Northern Region Manager Michael Oliver	Midlands Region Manager David Peters	Southern Region Manager Brian Quick	Western Region Manager Tom Roberts
8 Showgrounds	13 Showgrounds	9 Showgrounds	6 Showgrounds
*1 Chapman 2 Jarrett 3 Scott 4 Ingles	6 Brown 7 King 8 Green 10 Fisher 11 Moon	14 Noble 15 Allen 16 Evans 19 Lander	21 Hewitt 22 Driscoll

* Numbers refer to the areas.

Exhibit 6.1 Upton, Vance and Wells Ltd, company organization

about 150,000 sq. ft (14,000 sq. m) of machinery workshops and covered storage. At Romford, where Upton had started making greenhouses with a few hand tools, obtaining timber and glass from local merchants, they have smaller production facilities but a sizeable timber mill, which is ideally situated to receive and process their imported timber. Gravesend is the site of their concrete productions — modular garages, garden workshops, small business buildings, coal bunkers and all the bases required for their greenhouses and certain portable buildings.

Products from their Stevenage and Romford factories are distributed all over the U.K., and (since 1969) to Holland, Belgium and France, where it is accepted the U.V.W. productions are better value than can be obtained locally. Concrete products from Gravesend represent only about 5 per cent of their total sales, and a large proportion of Gravesend output is for the interlocking concrete bases for timber buildings.

Their range includes many types of portable wooden, concrete, flat and corrugated asbestos sheet, garages, garden rooms, sunhouses, offices, workshops, warehouses, house extensions, Dutch-type greenhouses with wood or aluminium frames, wooden fencing, and prefabricated industrial buildings for use as stores, factories, schools, churches, libraries, farm buildings, etc. They also supply accessories for use with sheds, garages and greenhouses — heating systems (electric, oil-fired and solid fuel), watering systems, concrete and asbestos containers, water butts and ventilation control mechanisms for greenhouses.

On the first Monday in January 1973 John Upton was presiding over the regular monthly meeting of the Board at Stevenage. Other directors present were Charles Vance, Bill Talbot and Martin Wells.

'Before we look at routine matters', said John Upton to his three colleagues, 'I have some sad news.'

'About Ted Young?' enquired Vance.

'Yes', replied Upton, 'he really is unable to carry on and, over the weekend, his doctor has advised him to retire now – in fact, when I saw him on Saturday, he looked as though he needed a long holiday.'

'He hasn't been well for some time', put in Martin Wells, 'and we've tried to get him to take on a deputy. After all, he's over sixty, isn't he.'

'Hm', agreed John, 'and the problem now is what are we going to do about his replacement?'

The four directors discussed the merits of all likely candidates in the company, but there was certainly no one at head office, Stevenage, who could possibly be groomed for the job, especially as there were so many other different projects under consideration at that time. For example, the company was looking into the possibility of buying a small factory at Treforest in South Wales to increase their production of sheds and garages. The directors considered the possibility of promoting one of the regional managers, but were agreed that the only man who could possibly cope with the job was Brian Quick, the Southern region manager, whose region contributed about 35 per cent of total company sales. However, Brian was 62 years old and unlikely to accept the sales director's job at his age. He lived with his wife in Croydon, London, and both were looking forward to his retirement in 1976. Michael Oliver, the Northern region manager, was 35, lived in Manchester and did not possess the character that the Board considered was needed at that time. David Peters, 38, of the Midlands region lived in Shrewsbury and was trying to handle the problems of a large scattered region that had been, until a year or two previously, two regions – East Midlands and West Midlands. The West Midlands manager had left to take up an appointment with another company and Peters had been asked by Ted Young to look after the nine areas. Naturally it had meant increased income for Peters in the form of increased commission. The Western Region manager, Tom Roberts, aged 32, lived in Bristol and had only been promoted to regional manager in 1971 from representative in area 15 – Greater London south of the Thames – where he had worked under Brian Quick. Allen was the new representative appointed to area 15 in 1971 and was showing great promise, not only because of his enthusiasm but also because of his wide experience in the industry.

'We'll have to get someone from outside the company', said John Upton.

'At least he'll have an opportunity of liaising closely with Ted', added Bill Talbot.

'I'm afraid not', returned Upton slowly, yet with emphasis. 'Ted's condition is a little more serious than we thought. His doctor, Edwards, had a word with me and stressed that Ted must give up work completely. There must be no question of his even being worried with any of our problems. He's got to have rest and lots of it. In short, he's got to cut himself off from U.V.W. and concentrate on getting well, and it's going to take a long time.'

The other three were obviously a little shocked at the seriousness of Ted's condition, and there could be no doubt but that they were going to miss his cheery presence in the company.

'If we start looking now', suggested Martin, 'we might find someone by May or June.'

'Or July, or August', added Bill disconsolately.

'Well gentlemen', said John, 'I think we'd better adjourn now and see how this business of Ted is going to affect us over the next few weeks. Meanwhile I'll ask young Cliff Raven to 'hold the fort' for the time being. I won't say too much to him, except that Ted's taking a few months' holiday.'

Cliff Raven, 24, was a sales office assistant to Ted Young and handled most of the routine matters in Stevenage. He also helped Vic Ainge, who was responsible for factory liaison and particularly for export documentation and shipping. Export orders were mainly the result of the efforts of Noble and Allen in London. These two representatives made regular trips to the continent in search of business and also called on prospects in the city (of London).

U.V.W. shares were held by the directors and members of their families. The major shareholder was John Upton's mother, who held 100,000, but she was not a director of the company. The other holdings as at December 1972 were as follows:

John Upton	60,000
Charles Vance	50,000
Martin Wells	45,000
Ted Young	5,000
Bill Talbot	5,000
Others	35,000

The remuneration of the directors in 1972 amounted to a total of £25,500. The regional managers received salaries as follows: Roberts £2,250, Quick £3,760, Peters £3,150 and Oliver £2,890. In addition, they received one half of one per cent commission on all sales over quota in their regions. The representatives received an average salary of £1,860 and 5 per cent commission on sales over quotas that were accredited directly to them. They received no commission on sales made from the showgrounds, whereas the regional managers received commission on the total sales in the regions. Targets for 1973 had been set by Ted Young and are given in Table 6.1.

The production director, Talbot, controls all three factories — Stevenage, Romford and Gravesend — but this organizational structure is not detailed in the main organization chart in Exhibit 6.1. Similarly, the financial director, Vance, has cost accountants attached to the factories, but these are not shown in the chart. Buying for all factories is carried out at Stevenage by the purchasing department, which is controlled partly by the production director and partly by the finance director.

The four regional managers report to the sales director, and each regional manager is responsible for controlling and motivating his whole region — representatives and showgrounds. The representatives receive 'leads' from Stevenage and also have their own accounts, mainly institutional and industrial customers. They are also expected to help at the showgrounds with regular attendance, receiving or meeting potential customers, arranging demonstrations, following up enquiries etc. Most of them find it invaluable to maintain very strong links with the showground staff, as they can often obtain a sale which is credited to them and on which commission is paid. This had not been regarded as an entirely satisfactory situation, and, as the regional managers received a commission irrespective of whether the showground or the representatives obtained the order, the matter had so far remained unsolved — to the dissatisfaction of many of the representatives.

There are thirty-six showgrounds, all owned by the company — eight in the Northern region, thirteen in the Midlands, nine in the South and six in the West. Their locations are detailed in Table 6.2. The largest is at Watford, where nearly 100 portable buildings are on display; the smallest is at Wellingborough, which was opened in 1972 and, in view of its location and size, is not exactly ideal. Ted Young

Table 6.1 Sales Targets for Regional Managers and Representatives for 1973

Name	Region/Area	Target (£)
Oliver	Northern	265,000
Peters	Midlands	325,000
Quick	Southern	450,000
Roberts	Western	100,000
Chapman	1	10,000
Jarrett	2	35,000
Scott	3	30,000
Ingles	4	20,000
Brown	6	20,000
King	7	20,000
Green	8	20,000
Fisher	10	25,000
Moon	11	23,000
Noble	14	90,000
Allen	15	80,000
Evans	16	25,000
Lander	19	20,000
Hewitt	21	20,000
Driscoll	22	25,000

Regional managers are paid one half of one per cent on all sales over their respective sales targets; representatives are paid five per cent on all sales accredited to them over their respective targets.

is, or rather was, thinking of moving the location to another district nearby — possibly Kettering. Aberystwyth and Marlow were opened in 1971, and are both well established. Each showground has a person in charge, most of them being women. At twenty of the largest grounds there is an assistant to help with the clerical work, answer the telephone, maintain records, etc. Generalizing, the larger the showground, the greater the annual sales, but no detailed investigations had been conducted by U.V.W. because the value of the showground land varied so widely throughout the country; some sites were better located than others, and staff effectiveness varied.

Table 6.2 Regions, Areas and Showgrounds

Areas	Showgrounds
Northern region	
1 Scotland	Glasgow, Edinburgh
2 Yorkshire	Bradford, Hull
3 Cheshire, Lancashire	Liverpool, Manchester
4 Westmorland, Durham, Cumberland, Northumberland	Newcastle, Penrith
Midlands region	
5 Norfolk, Suffolk	Norwich, Ipswich
6 Lincoln, Nottinghamshire	Lincoln, Nottingham
7 Leics, Northants., Rutland	Leicester, Wellingborough
8 Essex	Chelmsford
9 Cambs, Hunts.	Cambridge
10 Derbs, Staffs, Salop	Derby, Shrewsbury
11 Warwicks, Worcs, Herefordshire	Worcester
12 Radnor, Brecon, Carms, Pembroke, Cardiganshire	Aberystwyth
13 Montgy, Merioneth, Denbigh, Caerns, Anglesey, Flint	Bangor (North Wales)
Southern region	
14 Greater London, North of Thames	Palmers Green
15 Greater London, South of Thames	Croydon
16 Kent, Surrey, Sussex	Weybridge, Canterbury, Brighton
17 Hants, Isle of Wight	Portsmouth
18 Herts, Beds	Watford
19 Oxon, Berks, Bucks	Oxford, Marlow
Western region	
20 Glos, Somt, Wiltshire	Bristol, Cheltenham, Swindon
21 Dorset, Devon, Cornwall	Barnstaple, Plymouth
22 Glamorgan, Monmouthshire	Swansea

The county names refer to the old counties, before the reorganization of 1973.

U.V.W. has a number of competitors in the U.K. and a selection of competitive products is listed with prices in Tables 6.3 to 6.6. It is not practicable to list the prices and ranges of all the company's products, because there are so many, but a selection is given in Tables 6.7 to 6.10. The company issued a great many full-colour catalogues, which accounted for a large proportion of the annual advertising appropriation. This was maintained at approximately 5 per cent of annual sales. The forecast made by Ted Young for 1973 was £1,508,400 — the details of how this is broken down over regions, areas, salesmen and showgrounds is shown in Table 6.11. An estimate of the advertising budget for the year is between £90,000 and £93,000, of which about £50,000 to £60,000 will be spent on catalogues and other promotional literature. Management were convinced that such sales literature was vital in maintaining and increasing sales, and results certainly supported this contention. In 1964 the annual sales of the company — then based only at Romford — was £250,000, and in four years sales had more than trebled. In 1969 there was a downturn in sales, which was attributed by management mainly to the rapid rise and over-extension in the previous three or four years. They had been short of production capacity, delivery times had become protracted and orders had been lost. The directors had learned a hard lesson and were determined never again to be in such a position. It was for this very reason that they had been looking for additional production capacity and had become interested in a factory in South Wales, on Treforest Trading Estate, which was for sale as a going operation. It was ideally suited to U.V.W.'s needs, as it was equipped with plant and machinery to manufacture caravans. The owner had died and his executors wanted to dispose of the entire operation. Ted Young and Bill Talbot had carried out a fairly thorough investigation and were satisfied that, with the same staff, and with very little alteration, they could start producing portable buildings within a week or so of taking over. Charles Vance was satisfied that the asking price would not be beyond their financial capabilities. Bill Talbot had calculated the maximum weekly output based on their two most popular lines — a shed and a garage. His findings are shown in Table 6.12 (p. 149).

Table 6.3 Competitors' Prices for a Range of Comparable Sheds

Sheds with floors and bearers Maker and size	Softwood price (£)	Cedar price (£)
HALLS		
7 ft x 5 ft		59·30
9 ft x 6 ft		77·00
PRATTENS		
6 ft x 5 ft	45·05	
8 ft x 5 ft	54·08	
10 ft x 5 ft	59·15	
CASES		
6 ft x 6 ft 4 in	35·90	
9 ft x 6 ft 4 in	45·20	
15 ft x 6 ft 4 in	69·00	
12 ft x 9 ft 4 in	72·60	
REDWORTH		
6 ft x 4 ft	39·00	
7 ft x 5 ft	45·00	
9 ft x 6 ft	59·00	
REGAL		
6 ft x 5 ft	28·50	
10 ft x 6 ft	42·10	
14 ft 10 in x 6 ft	86·40	97·10
KENKAST		
6 ft x 4 ft	41·50	49·50
7 ft x 5 ft	50·75	57·75
8 ft x 6 ft	59·00	65·00

Table 6.4 Competitors' Prices for a Range of Comparable Garages

Maker and Size	Softwood/Asbestos (£)	Cedar/Asbestos (£)
HALLS		
14 ft x 9 ft		199·50 (all cedar)
16 ft x 9 ft		215·00 (all cedar)
REGAL		
14 ft x 9 ft 4 in	65·90	
16 ft x 9 ft 4 in	70·40	
KENKAST		
14 ft 4 in x 8 ft	67·00	
16 ft 4 in x 9 ft	84·00	

Table 6.5 Competitors' Prices for Comparable Fencing

Maker (6 ft lengths)	Interwoven (£)	Waney Edge (£)	Post (£)
REGAL			
3 ft high	1·40	1·95	0·50
4 ft high	1·85	2·45	0·55
5 ft high	2·35	2·95	0·60
6 ft high	2·85	3·30	0·65
KENKAST			
3 ft high	1·65	2·00	0·60
4 ft high	2·00	2·30	0·65
5 ft high	2·35	2·65	0·70
6 ft high	2·65	2·95	0·75

Table 6.6 *Competitors' Prices for a Range of Comparable Glasshouses*

Dutch type glasshouses complete with glass but no staging

Maker and size	Softwood price (£)	Cedar price (£)	Aluminium price (£)
HALLS			
8 ft 7 in x 8 ft		58·00	
10 ft 7 in x 8 ft		63·00	
12 ft 8 in x 8 ft		69·80	
ALTON			
8 ft x 8 ft	48·30	51·50	
10 ft 6 in x 8 ft	56·60	59·75	
13 ft x 8 ft	66·45	72·50	
PRATTENS			
8 ft 6 in x 7 ft	53·50		
10 ft 7 in x 8 ft 6 in	70·25		
REGAL			
10 ft x 6 ft	45·90		
12 ft 9 in x 6 ft	58·90		
10 ft x 10 ft	59·80		
WORTH (NON-DUTCH TYPE)			
8 ft x 6 ft 9 in		53·50	
13 ft x 6 ft 9 in		69·50	
13 ft x 8 ft		78·00	
EDEN (NON-DUTCH TYPE)			
8 ft 4 in x 6 ft 3 in			53·50
8 ft 4 in x 8 ft 4 in			62·50
10 ft 4 in x 8 ft 4 in			78·50
12 ft 5 in x 8 ft 4 in			87·50

Table 6.7 Prices of Selected Range of Sheds

Ridge or pent roof sheds. Interior headroom 220 cm at highest and 193 cm at lowest points. All sheds are supplied with wooden floors and bearers. There are windows along one side — to choice — with a two-window opening. The door, 80 cm wide, can be placed at either end. Prefix 'R' is for ridge and 'P' for pent roof.

Code*	Size in cm	Price softwood (£)	Code	Price cedar (£)
RSS66/PSS66	182 x 182	28·80	RCS66/PCS66	55·80
RSS86/PSS86	243 x 182	38·40	RCS86/PCS86	74·40
RSS106/PSS106	304 x 182	48·00	RCS106/PCS106	93·00
RSS88/PSS88	243 x 243	48·60	RCS88/PCS88	99·20
RSS108/PSS108	304 x 243	60·80	RCS108/PCS108	124·00
RSS128/PSS128	365 x 243	72·90	RCS128/PCS128	148·80
RSS1210/PSS1210	365 x 304	84·00	RCS1210/PCS1210	186·00
RSS1410/PSS1410	426 x 304	98·00	RCS1410/PCS1410	217·00
RSS1610/PSS1610	487 x 304	112·00	RCS1610/PCS1610	248·00

*The codings are given to illustrate the manner in which the company attempts to describe the product for readiness of understanding internally. For example, PCS1610 is a pent roof cedar shed 16 ft x 10 ft — P is for pent roof, C for cedar wood, S for shed and the figures are the dimensions in feet. Because an increasing amount of production is being exported, and because the country will be changing to metric measurements, all sizes are given primarily in the metric system.

Table 6.8 Prices of Selected Timber and Asbestos Garages

Planed timber construction; walls covered with asbestos sheeting. Roof, either ridge or pent, of corrugated asbestos on timber purlins to BS 690 (1963). Two side or four rear windows included in price. External timber coated with preservative. Height 243 cm at highest and 182 cm at lowest points. Door opening 208 cm wide and 175 cm high. Double garages have either two single garage doors or 'upandover' door at extra cost. Single garages can be supplied with 'upandover' doors at extra cost.

Single timber and asbestos garage

Size in cm and (feet)		Price Softwood (£)	Cedar (£)
426 x 274	(14 x 9)*	69·30	75·50
487 x 274	(16 x 9)	79·20	86·30
548 x 274	(18 x 9)	89·10	97·10
426 x 304	(14 x 10)	77·00	83·90
487 x 304	(16 x 10)	88·00	95·90
548 x 304	(18 x 10)	99·00	107·90

Double timber and asbestos garage

487 x 518	(16 x 17)	176·80	192·70
548 x 518	(18 x 17)	198·90	216·80
609 x 518	(20 x 17)	221·00	240·80
487 x 579	(16 x 19)	197·60	212·30
548 x 579	(18 x 19)	222·30	240·30
609 x 579	(20 x 19)	247·00	265·00

*Coding combines dimensions in feet, e.g. G169 = softwood garage 16 ft x 9 ft.

Table 6.9 Prices of Selected Dutch-type Greenhouses

Red deal or cedar timber with main framework, glass bars, etc., in 45 x 45 mm section. Ridge heights vary with size of glasshouses but not less than 198 cm. Glass: 3 mm clear horticultural supplied cut to size ready for glazing or ready-glazed.

Code	Size in cm (ft)		Price Red deal (£)	Cedar (£)
DH86	243 x 182	(8 x 6)	36·00	38·40
DH106	304 x 182	(10 x 6)	45·00	48·00
DH126	365 x 182	(12 x 6)	54·00	57·60
DH146	426 x 182	(14 x 6)	63·00	67·20
DH108	304 x 243	(10 x 8)	52·00	56·00
DH128	365 x 243	(12 x 8)	62·40	67·20
DH148	426 x 243	(14 x 8)	72·80	78·40
DH168	487 x 243	(16 x 8)	83·20	89·60
DH1210	365 x 304	(12 x 10)	72·00	84·00
DH1410	426 x 304	(14 x 10)	84·00	98·00
DH1610	487 x 304	(16 x 10)	96·00	112·00
DH1810	548 x 304	(18 x 10)	108·00	126·00

Table 6.10 Prices of Selected Range of Fencing

Interwoven fencing	Size	Cost (£)
IF36	90 cm high 182 cm wide (3 ft x 6 ft)	1·55 a panel
IF46	120 cm high 182 cm wide (4 ft x 6 ft)	1·90
IF56	150 cm high 182 cm wide (5 ft x 6 ft)	2·35
IF66	182 cm high 182 cm wide (6 ft x 6 ft)	2·75
Waney Edge fencing (Overlapped)		
WF36	90 cm high 182 cm wide (3 ft x 6 ft)	1·95 a panel
WF46	120 cm high 182 cm wide (4 ft x 6 ft)	2·35
WF56	150 cm high 182 cm wide (5 ft x 6 ft)	2·80
WF66	182 cm high 182 cm wide (6 ft x 6 ft)	3·15
Posts for fencing 7 cm x 7 cm		
P3	150 cm for IF 36 and WF36 (5 ft)	0·55 each
P4	182 cm for IF46 and WF46 (6 ft)	0·60
P5	210 cm for IF56 and WF56 (7 ft)	0·65
P6	240 cm for IF66 and WF66 (8 ft)	0·70

Table 6.11 Sales Estimates for 1973

Northern Region		Salesman (£)	Showground (£)	Total (£)
1	Scotland			60,000
	Chapman	18,000		
	Edinburgh		22,000	
	Glasgow		20,000	
2	Yorkshire			117,500
	Jarrett	44,500		
	Bradford		35,000	
	Hull		38,000	
3	Lancs, Cheshire			104,000
	Scott	37,000		
	Manchester		35,000	
	Liverpool		32,000	
4	Westmorland, etc.			81,500
	Ingles	29,500		
	Penrith		22,000	
	Newcastle		30,000	
	Total Northern Region	129,000	234,000	£363,000

Midland Region (East)

5	Norfolk, Suffolk			34,600
	Norwich		24,000	
	Ipswich		10,600	
6	Lincoln, Notts			64,150
	Brown	25,150		
	Lincoln		17,000	
	Nottingham		22,000	
7	Leics, Northants			40,250
	King	23,250		
	Wellingborough		2,000	
	Leicester		15,000	
8	Essex			56,500
	Green	28,000		
	Chelmsford		28,500	
9	Cambs, Hunts			24,750
	Cambridge		24,750	

Midland Region (West)

10	Derbs, Staffs			85,300
	Fisher	30,000		
	Derby		30,600	
	Shrewsbury		24,700	
11	Warks, Worcs			58,200
	Moon	28,000		
	Worcester		30,200	
12	Radnor, etc.			19,750
	Aberystwyth		19,750	
13	Montg, etc.			30,400
	Bangor		30,400	
	Total Midland Region	134,400	279,500	£413,900

Table 6.11 (Continued)

		Salesman (£)	Showground (£)	Total (£)
Southern Region				
14	North of Thames			135,000
	Noble	97,000		
	Palmers Green		38,000	
15	South of Thames			125,000
	Allen	85,000		
	Croydon		40,000	
16	Kent, Sy, Sussex			111,000
	Evans	31,000		
	Weybridge		26,000	
	Canterbury		24,000	
	Brighton		30,000	
17	Hants			50,000
	Portsmouth		50,000	
18	Herts, Beds			55,000
	Watford		55,000	
19	Oxon, etc.			63,000
	Lander	29,000		
	Oxford		20,000	
	Marlow		14,000	
	Total Southern Region	242,000	297,000	£539,000
Western Region				
20	Glos, etc.			80,800
	Bristol		36,800	
	Cheltenham		20,000	
	Swindon		24,000	
21	Dorset, etc.			57,000
	Hewitt	15,000		
	Plymouth		20,000	
	Barnstaple		22,000	
22	Glam, etc.			54,700
	Driscoll	23,000		
	Swansea		31,700	
	Total Western Region	38,000	154,500	£192,500

County names refer to the old counties, before the reorganization of 1973.

Table 6.12 New Factory Potential (see p. 143)

Bill Talbot had based his calculations of maximum weekly output of sheds and garages on their most popular models. These were the RSS/PSS 106 shed, 304 x 182 cm, and the G169 garage, 487 x 274 cm. The '106' shed sold at £48 and had a profit of £14.40; the '169' garage sold at £79.20 and had a profit of £23.75. Production would be organized in the woodworking and fabricating shops, where the sections for both sheds and garages would be made and assembled. The shed finishing shop is different from the garage finishing shop, because of the different materials, somewhat different processes and different labour requirements. The limitations on output are as follows:

	Maximum weekly production		
Production operation	'106' sheds		'169' garages
Woodworking	200	or	70
Fabricating, assembling	125	or	95
Finishing sheds	110		
Finishing garages			65

On 5 February, while waiting for his colleagues, John Upton was bringing himself up to date on the economic situation in Europe in general and in the U.K. in particular. He read the following passage:

The big question in Europe is inflation. Since the beginning of the cycle, twists in the price-wage spiral have followed one another at increasing speed, perhaps because the mildness of the preceding recession left the rate of capacity utilization unusually high, and labour unusually scarce, for the start of a recovery phase (Britain and Italy are exceptions: both have unused physical production capacity and high unemployment). In contrast to the experience of recent years, the British economy is experiencing a period of growth. The first area to see a revival was private consumption and the recovery has spread. Investment demand has at last emerged, if the longer order books in the capital industries are anything to go by. Export prospects have likewise improved, aided by devaluation. Further expansion is expected in 1973, especially as there is plenty of production capacity available. Unfortunately there have been, yet again, many strikes that have hampered steady recovery — the mineworkers in the first half of 1972, the dockers in the early summer and, more recently, the building trades. As a result, the third quarter GNP rose by only 0·5 per cent, while over the full year GNP has risen by 4 per cent, which is one per cent below the government target. Prices are now 8 per cent higher than a year ago while average wages have risen by 17 per cent. A disturbing feature is the unprecedented intensity of inflation, which, so far, has not been checked. The government were unable to secure a voluntary agreement with the unions and management on wage and price restraints and therefore decreed a 90-day freeze of prices, wages and dividends. Since the pound was floated, it has lost 10 per cent of its value.

John stopped reading as his co-directors came in, but he commented on the report he had been reading, saying that it looked as though they had better concentrate on exports for the next year or two. The main topic of their conversation, however, was the appointment of a new sales manager, and, in the previous four weeks, Martin Wells had been very busy advertising and sounding out possible sources in an endeavour to secure the services of the 'right' man. A number of applications had been received, and the real problem was the exact nature of the duties that the new man would be asked to carry out. It was unreasonable to expect him to be able to take on Ted Young's responsibilities 'lock, stock and barrel', and the board wished to avoid creating unnecessary friction with any of their 250 employees, especially with any of the regional managers and sales staff. In addition, the new sales manager would not be made a director of the company initially, but would have to prove himself.

'The way applications are coming in', said Martin Wells, 'we should be able to draw up a short list in a week or so — and some of them look very good.'

They discussed the merits of various applicants, indicating their preferences, and then turned to other matters. Some of the sales returns for January had already been reported, and, as sales appeared to be near to the estimates made originally by Ted Young, they agreed that the new man would have to work with these estimates and targets for 1973 — unless sales took a definite turn one way or the other.

A few months earlier they had discussed the stock levels carried. All wood imported or bought in the U.K. was held by another company in Romford owned by the Upton family, but bought-in components formed a high proportion of stocks

Table 6.13 Result of the 10 Per Cent Sample Stocktaking on 1 February 1973

Item	Cost per item (£)	Average stock	Average annual usage	Stockholding cost (£)
1	16·20	100	112	113
2	9·80	60	72	83
3	80·00	20	1,500	400
4	2·20	548	540	84
5	5·40	1,320	828	500
6	6·80	808	660	385
7	3·20	768	152	334
8	2·30	225	330	363
9	4·00	148	275	85
10	0·40	612	780	17
11	0·70	680	440	33
12	2·00	600	575	84
13	3·00	630	280	143
14	2·00	720	900	102
15	0·85	580	750	70

carried by U.V.W. Young had been given the task of looking into the problem, and Vance had looked at the cost of ordering, which was estimated to be £5 per order, irrespective of the size or frequency. A 10 per cent sample stocktaking in February had resulted in the report shown in Table 6.13. As Ted was absent, the report had been sent through to John Upton, who now invited comment. It was agreed that, as this was really a marketing problem rather than a production or financial problem, as such, they would leave it 'on the table' until the new sales manager joined the company. The operation of the transport fleet was next discussed, and, although they agreed that this should also fall within the province of the sales manager, they had to take a decision to buy three more lorries of the same make they had been using for several years — two for normal replacement and one extra. At the end of the formal business the progress of Ted's health was discussed, but all agreed that it was not very encouraging.

With the introduction of value added tax (VAT) a lot of extra work was being placed on all departments, and therefore their March meeting was cancelled. Bill was also busy with the Treforest factory negotiations, John spent five days on a VAT course and Martin was engaged in processing the applicants and conducting preliminary interviews.

Early in April, Cliff Raven received an enquiry from Bob Hewitt in Dorset for 5,000 panels of IF66 fencing to be supplied in lots of 100 a week, delivery to start in July. The customer wished to collect the goods and was prepared to place the order with U.V.W. at list price (£2.75) less a discount, which the customer had suggested should be 10 per cent. Tom Roberts had told Cliff Raven that he was prepared to recommend a discount of 5 per cent, and, when the facts were reported to John Upton, he agreed, adding that, if necessary, Hewitt could go to $7\frac{1}{2}$ per cent. From the telephone conversations that had taken place between company personnel, it was expected that the customer would place the order at list less $7\frac{1}{2}$ per cent. The total order value was between £12,000 and £13,000, and certainly worth pursuing. The costing for this particular fencing panel is as follows:

Materials	£1·70
Labour	0·30
Overheads	0·13
Warehousing and distribution	0·07
	£2·20

Bill Talbot was told by the Stevenage production manager that they could produce up to 500 of the panels a week up to July or August without seriously affecting other manufacture, but this particular order would have to be made on one of their newer machines. Each time a new batch of fences was started on the machine, a setting-up operation costing £12 was required. The manager recommended that they should produce the total amount in lots of 500 to save on setting-up costs. As he explained, if the runs were in lots of 100 a week, this would mean £12 a week for setting-up. Another factor was the storing of these panels until required by the customer, because it was not possible to keep them all in the Stevenage production workshop. In the 7p for warehousing and distribution, approximately 1p was for normal production storage, which was usually for up to a week. They could not carry finished stocks in the factory, and extra storage was required. This was available in the nearby finished goods store, where the annual square footage rental was 10p. Thus, to store one panel on edge for a year would cost 20p. The number of panels being made at any one time determined the method of stacking. If this was done by hand, the panels were stacked upright; if a large run was being produced, a forklift truck stacked them nine at a time to a height of eighteen, which, with the pallets, made this an acceptable height.

At their Board meeting in April the four directors were able to finalize their choice of man to succeed Ted Young. They were unanimous that the best man for the job would be Mike Parsons. He was the right age and had had an extensive experience of their industry in the U.K. and abroad. He had also followed a regular course of marketing training over the years, which included a diploma in marketing and post-diploma work with certain universities specializing in such activities. He was sensible enough to know that success in business ultimately depended on capable management rather than on a variety of tools and techniques — in short, he 'spoke the language' of the U.V.W. directors. He was offered the position and accepted.

The Board continued with their meeting, and looked at the sales figures for the first quarter, which had been compiled by Cliff Raven (Table 6.14). Sales were below the level they had expected, and, undoubtedly for this reason, Raven had decided to look at the sales returns for one showground in particular. His analysis of the Lincoln showground for the period is given in Table 6.15.

Table 6.14 Breakdown of Sales, January to March 1973

Salesman/Showground	Jan. (£)	Feb. (£)	Mar. (£)
1 Chapman	1,416	1,480	1,600
Edinburgh	1,731	1,755	1,435
Glasgow	1,575	1,485	1,760
2 Jarrett	3,460	3,250	3,404
Bradford	2,750	2,652	2,870
Hull	2,951	3,420	3,210
3 Scott	2,951	2,990	3,045
Manchester	2,800	2,830	2,550
Liverpool	2,520	2,600	2,964
4 Ingles	2,454	2,500	2,530
Penrith	1,678	1,740	1,770
Newcastle	2,535	2,549	2,600
5 Norwich	1,945	2,062	2,317
Ipswich	750	630	420
6 Brown	1,864	2,360	2,881
Lincoln	980	448	300
Nottingham	1,120	975	410
7 King	2,180	2,010	2,500
Wellingborough	400	500	310
Leicester	561	590	406
8 Green	1,862	2,346	2,500
Chelmsford	1,190	540	480
9 Cambridge	1,929	1,925	1,960
10 Fisher	2,375	2,609	2,611
Derby	1,730	1,420	1,000
Shrewsbury	1,690	1,670	1,500
11 Moon	2,485	2,897	2,962
Worcester	1,650	1,220	990
12 Aberystwyth	1,540	1,581	1,611
13 Bangor	2,321	2,414	2,478
14 Noble	7,898	8,048	8,264
Palmers Green	2,982	3,039	3,006
15 Allen	7,060	7,100	7,500
Croydon	2,970	3,110	2,885
16 Evans	2,544	2,590	2,636
Weybridge	1,070	1,106	900
Canterbury	1,907	2,040	2,000
Brighton	3,306	3,250	3,600
17 Portsmouth	4,092	4,165	4,230
18 Watford	4,512	4,570	4,655
19 Lander	2,019	2,000	1,720
Oxford	2,103	2,200	2,368
Marlow	1,180	1,195	1,400

154   *Business Analysis for Marketing Managers*

Table 6.14 *(Continued)*

Salesman/Showground	Jan. (£)	Feb. (£)	Mar. (£)
20 Bristol	3,100	3,150	3,298
Cheltenham	1,582	1,450	1,294
Swindon	1,740	1,940	2,056
21 Hewitt	1,100	1,040	1,000
Plymouth	1,578	1,609	1,630
Barnstaple	1,810	1,920	2,016
22 Driscoll	1,872	1,980	2,421
Swansea	2,395	2,360	1,994

'I think we should leave some of these problems for Parsons to have a look at', said Vance with a smile.

'That's dodging the issue', laughed Wells.

'No', interjected Upton, 'that's a good idea. It's not passing the buck — just the opposite. It's showing him that he has our confidence. He's able and willing to look at any marketing problems we have before he actually joins us, so let's start as we intend to continue — take him into our confidence.'

The others agreed, on reflection, that it made sense to allow Parsons to suggest courses of action and to make decisions now on matters that would probably have

Table 6.15 *Sales at the Lincoln Showground, January to March 1973*

Week ending	Sales (£)
Jan 6	262·70
Jan. 13	224·00
Jan. 20	249·40
Jan. 27	244·10
Feb. 3	163·50
Feb. 10	148·80
Feb. 17	11·75
Feb. 24	123·60
Mar. 3	89·10
Mar. 10	62·40
Mar. 17	72·00
Mar. 24	38·40
Mar. 31	38·40

effect in a few months' time when he was with the company. The meeting was then concluded.

We conclude the data with a profit and loss account and balance sheet for 1972, fixed assets 1971 and 1972, profit and loss and balance sheet summaries 1968—72, and company sales 1970—72 (Table 6.16).

Upton, Vance and Wells Ltd

Profit and Loss Account for year ended 31 December 1972

Sales		£1,206,460
Materials	£458,450	
Wages	198,560	
Factory overheads	54,800	
		711,810
		494,650
Less expenses:		
Salaries	65,450	
Commission	4,970	
Travelling	25,400	
Warehousing, transportation	144,440	
Showgrounds — wages, etc.	45,250	
Advertising	68,000	
Financing, insurance, audit	9,650	
General administration	18,750	
Depreciation	15,000	
		396,910
Net profit		97,740
Taxation		42,040
		55,700
Dividend		30,000
		25,700
Profits brought forward		169,300
		£195,000

Balance Sheet as at 31 December 1972

Freehold land, buildings, (written down value)			£105,690
Plant and equipment (written down value)			24,885
Motor vehicles (written down value)			37,425
			168,000
Current Assets:			
Stock and finished goods	128,700		
Debtors	175,900		
Prepayments	26,840		
Securities	50,000		
Cash on deposit	10,300		
Cash in hand	1,700	393,440	
Current Liabilities:			
Creditors	154,900		
Accrued charges	19,500		
Tax	42,040		
	216,440		
			177,000
			£345,000
Financed by:			
300,000 issued and fully paid up 50p shares			150,000
Unappropriated profits			195,000
			£345,000

FIXED ASSETS, 1971 AND 1972

The company's fixed assets are stated in the books at an independent valuation, and, if the properties were sold at the net value, there would be a capital gains tax liability. No provision has been made for this liability, as the directors have no intention in the near future of selling those properties.

	1971			1972		
	Cost or valuation (£000s)	Depreciation (£000s)	Net (£000s)	Cost or valuation (£000s)	Depreciation (£000s)	Net (£000s)
As at 1 January	159	52	107	200	65	135
Additions	41	–	41	48	–	48
Depreciation for year	–	13	(13)	–	15	(15)
	200	65	135	248	80	168
Comprising:						
Land and buildings	90	6	84	122	16	106
Plant and equipment	45	23	22	48	23	25
Motor vehicles	65	36	29	78	41	37
	200	65	135	248	80	168

PROFIT AND LOSS ACCOUNT SUMMARIES, 1968–72

	1968		1969		1970		1971		1972	
	(£)	(£)	(£)	(£)	(£)	(£)	(£)	(£)	(£)	(£)
Sales		895		878		958		1,012		1,206
Inc./dec. in stocks		−17		+18		−14		+3		−
		878		896		944		1,015		1,206
Materials	334		348		378		396		458	
Wages	176		160		152		171		199	
Factory overheads	44		44		47		52		55	
		554		552		577		619		712
Gross profit		324		344		367		396		494
Less expenses:										
Salaries	41		45		47		51		65	
Commission	3		4		4		4		5	
Travelling, etc.	18		18		20		21		25	
Trans. and Wareh.	79		80		104		102		144	
Showgrounds	43		24		35		39		45	
Advertising	39		20		57		60		68	
Fin., insur.	7		7		7		8		10	
Gen. admin.	12		13		14		17		19	
Depreciation	9		8		10		13		15	
		251		219		298		315		396
Net profit		73		125		69		81		98
Taxation		33		56		32		34		42
		40		69		37		47		56
Dividend		30		30		15		30		30
		10		39		22		17		26
Profit B/F		81		91		130		152		169
Retained profit		91		130		152		169		195

BALANCE SHEET SUMMARIES, 1968–72

	1968 (£)	(£)	1969 (£)	(£)	1970 (£)	(£)	1971 (£)	(£)	1972 (£)	(£)
Net fixed assets:										
Land, bldgs. (W.D.V.)*	44		50		68		84		106	
Plant, etc. (W.D.V.)	8		12		19		22		25	
Motor vehicles (W.D.V.)	10		17		20		29		37	
		62		79		107		135		168
Current assets:										
Stock, etc.	122		140		126		129		129	
Debtors	62		72		101		122		176	
Prepayments	20		30		38		40		27	
Securities	40		50		25		50		50	
Cash deposits	26		25		20		15		10	
Cash in hand	1		4		8		3		2	
	271		321		318		359		394	
Current liabilities:										
Creditors	99		104		127		131		155	
Acc. charges	10		10		14		10		20	
Tax	33		56		32		34		42	
	142		170		173		175		217	
		129		151		145		184		177
		191		230		252		319		345
Financed by:										
Share capital	100		100		100		150		150	
Retained profits	91		130		152		169		195	
		191		230		252		319		345

*W.D.V. = Written down value.

Table 6.16 Company Sales from 1970 to 1972

	1970 (£)	(£)	1971 (£)	(£)	1972 (£)	(£)
Northern Region						
1 Chapman	11,400		12,050		14,390	
Edinburgh		13,850		14,600		17,500
Glasgow		12,600		13,250		15,900
2 Jarrett	28,200		29,800		35,610	
Bradford		22,330		23,750		28,290
Hull		24,300		25,700		30,300
3 Scott	23,500		24,850		29,590	
Manchester		22,350		23,560		28,000
Liverpool		20,400		21,500		25,600
4 Ingles	18,750		19,800		23,580	
Penrith		14,100		14,850		17,680
Newcastle		19,080		20,160		23,890
	81,850	149,010	86,500	157,370	103,170	187,160
Midland Region						
5 Norwich		18,670		19,680		21,680
Ipswich		8,130		7,900		8,690
6 Brown	13,900		14,640		17,640	
Lincoln		17,250		14,400		14,940
Nottingham		20,600		19,000		20,000
7 King	12,840		13,520		16,300	
Wellingborough		–		–		2,000
Leicester		14,050		11,300		12,670
8 Green	15,480		16,300		19,650	
Chelmsford		22,030		22,150		25,000
9 Cambridge		23,500		20,070		22,300
10 Fisher	15,750		17,400		21,050	
Derby		23,850		25,200		28,000
Shrewsbury		18,400		19,550		22,000
11 Moon	14,800		16,010		19,630	
Worcester		20,890		22,100		24,750
12 Aberystwyth		–		14,600		16,200
13 Bangor		23,600		24,850		26,900
	72,770	210,970	77,870	220,800	94,270	245,130
Southern Region						
14 Noble	70,300		61,500		76,080	
Palmers Green		19,830		24,180		29,800
15 Allen	62,000		54,000		66,700	
Croydon		21,640		25,290		31,300
16 Evans	18,400		19,600		24,310	
Weybridge		14,390		16,360		20,250
Canterbury		13,230		15,150		18,750
Brighton		17,300		19,000		23,530
17 Portsmouth		26,230		31,750		39,200
18 Watford		30,450		35,600		44,150

(continued overleaf)

Table 6.16 (Continued)

		1970 (£)	(£)	1971 (£)	(£)	1972 (£)	(£)
19	Lander	17,300		18,300		22,720	
	Oxford		11,370		12,650		15,680
	Marlow		–		8,300		10,300
		168,000	154,440	153,400	188,280	189,810	232,960
Western Region							
20	Bristol		23,560		25,060		30,180
	Cheltenham		12,200		12,800		15,490
	Swindon		15,100		15,850		19,000
21	Hewitt	9,230		9,760		12,000	
	Plymouth		12,590		13,300		16,000
	Barnstaple		13,960		14,750		17,600
22	Driscoll	14,450		15,260		18,390	
	Swansea		19,870		21,000		25,300
		23,680	97,280	25,020	102,760	30,390	123,570

Total company sales 1970 – £958,000   1971 – £1,012,000   1972 – £1,206,460

6.2 Analysis

With Upton Vance and Wells Ltd we are faced with a sales forecast, prepared by Ted Young, that is 25 per cent above the sales of 1972. It is broken down in Table 6.11, but you should assess it very carefully before accepting it. The Northern and Western regions each show an increase of about 25 per cent over 1972, and the Southern region has an average of about 27·5 per cent increase. The Midlands region has one or two oddities: all the salesmen's forecasts have been increased by over 42 per cent each above their 1972 figures, while the estimates for the showgrounds have been increased from 9 per cent to 22 per cent with an average of 14 per cent. Wellingborough has no increase in its sales estimate.

Table 6.17

North	Per cent	South	Per cent
Chapman	25	Noble	27·5
Edinburgh	25·7	Palmers Green	27·5
Glasgow	25·8	Allen	27·4
Jarrett	25	Croydon	27·8
Bradford	23·7	Evans	27·5
Hull	25·4	Weybridge	28·4
Scott	25	Canterbury	28
Manchester	25	Brighton	27·5
Liverpool	21·5	Portsmouth	27·5
Ingles	25·1	Watford	24·6
Penrith	24·4	Lander	27·6
Newcastle	25·6	Oxford	27·5
Northern salesmen	25	Marlow	35·9
Northern showgrounds	25	Southern salesmen	27·5
		Southern showgrounds	27·5

Table 6.17 (Continued)

Midlands	Per cent	West	Per cent
Norwich	10·7	Bristol	22
Ipswich	22	Cheltenham	29
Brown	42·6	Swindon	26·3
Lincoln	13·8	Hewitt	25
Nottingham	10	Plymouth	25
King	42·6	Barnstaple	25
Wellingborough	0	Driscoll	25
Leicester	18·4	Swansea	25·3
Green	42·5	Western salesmen	25
Chelmsford	14	Western showgrounds	25
Cambridge	11		
Fisher	42·5		
Derby	9·3		
Shrewsbury	12·3		
Moon	42·6		
Worcester	22		
Aberystwyth	22		
Bangor	13		
Midlands salesmen	42·6		
Midlands showgrounds	14		

Over the past three years (1970, 1971 and 1972) the sales turnover has increased by 9 per cent, 5 per cent and 19 per cent respectively. Therefore, you are faced with a considerable increase estimated by Mr Young for 1973, and Tables 6.1 and 6.11 should be given very close inspection.

The sales estimates for 1973 as increases over 1972 (taken from Tables 6.1 and 6.11) are given in Table 6.17.

Occasionally it is useful to obtain information additional to the case material, and it may be of value to determine the population for each of the areas listed in Table 6.2 and calculate the sales per 100 head of population. This has been done in Table 6.18.

From Table 6.18 it appears that area 9 is the best area and area 1 the worst. If we take a purely arbitrary figure for the sales per 100 head of population — say the average, which is £59·54 divided by 22 = £2·71 — and recalculate all those areas below this average sales per 100, the exercise would provide a new sales forecast based purely on a statistical calculation.

Q.6.1 By recalculating all the areas with turnovers below this average of £2·71 per 100, so that they equate to this average per 100 population, what is the new sales total?

From the profit and loss account summaries (p. 157) percentages have been calculated in Table 6.19 to help us to project a profit and loss account for 1973.

The percentages in Table 6.19 have been taken of the goods manufactured during the year. The percentages in Table 6.20 have been taken of goods sold during the year.

Business Analysis for Marketing Managers

Table 6.18 Sales per 100 Population in 1972

Area	Sales (£)	Approximate population	Sales per 100 (£)
1	47,790	4,212,400	1·13
2	94,200	5,047,600	1·87
3	83,190	6,648,700	1·25
4	65,150	2,567,800	2.54
5	30,370	1,161,100	2·62
6	52,580	1,783,000	2·95
7	30,970	1,266,500	2·45
8	44,650	1,353,600	3·30
9	22,300	504,800	4·42
10	71,050	3,078,200	2·31
11	44,380	2,910,800	1·52
12	16,200	393,600	4·12
13	26,900	618,200	4·35
14*	105,880	3,689,500	2·87*
15*	98,000	3,689,500	2·66*
16	86,840	3,636,900	2·39
17	39,200	1,670,900	2·35
18	44,150	1,385,700	3·19
19	48,700	1,600,500	3·04
20	64,670	2,237,500	2·89
21	45,600	1,637,300	2·79
22	43,690	1,716,800	2·54

*Greater London population is split arbitrarily into two equal amounts; this calculation is suspect, however, because the export sales figure is not known.

Table 6.19

Percentage during the year

	1968	1969	1970	1971	1972
Materials	38	39	40	39	38
Wages	20	18	16	17	17
Overheads	5	5	5	5	5

Table 6.20

Percentage during the year

	1968	1969	1970	1971	1972
Salaries	4·6	5·1	4·9	5·0	5·4
Commission	0·3	0·5	0·4	0·4	0·4
Travelling etc.	2·0	2·0	2·1	2·0	2·0
Trans. and W'h'sing	8·8	9·1	10·8	10·0	11·9
Showgrounds	4·8	2·7	3·7	3·8	3·7
Advertising	4·4	2·3	5·9	5·9	5·6
Finance, insurance	0·8	0·8	0·7	0·8	0·8
Gen. admin.	1·3	1·5	1·5	1·7	1·5
Depreciation	1·0	0·9	1·0	1·3	1·2
Net profit	8·0	14·0	7·2	8·0	8·0

Salaries and commission for 1973 will have to comply with the restrictions placed on companies during that year — that pay increases must not exceed 4 per cent plus £1 per week per employee. It will be as well to look into this figure before proceeding further with this analysis.

We may assume that Ted Young will receive some portion of this salary at least for 1973, and, although it is not known what this might be, we can include a whole year's salary for Parsons, despite the fact that he will not be working for the whole of 1973 for the company. As he will probably only receive half of his salary rate for 1973, the other half can be considered as a contribution towards Ted Young's remuneration, and therefore our budgeting will be that much more accurate.

We can estimate salaries and commission for 1973 as follows:

Directors' salaries		£25,500
Oliver	£2,890	
Peters	3,150	
Quick	3,760	
Roberts	2,250	
		12,050
Salesmen 15 x £1,860		27,900
Mike Parsons		4,000
		69,450
4 per cent of £69,450		2,778
25 employees under consideration —		
25 x 52 x £1		1,300
		£73,528

While Parsons may only work for about six months, his total salary is shown, since there will be some portion of Ted Young's salary to be paid.

Commission can be calculated by combining the information in Tables 6.1 and 6.11 in Table 6.21.

Q.6.2 With the information now prepared, are you able to construct a projected profit and loss account for 1973?

A number of problems appear to have been left for Mike Parsons to deal with. The total sales for the first three months, shown in Table 6.14, is £351,770, which is 23·32 per cent of the total sales estimate. What we do not know is the seasonality of sales over the year, but it is likely, in view of the product, that higher sales will be achieved during spring and summer than in autumn and winter. It is unlikely, therefore, that the first quarter's sales will amount to 25 per cent of the year's total. Nevertheless it is disturbing to see the low sales for the Lincoln showground — £1,728. If Lincoln reflects the sales pattern for the rest of the country, then we could expect 23 per cent of the total sales estimate for the year to be achieved in the first three months. In that case 23 per cent of £17,000 (from Table 6.11), which is £3,910, should be achieved in the first three months instead of only £1,728.

The future operation of the salesmen and the showgrounds needs careful consideration. At present the salesmen have no responsibility for the showgrounds and receive no commission on showground sales. This has undoubtedly contributed to considerable dissatisfaction among salesmen, but, to take the decision to credit

Table 6.21

Name	Estimate (£)	Commission payable on* (£)	Commission (£)
Oliver	363,000	98,000	490
Peters	413,900	88,900	444·50
Quick	539,000	89,000	445
Roberts	192,500	92,500	462·50
Chapman	18,000	8,000	400
Jarrett	44,500	9,500	475
Scott	37,000	7,000	350
Ingles	29,500	9,500	475
Brown	25,150	5,150	257·50
King	23,250	3,250	162·50
Green	28,000	8,000	400
Fisher	30,000	5,000	250
Moon	28,000	5,000	250
Noble	97,000	7,000	350
Allen	85,000	5,000	250
Lander	29,000	9,000	450
Evans	31,000	6,000	300
Hewitt	15,000	–	–
Driscoll	23,000	–	–
			£6,212

*The estimates in Table 6.11 are deducted from the targets in Table 6.1 to determine the amount on which commission is payable.

them with commission on all showground sales would necessitate not only a recalculation of targets and commission but also the agreement of the Board.

A decision is required on the enquiry for fencing. The customer is prepared to collect 100 pieces of IF66 fencing a week for 50 weeks and therefore a rate of production must be requested that will satisfy the customer and also minimize costs some of which are pure production costs, and some of which are sales costs. There are three main costs to be considered: the setting up charge which is a production cost, and the costs of storing (see p. 152) and investment in finished stock which are sales costs. The position is illustrated in Table 6.22.

Table 6.22 Batch size

	500	400	300	200	100
No. of weeks	10	13	17	25	50
Setting up charge (£)	120	156	204	300	600
Average stock	2,000	1,950	1,700	1,250	–
Storage at 10p sq. ft (£)	400	390	340	250	–
Production and storage cost (£)	520	546	544	550	600
Stock value* (£)	4,400	4,290	3,740	2,750	–
Cost of investment in stock @ 12 per cent p.a. (£)	528	515	449	330	–
Total cost (£)	5,448	5,351	4,733	3,630	600

*Valued at £2.20 each.

Therefore the lowest cost comes from producing at 100 per week, which is the same rate as the collection required by the customer. Before issuing requests to the production department, however, it would be advisable to consider one or two other important points. For example, will this rate of 100 a week interfere with normal production requirements? Would it be more convenient to produce at the rate of 500 every five weeks?

The stockholding problem in the case is very complicated, because we do not know exactly what the items are. Some items seem to be considerably overstocked: for instance, there is over five years' supply of item 7. Others, notably item 3, appear to have less than one week's supply in stock. Such anomalies have doubtless stimulated the investigation, but you are advised to treat this stockholding problem with care.

Q.6.3   Does the value of the stock held by U.V.W., as indicated in the balance sheet, agree with that indicated by the 10 per cent sample stock take?

There is a simple formula for the minimizing of stock held by a company. It is,

$$N = \sqrt{\frac{VS}{2C}}$$

where,

N = the optimum number of orders to be placed a year
V = the total sterling value of the items used a year
C = the cost of ordering (which is £5 in this case)
S = the cost of carrying stock and is expressed as a percentage of average stock.

The aim is to keep as little as possible in stock, bearing in mind the usage rate and cost of ordering. For the moment we will omit the delivery rates. The less that is kept in stock, the more frequently will there be a need to order and to accept deliveries. This means more orders, more checking, more progressing and so on. Conversely, the less frequently we order, the more has to be kept in stock. The ideal number of orders to place a year will be when N (the optimum) is at a minimum, that is,

$$\text{total ordering cost per year} = \text{total carrying cost per year}$$

or,

$$N \times C = V/N \times \tfrac{1}{2} \times S$$

Note that V/N is the value per order and, assuming that there is fairly regular usage of stock, then the average stock will be half of V/N. S is the percentage carrying cost. Simplifying,

$$NC = \frac{V/N}{2} \times S$$

that is,

$$NC = \frac{VS}{2N}$$

$$2N^2C = VS$$

$$N^2 = \frac{VS}{2C}$$

$$N = \sqrt{\frac{VS}{2C}}$$

Table 6.23 Calculation of Values of V and S

Item	Cost (£)	Usage	V (£)	Present average stock cost (£)	Stockholding cost (£)	S (per cent)
1	16·20	112	1,814	1,620	113	7
2	9·80	72	705	588	83	14
3	80·00	1,500	120,000	1,600	400	25
4	2·20	540	1,188	1,206	84	7
5	5·40	828	4,471	7,128	500	7
6	6·80	660	4,488	5,494	385	7
7	3·20	152	486	2,458	334	14
8	2·30	330	759	518	363	70
9	4·00	275	1,100	592	85	14
10	0·40	780	312	245	17	7
11	0·70	440	308	476	33	7
12	2·00	575	1,150	1,200	84	7
13	3·00	280	840	1,890	143	8
14	2·00	900	1,800	1,440	102	7
15	0·85	750	637	493	70	14

We can now start to analyse the 10 per cent sample stock take (Table 6.23).
With Table 6.23's values for V and S we can now calculate the optimum number of orders per year per item to minimize costs (Table 6.24).

Table 6.24

Item	N = optimum no. of orders	Usage	Units per order
1	$\sqrt{1,814 \times 0 \cdot 07/2 \div 5} = \sqrt{12 \cdot 69} = 4$	112	28
2	$\sqrt{705 \times 0 \cdot 14/2 \div 5} = \sqrt{9 \cdot 87} = 3$	72	24
3	$\sqrt{120,000 \times 0 \cdot 25/2 \div 5} = \sqrt{3,000} = 54$	1,500	28
4	$\sqrt{1,188 \times 0 \cdot 07/2 \div 5} = \sqrt{8 \cdot 3} = 3$	540	180
5	$\sqrt{4,471 \times 0 \cdot 07/2 \div 5} = \sqrt{31 \cdot 3} = 6$	828	138
6	$\sqrt{4,488 \times 0 \cdot 07/2 \div 5} = \sqrt{31 \cdot 4} = 6$	660	110
7	$\sqrt{486 \times 0 \cdot 14/2 \div 5} = \sqrt{6 \cdot 8} = 3$	152	51
8	$\sqrt{759 \times 0 \cdot 70/2 \div 5} = \sqrt{53 \cdot 1} = 8$	330	42
9	$\sqrt{1,100 \times 0 \cdot 14/2 \div 5} = \sqrt{15 \cdot 4} = 4$	275	69
10	$\sqrt{312 \times 0 \cdot 07/2 \div 5} = \sqrt{2 \cdot 2} = 2$	780	390
11	$\sqrt{308 \times 0 \cdot 07/2 \div 5} = \sqrt{2 \cdot 2} = 2$	440	220
12	$\sqrt{1,150 \times 0 \cdot 07/2 \div 5} = \sqrt{8 \cdot 0} = 3$	575	192
13	$\sqrt{840 \times 0 \cdot 08/2 \div 5} = \sqrt{6 \cdot 7} = 3$	280	94
14	$\sqrt{1,800 \times 0 \cdot 07/2 \div 5} = \sqrt{12 \cdot 6} = 4$	900	225
15	$\sqrt{637 \times 0 \cdot 14/2 \div 5} = \sqrt{8 \cdot 9} = 3$	750	250

The carrying costs can now be minimized by the application of the formula (Table 6.25).

In this calculation to minimize stockholding costs note that the average stock cost is approximately 50 per cent of the cost of the largest order: for example, item 1 is 28 x £16·20/2 = £227; and item 2 is 24 x £9·80/2 = £117·60. This is assuming that there will be a regular usage of stock, though this is unlikely, and variations in actual usage will need to be considered. The ordering cost has been inserted at £5 per order: thus item 1 requires three orders, which is 4 x £5 = £20. The cost of holding stock has been charged at 12 per cent, although this figure would need to be reviewed in the light of actual interest charged.

We can now compare the total cost of average stock of the 10 per cent sample in Table 6.13 with the total cost of the minimized stock in Table 6.25 — £26,946·90 compared with £3,497 — a drastic reduction. Furthermore, if the average stock shown in Table 6.13 has interest of 12 per cent per annum applied, this would require another £3,233·63 a year.

Q.6.4 From this calculation of the stockholding what action would you consider?

Table 6.12 — the new factory potential — is on the face of it a simple linear programming exercise, but you should appreciate that many more questions have to be asked before a simple mathematical solution can be adopted. Apart from the woodworking and fabricating constraints, it is possible to complete either 110 sheds or 65 garages a week, showing similar profit: 110 x £14·40 = £1,584 and 65 x £23·75

Table 6.25 Application of formula to reduce Stockholding Cost

Item	No. of orders	Units per order	Average stock cost (£)	S (per cent)	S (£)	Ordering cost (£)	Interest on investment @ 12 per cent p.a. (£)	Total cost (£)
1	4	28	227	7	16	20	27	63
2	3	24	118	14	17	15	14	46
3	54	28	1,120	25	280	270	134	684
4	3	180	198	7	14	15	24	53
5	6	138	373	7	26	30	45	101
6	6	110	374	7	26	30	45	101
7	3	51	82	14	11	15	10	36
8	8	42	48	70	34	40	6	80
9	4	69	138	14	19	20	17	56
10	2	390	78	7	5	10	9	24
11	2	220	77	7	5	10	9	24
12	3	192	192	7	13	15	23	51
13	3	94	141	8	11	15	17	43
14	4	225	225	7	16	20	27	63
15	3	250	106	14	15	15	13	43
			£3,497					£1,468

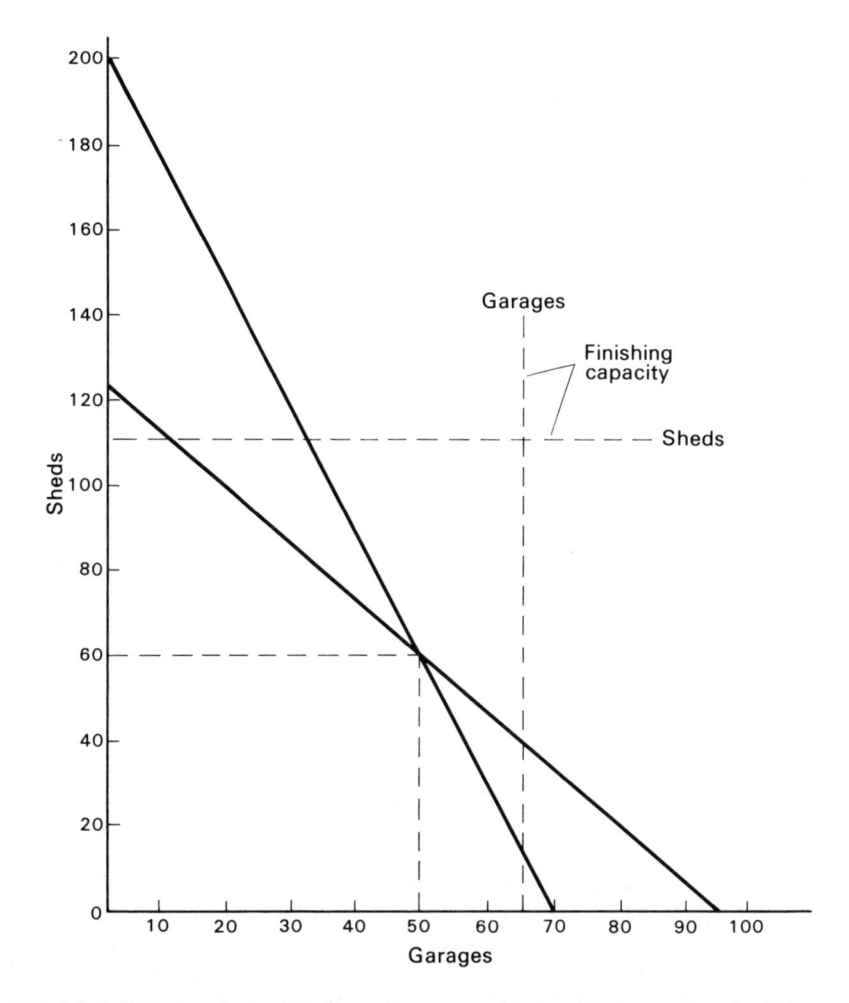

Exhibit 6.2 Graphical analysis of Treforest factory production. Maximum output will be achieved with about sixty sheds and fifty garages, but this would leave finishing capacity for fifty sheds or seventeen garages. Therefore, the simple mathematical solution is probably not the best answer.

= £1,543. Until you possess much more information about company objectives, alternative products or perhaps different production options, it is difficult to see how you can make anything more than an intelligent mathematical guess.

Q.6.5 What actions do you consider Mike Parsons would have to take on assuming the appointment of sales manager?

6.3 Report

A report may recommend the following:

Aim. The marketing aims of the company should be directed towards portable buildings, but consideration must be given to the current consumer market and the potential industrial market.

Objectives. Specific objectives need to be made about such items as the proposed order for fences, the production scheduling for the new factory at Treforest, the organization of the sales areas, commission arrangements for salesmen, the showgrounds' activities and, not least, the sales forecast for the next year.

Actions necessary to achieve these objectives have been fully discussed and assessed in the analysis, but you must remember that, if you argue your case from the assumed role of Mike Parsons, you do not possess the authority of the man you are supposed to have replaced.

ANSWERS TO QUESTIONS

A.6.1 If you have accepted the arbitrary figure of £2·71 per 100 head of population, then a new forecast would mean that all areas except 6, 8, 9, 12, 13, 14, 18, 19, 20 and 21 have to be recalculated at £2·71 per 100. This will give a figure of approximately £1,490,748 for all areas, which is only £17,616 short of the 1973 forecast. However, the figure of £2.71 is suspect, and is but a crude estimate of sales per 100. A better method is to sum the sales for 1972 in Table 6.16, sum the population given in the analysis and calculate a new figure per 100 head: £1,206,460 divided by 52,810,900 (i.e. 528,109 100's) gives a figure of £2·28 sales per 100 head of population.

When this figure is regarded as the average sales per 100 head, only four areas — 1, 2, 3, and 11 — fall below this figure. A recalculation will give a new total of £1,365,985, which is £142,415 short of the 1973 estimate. While these calculations are but estimates, it is important to understand the implications of the sales forecast made by Ted Young.

A.6.2 A projected profit and loss account can be prepared with a minimum-maximum approach — that is, by estimating the lowest and highest expenses to determine the largest possible range of profit:

		£1,508,400
Sales estimate		
Materials 38–39 per cent	£573,192–588,276	
Wages 16–18 per cent	241,344–271,512	
Overheads 4–5 per cent	60,336– 75,420	
		874,872–935,208
		633,528–573,192
Less expenses:		
Salaries (calculated)	£73,528	
Commission (calculated)	6,212	
Travelling (2 per cent)	30,168	
Warehousing etc.		
(10–12 per cent)	150,840–181,008	
Showgrounds (3½–4 per cent)	52,794– 60,336	
Advertising (given)	93,000	
Finance (say 0·8 per cent		
as before)	12,067	
General administration		
(1·5–1·7 per cent)	22,626– 25,643	
Depreciation (say)	15,000	
		456,235–496,962
	Projected net profit	£177,293– 76,230

A.6.3 The balance sheet (p. 155) gives the year-end stock of materials, components and finished goods as £128,700. Even taking a simple tenfold expansion of the sample stock-take would indicate that there should be well over £250,000 stock of materials and components. This leads one to suspect the 10 per cent sample, and an investigation seems to be indicated to determine how the fifteen items were selected and what is actually meant by a '10 per cent sample'.

A.6.4 To minimize costs of stockholding is one thing, but we must then look more closely at the items held in stock. We need to know a lot more about delivery times, buying opportunities and discounts and the length of time required for some of the items to season. The amount of physical storage space will also tend to influence decisions taken on stockholding. Above all, you must avoid applying simple (or complex) mathematical calculations to business decisions without assessing all the raw data.

A.6.5 On taking over the appointment, Mike Parsons has a number of actions to institute. A major problem is the declining performance of the Midlands region. The fact that the regional manager — Peters — lives well to the west of his territory is an important fact, which may contribute to the poor performance. It is no certain solution to require him to move to a more central residence, but to revert to the original east and west Midlands regions may be a possible solution. To do this would doubtless disrupt present arrangements and would cost perhaps another £4,000 to £6,000 a year. It is vital that the costs of decisions are included in your thinking.

A general weakness in the operation seems to be in the company's sales forecasting methods and some amendment appears to be advisable if the Midlands men are not going to be saddled with the responsibility of obtaining over 40 per cent increases in sales. It might be as well to make the showgrounds the important sales outlets, review the salesmen's activities and bring their operations closer to the showgrounds. This cannot be done on a sort of 'blanket' approach. For example, area 20 has three showgrounds and no salesman, area 21 has two showgrounds and the salesman living in Dorset, while the regional manager lives in Bristol. Clearly the men and showgrounds cannot be treated as chess pieces that may be moved around at will.

Parsons should take the opportunity of building up a marketing plan for 1974, while doing as much as possible for 1973. More control of the sales operation, both men and showgrounds, is essential; some review of product policy for the future is also desirable; advertising can be retained for 1973, as it is probably too late in the year for alterations. One technique that might be introduced fairly quickly is sales budgeting, the regional managers being required to plan for profit rather than for sales, if they are not already doing so, and to monitor and control regional operations.

The operation of value added tax will need to be examined, and the impending change to metrication will require careful consideration of all portable buildings. Customers can readily understand what a 10 ft by 8 ft shed is, but not necessarily a 304 cm by 243 cm shed. The timber trade has been using metric units for some years and is therefore conditioned to them. Only the consumer market remains to be educated, though this is not a simple operation.

Index

'Acid test ratio', 71
Actions proposed, 5, 7
Aim of company, 5
Allocation of expenses, 74, 75, 80, 81
Analysis and synthesis, 2
Area profitability, 74–6, 102, 103
Assessment of actions, 5, 11
Average deviation of series, 17
Average stock, 80

Balance sheet projection, 43, 46, 105, 113
'Bench marks', 107, 126
Break-even, 126, 127

Case analysis, schematic representation, 4
   history, 2
   project, 2
   study, 2
Cash flow projection, 46, 47, 109, 132
Cash or overdraft projection, 44
Check list, 8
Coefficient of determination, 36, 130
Complexity analysis, 25, 27
Conjectural analysis, 4, 5
Correlation analysis, 33–40, 82, 83, 129
Credit management, 106
Creditors' ratio, 42, 43
Current position check list, 8
Current ratio, 71
Cycle estimation, 17

Debt ratio, 72
Debtors' ratio, 41, 72
Decision making, 7, 11
Depreciation, 71
Deviation from trend, 17, 19

Dichotomous data and *phi* (Φ), 39, 40
Discount effect on profit, 27, 28
Distribution check list, 9

Estimate of cycle, 17
Estimating trends, 13
Evaluation of actions, 11
Exponential trends, 21–5
Extrapolation, 15

Financial analysis, 40–8
Fixed assets determination, 70, 71
Flexible budgeting, 15

Game theory, 28–33
Gompertz curve, 18, 22–5
Graphical analysis of linear program problem, 169

Intangible assets, 71
Inter-firm comparison index, 40
Investments, 71

Least squares method, 13, 26
Line of best fit, 13
Linear programming, 167–9
Linear trend, 14, 27
Liquidity ratio, 71
Location of problems, 6
Logarithmic curve, 18
Logarithmic trend, 19, 26

Management ratios, 41, 70, 71
Market share, 73
Marketing, meaning of, 1
   mix components, 3
   segment analysis, 84
   share, 73

Mean square contingency coefficient
    phi (Φ), 34, 39, 40
Method of least squares, 18
Mixed strategies in game theory, 29

Non-linear trends, 18
Non-operating assets, 71

Objectives to be achieved, 5, 78, 79
Optimum order quantities, 42, 165–7
Optimum strategy in game theory, 32
Organizational analysis, 6, 48, 49
Overdraft or cash projection, 44

Pearson's coefficient of correlation, 36
Percentage trend, 14
phi (Φ) – mean square contingency
    coefficient, 34, 39, 40
Price check list, 10
Price structure, 124–6, 134, 135
Primary ratio (profit/funds), 40, 70, 73
Problem location, 6, 110
Procedural analysis, 6, 48, 49
Product check list, 8, 9
Profit, 1
    and loss account (revenue account)
        projection, 43, 45, 105, 113, 131,
        133, 136, 171
    on cost, profit on return, 123
Profitability of areas, 74–6, 102, 103
Promotion check list, 10
Pure strategy in game theory, 29
Purpose of operations, 5

Qualitative judgment, 33
Quarterly trend, 15

Ratio analysis, 41
Responsibility and authority, 8
Revenue account (profit and loss
    account), 43, 45, 105, 113, 131
    projection, 133, 136, 171
Role of case analyser, 2

Saddle point in game theory, 29
Sales calls analysis, 77, 84
Secondary ratios, 40
Selection of actions, 5, 12
Selling check list, 10
    patterns, 104
Sequential linking of analysis, 11
Service check list, 10
Shareholders' interest ratio, 72
Simple modified exponential, 18, 21–5
Spearman's rank correlation, 35
Stock control, 42, 73, 79, 80, 165
    turn ratio, 80
Straight line projection, 14
    trend, 14
Synthesis of report, 2

Three-point method for non-linear
    trends, 20
Trend estimation, 13–26

Uncontrollable factors, 7

Weak analysis, causes of, 4